E-learning 1.0, 2.0, and 3.0 in Higher Education

E-learning 1.0, 2.0, and 3.0 in Higher Education

Rhiannon Evans and Claus Nygaard

THE LEARNING IN HIGHER EDUCATION SERIES

First published in 2019 by Libri Publishing

Copyright © Libri Publishing

Authors retain copyright of individual chapters.

The right of Rhiannon Evans and Claus Nygaard to be identified as the editors of this work has been asserted in accordance with the Copyright, Designs and Patents Act, 1988.

ISBN 978-1-911450-39-9

All rights reserved. No part of this publication may be reproduced, stored in any retrieval system or transmitted in any form or by any means, electronic, mechanical, photocopying, recording or otherwise, without the prior written permission of the copyright holder for which application should be addressed in the first instance to the publishers. No liability shall be attached to the author, the copyright holder or the publishers for loss or damage of any nature suffered as a result of reliance on the reproduction of any of the contents of this publication or any errors or omissions in its contents.

A CIP catalogue record for this book is available from The British Library.

Cover design by Helen Taylor

Design by Carnegie Book Production

Libri Publishing
Brunel House
Volunteer Way
Faringdon
Oxfordshire
SN7 7YR

Tel: +44 (0)845 873 3837

www.libripublishing.co.uk

Contents

Foreword
Birgit Loch — vii

Chapter 1: An Introduction to e-learning in higher education: 1.0, 2.0, and 3.0.
Malinda Hoskins Lloyd, Willie McGuire, Reya Saliba, Rachid Bendriss, Flemming Meier, Rhiannon Evans, and Claus Nygaard — 1

Chapter 2: E-learning as a strategy for improving university students' learning outcomes
Claus Nygaard — 23

Chapter 3: Using a peer-centred online learning platform to support students' academic-professional transition
Willie McGuire and Olan Harrington — 45

Chapter 4: The effectiveness of e-learning in Business Communication at the University of Johannesburg? What students say!
Magas R. Pather — 73

Chapter 5: Using Wordpress, Canvas LMS, Dropbox and Facebook to enhance students' online engagement in postgraduate education
Anne Hørsted — 101

Chapter 6: Using e-learning to improve the student experience of lectures
Rhiannon Evans — 115

Chapter 7: The E-CIL framework: an instructional practice for promoting student engagement with content, the instructor, and other learners in online courses
Malinda Hoskins Lloyd — 137

Contents

Chapter 8: Experiential learning in premedical education: enhancing atudents' experience through e-learning
Reya Saliba & Rachid Bendriss   165

Chapter 9: Ten e-learning technologies to support problem-based collaborative work
Flemming Meier & Claus Nygaard   189

Chapter 10: Using e-learning to supervise students' project work in higher education: some pedagogical requirements
Flemming Meier   211

Foreword

When I think of e-learning, I find there are three questions that occupy my mind. The first is how we choose the most effective technologies, including latest e-learning trends such as learning from any device, but also the Internet of Things, artificial intelligence, as well as virtual and augmented reality. I believe particularly augmented reality has enormous potential as it merges physical and virtual learning spaces. To give an example, in anatomy teaching an interactive three-dimensional model of the human body, accessible to our students via a smart phone or tablet, may reduce the reliance on expensive and physical space-intensive cadaver teaching. It allows students to undertake assessment tasks without waiting for their next class, wherever they are and whenever they like. And it allows design of new forms of assessment we may not have thought of before. The second question I think of is how best to engage teaching staff in e-learning, and the third, how we can involve our students in the design of e-learning environments. I will pick up these two points again in a moment. Particularly, I will address a couple of chapters in no particular order and share the thoughts that went through my mind while reading.

E-learning 1.0, 2.0 and 3.0 are introduced in Chapter 2 by Claus Nygaard, together with a curriculum design model, commencing with the question how we perceive learning, then how we perceive e-learning, and finally how we perceive curriclulum. I wholeheartedly agree with Nygaard's views that most current e-learning practice is aligned with E-learning 1.0, Distribution of information to students, as this is the traditional model that most current lecturers have learnt through, and it is the safest model as the teacher is the authority and remains in control. One also needs to keep in mind that most lecturers have been appointed on the basis of their research, with very few holding formal qualifications in adult learning or other forms of engagement with educational theory. I would be interested to see current e-learning approaches analysed using this model, to inform curriculum reform projects. One could commence with the question how curriculum is perceived in the current design, how e-learning is designed, what this tells us about how we perceive learning,

Foreword

to then question if this was the intention and if this is how learning should be perceived.

In Chapter 6, Rhiannon Evans discusses the low student engagement with lecture recordings that are automatically produced in larger lecture theatres. The availability of these recordings has reduced student attendance in the classes that are being recorded. While reading this chapter I was very much reminded of the work undertaken by one of my PhD students, Maimuna Musarrat, at a different university. In an effort to identify barriers and enablers to the adoption of educational technology by lecturers, she investigated lecturer attitude towards voluntary use of technology in higher education, and mandatory (or automatic) use. The voluntary technology was the tablet PC, provided to the lecturers who volunteered and were offered professional development on how to use it and membership in a community of practice to ask questions and share approaches. The mandatory technology was lecture recording technology, by default set to automatically record a full lecture-duration of content projected onto the screen with input from the document camera or computer, with the recording made available on the LMS shortly after. The introduction of this technology had not included professional development. Maimuna surveyed lecturers and followed up in more depth via focus groups. She identified four types of lecturers: those who are "willing users" of lecture recording and encourage their students to engage with the recordings; the "non-willing users" who didn't know they could have opted out, don't think it provides benefits to students and are not encouraging their students to access the recordings; the "non-willing non-users" who have opted out or are glad they are allocated teaching spaces that do not provide recording facilities; and finally the "willing non-users", those who can see benefits for their students and for themselves but are scheduled in spaces where recordings are not produced. Representatives of this latter group were requesting to be scheduled in lecture recording enabled rooms. Maimuna found that the main motivator for adoption of lecture recording is the value perception, where those who can see a benefit to learning will embrace a technology. A very fitting quote from Chapter 1 of this book is: *The role of faculty, we shall argue, is more important for the success of e-learning than technology itself.*

Of course, this brings me back to this book, where much of the discussion is around the pedagogy, and how it should be driving the use of technology. I like Evans' suggestion to use availability of automated lecture recording as a trigger to rethink teaching, abandon typically teacher-centred lectures and produce good quality bite-size videos instead. I would then argue that this would be a constructive way to move to blended learning where face to face time remains and is used in a more engaging way, to co-construct knowledge and aid understanding. Key to this development is the careful alignment of the online and the face to face components, so they complement each other and students benefit from the best each can offer. I will pick up on this again a bit later where I describe my own approach to avoiding live lecture recordings.

In reading through the chapters of this book, I would like to propose one additional approach to e-learning 3.0 that I believe has not been covered in a chapter: the inclusion of students as partners. This, at its most basic level, means seeking the input of students into the design of curriculum, e.g. before design commences, or during design. Most studies investigate student perception of their learning environment and curriculum while they are studying, or at the end of semester. But what about consulting with a group of students on what would work best, before the curriculum is (re)designed? I took this approach when redesigning a traditionally-taught mathematics course into blended mode. Students who had just completed the course were invited to a focus group where we sought ideas on improvements to the course. We carefully steered them towards the idea of an online component. Perhaps this should have been expected: students wanted more online material on one hand, so they could catch up if they missed a class. On the other hand, they did not want all learning to be online, as they appreciated the benefits of face to face contact with a lecturer or tutor, and other students. They wanted lecture recordings, but at the same time admitted they would most likely not watch long recordings. They wanted to be able to find relevant material on the LMS, quickly. As a consequence, in the new blended design we opted out of live lecture recordings and, as Evans suggested earlier, instead embedded short videos explaining concepts or showing worked examples in the weekly schedule. We explained why we had made certain changes, and how these aligned with what the focus group had suggested. Feedback after the course had been taught in blended mode for the first couple of times was extremely positive, towards the easy of navigation, as well as the availability of online resources. But feedback also clearly stated that students would not want to give up any of the existing face to face hours. We did receive negative feedback from the students who really wanted live lecture recordings and didn't understand that our design had been such that these live recordings were not needed.

The more advanced level of working with students as partners is their active inclusion in curriculum design. I was privileged to be visiting Loughborough University in the UK a few years ago, where students were working on an internship to improve a second year mathematics course that had been regarded as difficult by students. These students had just completed the course and were creating additional resources for the next cohort of students. For example, they recorded screencasts, video of handwritten explanation on a tablet PC with audio narration, as support resources that they felt were missing to understand concepts. I was able to interview these students and their supervising lecturers. The students admitted that for the first time, they had learnt what it means to study a topic properly, to completely understand it, as they felt they needed to before they could explain it to others. Involving students in the production of learning resources for their peers, or allowing them to actively be involved in the improvement of curriculum requires a rethinking towards e-learning 3.0, as I've indicated earlier. A concern from one of the lecturers in the Loughborough study was "but what about the correctness"? He was worried that students may not have the maturity and technical knowledge to influence curriculum.

In line with the above and on the topic of learning by teaching, I would like to pick up on an idea mentioned by Flemming Meier and Claus Nygaard in Chapter 9, where they compare e-learning tools for problem-based collaborative work. While Kahoot, an online quiz tool with in-built games-based learning, has scored very low against other tools, the idea of getting students to write quizzes and use these with other students has potential. By engaging with assessment and writing assessment tasks as well as correct and incorrect solution options, students will need to understand the content well and identify key concepts to assess. They will do this in an environment they regard as "fun" to work in. I have used Kahoot and other audience response systems in my own mathematics teaching to prepare students for exams: questions are extracted from past exam papers, with a typical (usually at least slightly incorrect) solution shown. Students are then asked how many marks they would provide, which allows for discussion of how we interpret what a student has written, and how we decide how many marks to give. This places the students in the position of the marker for the first time, and gives them the opportunity to understand our expectations of them in an exam.

This book includes perspectives from different continents and disciplines, but also ranges from the introduction of the model of e-learning 1.0, 2.0 and 3.0, to the comparison of e-learning tools, and accounts of student feedback on initiatives that have been taken at individual universities. This book is a welcome contribution to ongoing important discussions on improving learning and teaching with the support of e-learning.

Birgit Loch
December 2018

About the Author

Birgit Loch is Professor of Mathematics Education and Associate Pro Vice-Chancellor Coursework in the College of Science, Health and Engineering at La Trobe University, Melbourne, Australia. Her research interests are the effective use of educational technologies in STEM education with focus on tablet technology and learning from video, the role of students as partners, open educational resources and technology adoption by teaching staff.

Chapter 1

An introduction to e-learning in higher education: 1.0, 2.0, and 3.0.

Malinda Hoskins Lloyd, Willie McGuire, Reya Saliba, Rachid Bendriss, Flemming Meier, Rhiannon Evans, and Claus Nygaard

Why e-learning?

E-learning has been a practice and a buzzword in higher education since the 1980s. It has come in many forms matching the evolution of technology over time. Many scholars have written about various types of e-learning. With the existence of highly ranked international journals devoted to e-learning, much research has been published over the past decades. Some scholars have published about the differences between traditional teaching and online learning (Carliner, 2004; Hiltz & Turoff, 2005; Rhode, 2009; Shachar & Neumann, 2010). Some have published about the characteristics of distance learning or distance education (Keegan, 1996; Moore & Kearsley, 2011; Simonson *et al.*, 2015). Others have published on the crossover of traditional face-to-face teaching and online teaching and named this blended learning (Garrison & Kanuka, 2004; Ross & Gage, 2006; Helms, 2012; Graham *et al.*, 2013; Alammary *et al.*, 2014). Yet others published about the synchronous and asynchronous aspects of e-learning (Pilkington & Walker, 2003; Hrastinski, 2008).

One of the main debates in the field of e-learning, naturally, has focused on the effectiveness of e-learning, and the conclusions reached have been both contra and pro e-learning. In a recent bibliographical study of 761 papers discussing the effectiveness of e-learning, Noesgaard and Ørngreen (2015) showed that the effectiveness is measured differently. The five most dominant measures of effectiveness were "Learning Outcomes" (56%), "Perceived learning, skills or competency" (21%), "Attitude" (15%), "Satisfaction" (also 15%), and "Skills acquired" (9%). This shows us that the reasons for applying e-learning are varied, and the effectiveness, therefore, is measured differently. Based on a meta-analysis of studies of e-learning, Russell (1999) concluded that no significant difference could be found between the effect of e-learning and traditional face-to-face learning. McConnell (2000) also came to the conclusion that learning is not necessarily improved by the use of e-learning after a meta-analysis of studies of the effects of e-learning and face-to-face learning. Davies & Graff (2005), in their study, found that e-learning was not significantly correlated with higher grades. Hugenholtz et al. (2008) came to the same conclusion based on a study of two groups (e-learning and face-to-face).

However, other researchers have arrived at different and more positive conclusions in favour of e-learning. Keller & Suzuki (2004) came to the conclusion that e-learning shows a positive increase in students' motivation. Kim & Frick (2011) also showed such positive change in students' motivation when they are engaged in self-directed e-learning. Lou *et al.* (2017) surveyed 643 students and found that student-instructor interaction and student-student interaction significantly strengthen students' sense of membership and influence and promote their continuous use of the e-learning platform.

An obvious question to ask, after having consulted such past studies, on the effect of e-learning is: *Why e-learning?* If researchers are not certain about the effect, why spend our time implementing it in higher education? Why write a book about e-learning in higher education? Well, as you may imagine, the authors of this book all believe that e-learning has a positive effect – but only under certain circumstances, we should add. This is important, because adding the "e" to learning – that is introducing technology – does not necessarily lead to an increase in student learning. The effect on student learning comes from *the ways in which technology is used*. In this book, we use the terminology of e-learning 1.0 (distribution), 2.0 (dialogue), and 3.0 (construction) (Figure 1) (see also Nygaard, in this volume; Nygaard, 2015) to distinguish between e-learning as technology and e-learning as a pedagogical practice. In the following chapters showcasing the positive outcomes of using e-learning, we follow up on Nygaard's research and link it to our own experiences of using e-learning to enhance student engagement and student learning. The e-learning typology is presented in Figure 1.

E-learning typologies		
1.0: Distribution	2.0: Dialogue	3.0: Construction
E-learning is used to distribute information to students.	E-learning is used to facilitate a dialogue between students and teachers (and other relevant peers).	E-learning is used to enable construction of new knowledge or innovation of new methods/processes/products.

Figure 1: A typology for e-learning 1.0, 2.0, and 3.0.

'Distribution' is an approach to e-learning where the online component is used to distribute information to students. 'Dialogue' is an approach to e-learning where the online component is used to facilitate a dialogue between students as well as between students and teachers. 'Construction' is an approach to e-learning where the online component is used to help students construct new knowledge. In chapter 2, Nygaard explicitly links this typology with learning theory, so we will not go into further detail with the theoretical underpinnings here. However, we will focus on some of the ways in which e-learning 1.0 (distribution), 2.0 (dialogue), and 3.0 (construction) may both mirror existing e-learning practices and inspire new e-learning practices in higher education. We use this typology, because it enables us to look at the pedagogical *practice* of e-learning rather than the technology itself. In the next section, we shall go into more detail with what we mean by e-learning as pedagogical practice.

E-learning as pedagogical practice

One of the characteristics of our book is that we perceive e-learning as a pedagogical practice rather than a technological component. It means that we are interested in *how* e-learning is used to facilitate/ support/ scaffold/ enhance/ increase student learning rather than being interested in the technology itself. With the focus on learning first and technology second, we support the understanding that universities need to change from designing input-based to output-based curricula (Jarvis *et al.*, 1998; Rassow, 1998; Nygaard *et al.*, 2009), where students' learning outcomes, rather than the technology, are the focal point. This is important when we talk about e-learning. Whether we implement a CMS (content management system), an LMS (learning management system), use a plain website, web 2.0, or particular apps for computers, smartphones or tablets, or we augment reality with technology, is irrelevant to us. What is relevant here is how such technologies make e-learning possible as a pedagogical practice. This means that it is the pedagogical practice which is being enabled through the use of such technologies that interests us.

Therefore we go along with the original Greek definition of pedagogy, from the term *paidagogos*, comprised of child (*paidos*) and leader (*agogos*). The word describes the act of leading the way for the child. As it has now come to be used in professional educational contexts, it is often referred to as "the science of teaching", "the method of teaching", "the practice of teaching". Our focus on pedagogy enables us to discuss how we move from discipline-oriented teaching to learning-based student activities. For us the role of today's university is not to "give the right knowledge to its students". Universities need to provide students with the right possibilities to develop adequate competencies (Nygaard et al., 2009). Here we think of competencies which are relevant for the job market and are, at the same time, transformative (Harvey & Knight, 1996; Harvey, 2000).

With pedagogy at the centre of e-learning, the relevant point – we argue – is how e-learning leads the way for the student in his/her learning process. With that in mind, some obvious points of interest appear, which are important for universities to take into consideration when using e-learning. In fact, even before e-learning is implemented the university should take these points into consideration:

1. the e-learning strategy of the university;
2. the culture of teaching and learning at the university;
3. the role of faculty at the university;
4. the use of technology, materials, and resources at the university.

1. the e-learning strategy of the university

First of all, the overall e-learning strategy of the university should be taken into account. If this does not exist, it should be formulated. This is important because the university will hardly be able to trace an overall positive effect on students' motivation, students' engagement, and students' learning outcomes from implementing e-learning if it does not have an e-learning strategy which links *the pedagogy behind using technology* with *learning as a process*. Nygaard (2015:44) in his discussions of a university strategy for technology-enhanced learning presented eight statements about the use of technology, which he argued form the rudiments of a strategy for technology-enhanced university learning. As can be seen from the eight statements, they are much focused on the pedagogy behind the use of technology and learning as a process.

"1. *Technology should be used in such a way that students are inspired to construct and maintain meaning.*

2. *Technology should be used in such a way that students explicitly draw on their past experiences, because when doing so it becomes apparent to them how they can link new knowledge to their existing knowledge.*

3. *Technology should be used in such a way that it enables students to become aware of their new knowledge, skills and competencies, which arise from using technology-enhanced activities.*

4. *Technology should be used in such a way that it enables students to doubt and question their own assumptions, to invite them to further reflect on the use of their knowledge, skills and competencies.*

5. *Technology should be used in such a way that students are required to interact with other students, with cases, and with practice.*

6. *Technology should be used in such a way that it opens up for both engagement and flexibility over time, as student learning is an ongoing process.*

7. *Technology should be used in such a way that the students get immediate feedback on their learning outcomes and their progress as learners.*

8. *Technology should be used in such a way that it enables and/or requires students to interact with a large variety of other students.*"

It becomes apparent from these eight statements that the choice of e-learning has much more to do with learning and pedagogy than with technology. There are so many different technologies available, and picking the right one is not the key issue. It is from discussing technology as pedagogical practice that the university makes the right decisions about investment in and implementation of e-learning.

2. the culture of teaching and learning at the university

Second, the way that teaching and learning takes place at the university as an institutionalised practice is important for the effect of e-learning. This is because the institutionalised practices of teaching and learning lead to a certain kind of student (and staff) culture. E-learning will not be a success if it is in conflict with the existing teaching and learning culture. Technology will not do the trick alone if the existing culture is driven by didactic teaching and teacher-centric lecturing. Therefore, it is important to discuss how linking *the pedagogy behind using technology* with *learning as a process* will enable a certain type of teaching and learning culture to emerge over time. Löfvall and Nygaard (2012) compiled the results of an empirical study of the student culture at Copenhagen Business School and they introduced a model with four types of student culture: 1) students as pupils; 2) students as customers; 3) students as partners; 4) students as employees. Let us take a brief look at those four types of student culture. While reading on, think of the dominant student culture at your university.

A culture of pupils

Students as pupils perceive the university as school. They wait to be instructed by teachers who have designed the curriculum and decided which subjects are relevant to teach. When those students talk about university, they focus mainly on the role of the teacher, the syllabus, and the exam. Such students will engage in highly structured e-learning activities based on a teacher-driven instructional design. One of the main challenges to universities is that if they pick e-learning systems which are highly modularised and support this kind of student culture, they are in danger of reproducing a culture where students remain as pupils in school and do not take responsibility for their own learning process. A key question to ask is of course: *What proportion of your students perceives university as a school and therefore acts like pupils?* But an even more important question to ask is: *What proportion of your teachers perceive themselves* as domain experts and therefore practice mainly didactic teaching through teacher-centric lecturing?

A culture of customers

Students as customers perceive the university as a commoditised market place. They want value for money, meaning the best possible education. They think of the university as the place to go to get knowledge that will increase their future opportunities on the job market. When these students talk about the university, they focus mainly on the perceived quality of the deliveries: teachers, educational materials, work spaces, classrooms, canteen, gym, sports club, etc. Everything that you would evaluate as a customer is taken into account. Such students engage in highly structured e-learning activities based on teacher-driven instructional design, if they are professionally designed and live up to the expectations of the customer. One of the main challenges to universities is that if they commoditise their beautifully designed e-learning packages they are in the danger of branding their university as an over-the-counter provider of standardised e-learning material.

Within the culture of students as customers, the university conducts surveys on student satisfaction. In the U.S.A., we have the National Survey of Student Engagement (NSSE) and the Student Satisfaction Inventory (SSI) as leading surveys. In the UK, we have the National Student Satisfaction Survey and the Postgraduate Taught Experience Survey as leading surveys. On top of that most universities make their own standardised course, module, and program evaluations.

A key question to ask is of course: *What proportion of your students perceives university as a commoditised market place and therefore acts like customers?* But an even more important question to ask is: *What proportion of your teachers perceive themselves as domain experts who have to deliver prescribed content to commoditised modules?*

A culture of partners

Students as partners perceive the university as a platform for academic engagement and professional partnerships. They find that they learn through their personal use of the possible offerings that are available at the university. They see teachers, modules, resources, e-learning systems, etc. as only a part of what drives their learning. They believe that learning comes from personal engagement. They seek partnership relations and believe they can help create an integrative study culture by engaging in curricular and extracurricular activities. In their view, the university is a collective of like-minded students and staff rather than a school with expert teachers. When those students talk about university, they focus mainly on how the offerings that are available at the university fit or misfit the development of their own professional practice. Such students will engage in e-learning activities if they are considered to support their transition from university students to future professional practitioners. One of the main challenges to universities is that the future professional practices of their students are multiple, and therefore it may be difficult to design e-learning activities that appeal to all students.

Nygaard *et al.* (2008) found that inviting students to an e-learning platform did not by itself lead to enhanced online activities and improved learning. But when students were given specific roles as partners in collaborative work processes taking place in a blended learning environment, regulated by techniques such as collective feedback and peer-grading, the activity rate increased noticeably and student learning improved.

A key question to ask is of course: *What proportion of your students perceives university as a platform for academic engagement and professional partnerships and therefore acts like partners?* But an even more important question to ask is: *What proportion of your teachers perceives themselves as learning partners who have the main role of facilitating student engagement?*

A culture of employees

Students as employees perceive the university as a workplace where knowledge is created and shared. They define their own role as employees, and they invest in nurturing a workplace feeling and sense of community among fellow students and faculty. Studying at the university is a full-time job and not something you do just because you have to get a job once you have graduated. They invest their time in curricular and extracurricular activities organising and developing relationships that improve learning for themselves and fellow students. When those students talk about university, they focus mainly on how much they feel a part of university- and campus life. Such students will engage in e-learning activities if they support their everyday life as a student by, for example, tying together the academic studies with the social engagement at the workplace. One of the main challenges to universities is that the social engagement and workplace practices of their students are so varied and run across the different courses, modules, and programmes, and therefore it may be difficult to design e-learning activities that mirror the totality of the university as a workplace. It may be that the university then ends up having different e-learning systems for different types of curricular and extracurricular activities.

Andrews *et al.* (2013) showed how their work with student partnerships in nursing created a sense of workplace feel in university. This came about by students and staff participating in the setting of ground rules to identify accepted levels of behaviour, and by having students and staff recognise that learning is a two-way process where all are co-producers of knowledge and learning. Phillips *et al.* (2013) showed how students were engaged in their studies by combining performance practice with theory, thereby allowing students to train as performative practitioners. This was followed up with student placements, where they worked outside university to enhance their workplace skills and further develop as reflective practitioners. Newton (2015) showed how technology-enhanced learning can pave the way to a new performative teaching and learning culture. A key question to ask is of course: *What proportion of your students perceives university as a workplace and therefore acts like employees?* But an even more important question to ask is: *What proportion of your teachers perceives themselves as equal colleagues to students with the main role of engaging in students' knowledge creation and knowledge sharing?*

3. the role of faculty at the university

The student culture discussed above does not come out of nothing. It is shaped and further institutionalised by faculty when they design curricula and interact with students and technology. The role of faculty, we shall argue, is more important for the success of e-learning than technology itself.

Warmelink *et al.* (2012) reported from a decade of developing computer games for university students and came to the conclusion that games themselves are not sufficient to guarantee learning. Teachers need to support the process of reflection and theory building based on the gaming experience. Hardy and Totman (2012) showed how teachers' role changed when using an online simulation game to teach politics. During the four stages of their simulation game, the teachers' role changed according to Grow's (1991:129–136, cf. Hardy & Totman, 2012:192–193) four-stage model:

1. Student is dependent. Teacher is a coach/authority. The basic classroom situation of giving information and testing its retention. Rote learning and drilling.

2. Student is interested. Teacher is motivator/guide. A more inspiring lecture approach with guided discussion.

3. Student is involved. Teacher is a facilitator. Teacher has a more equal role in discussion. Group projects can take place with limited autonomy.

4. Student is self-directive. Teacher is a consultant/delegator. Independent research and autonomous group projects are viable.

Lenstrup (2013) showed how students became more engaged and motivated through the use of social-media learning environments. She argued that, with the adoption of social-media learning environments, new openings and challenges arose both for students and teachers, changing the role of the teacher from the traditional expert deciding the curriculum to one of a facilitator, supervisor or sparring partner for the students.

4. the use of technology, materials, and resources at the university

The use of technology, materials and resources is important for the result of e-learning activities. Gartmeier *et al.* (2015) measured the effects of e-learning featuring contrastive video cases and role-play including video feedback. They found that such use of e-learning helped improve students' communication competence, knowledge and cognitive ability in relation to a control group of students. DePew *et al.* (2015) showed how student learning is enhanced in nursing education by applying ApprenNet, which uses a three-phased learning model integrating video watching and self-recording (learning by doing), peer-feedback (learning from peers), and expert response (learning from experts). Hager (2013) showed how universities can use ePortfolios as a driver for the transformation from didactic teaching to interdisciplinary communities of learning, where students are supported in their development of twenty-first-century skills such as creativity and collaboration.

As we show in the chapters of the book, technology may be used in a variety of ways and so may the materials and resources made available to students. It is exactly what Nygaard's typology of e-learning 1.0, 2.0, and 3.0 reminds us. Technology may be used as a repository for materials and resources, which are then distributed to students online (e-learning 1.0). Technology may also be used as a forum for dialogue and exchange of information (e-learning 2.0). Finally, technology may be used as a platform for co-creating new knowledge (e-learning 3.0). Thinking of the university's e-learning strategy, as touched upon above, you can imagine what difference it will make for the e-learning activities and also investments in teaching and learning technology, if the university is clear about its e-learning strategy. At the same time, the e-learning strategy will have an effect on the teacher and student culture whether e-learning is used for distribution, dialogue, or co-creation of new knowledge. We are not the only ones discussing the effect of our uses of technology, materials, and resources on student engagement and learning.

We hope that we have succeeded in stating the important message that it is imperative to think about as diverse aspects as politics, people, and practices when considering the use of e-learning in university education. E-learning calls for an investment in technology, but what really drives e-learning to its success is the pedagogical practice underlying its implementation.

In this book: chapter by chapter

Following this introductory chapter, we present nine chapters all focusing on the pedagogy of e-learning in the light of e-learning 1.0, 2.0, and 3.0.

Chapter 2, *E-learning as a strategy for improving university students' learning outcomes*, is written by Claus Nygaard. He discusses the contributions of three different learning theories (behaviourist theory of learning, cognitive theory of learning, and social theory of learning) and links them to the typology of e-learning 1.0 (distribution), 2.0 (dialogue), 3.0 (construction) as we briefly introduced above. His main argument is that our choice of e-learning technology should be informed by our theoretical understanding of learning. This is so because the "e" in itself does not lead to learning. Should we improve students learning outcomes using e-learning, our strategy of using e-learning technologies has to be motivated by learning theory. The most important lesson from his chapter is that when you design curricula for e-learning there are three important questions which have to guide your work: 1) how do you perceive learning? 2) how do you perceive e-learning? 3) how do you perceive curriculum? Those three questions form the basis of your e-learning strategy and will help you design a curriculum using e-learning which improves students' learning outcomes. His chapter is an inspiring read, because it makes us reflect on the theoretical underpinnings of our choice of e-learning, technology and thus helps us make well considered decisions of how to design a curriculum for e-learning. Reading Claus' chapter, you will: 1) be presented with a central typology for e-learning, which distinguishes between e-learning 1.0, 2.0, and 3.0; 2) be introduced to learning theory and discussions of how different approaches to learning may have implications for your understanding of students' learning outcomes; 3) be invited to reflect on your own curriculum design, when using e-learning, to improve students' learning outcomes.

Chapter 3, *Using a peer-centred online learning platform to support students' academic-professional transition*, is written by Willie McGuire and Olan Harrington. They focus on an *alumni* project called Teaching-Jobs which focuses on an attempt to shift students from their current 2.0 state in Nygaard's typology to a condition closer to the construction level descriptive of the 3.0 state. This is particularly evident in one of the key aims of the project which was to create a self-sustaining support model for future *alumni* using peer mentoring to create student ownership of the resource and its future iterations. Their chapter addresses a current issue in the transition from initial teacher qualified status to fully qualified status. The authors conduct a literature review using two case studies to highlight two key aims: the need to develop an evidence-based rationale for the use of a blended learning constructivist pedagogy in supporting this transition and also the enhancement of subject specific knowledge essential to the transition. One of the key lessons echoes the words of Mick Jagger: *"You can't always get what you want,"* as the authors found that there was a considerable gap between their expectations of how students might use the e-learning resource and the reality of its deployment. Reading Willie's and Olan's chapter, you may take away three insights: 1) the reasons why they created the peer-centred online learning platform to support students' academic-professional transition; 2) two key modes of support: dialogue with peers and access to the online support materials; 3) learn about their attempts to create a self-perpetuating system, by which they mean a resource, which once established, would then be controlled exclusively by alumni for alumni.

Chapter 4, *The effectiveness of e-learning in Business Communication at the University of Johannesburg? What students say!*, is written by Magas Pather. He questions whether e-learning is fit for the purpose of teaching Business Communication where students feel that contact time is vital in acquiring Oral presentation skills and to stimulate an esprit de corps. E-learning in South Africa also faces challenges which hamper its implementation. These barriers are not insoluble and, in the near future, part of the Business Communication curriculum will be presented online. The chapter therefore concludes that a hybrid learning model is what is envisaged as the new platform for teaching and learning Business Communication, which promotes e-learning 3.0 (construction), where both teacher and lecturer participate collaboratively in the online environment. Hopefully, this implementation will lead to the creation of new knowledge which will ensure a seamless transition from campus to cyberspace. Reading Magas' chapter, you will gain an awareness of: 1) e-learning for Business Communication from an African perspective; 2) e-learning as a pedagogical and practical tool for Business Communication; 3) students' perceptions of the effectiveness of e-learning for the Business Communication course.

Chapter 5, *Using Wordpress, Canvas LMS, Dropbox and Facebook to enhance students' online engagement in postgraduate education*, is written by Anne Hørsted. She focuses on how a group of teachers in a postgraduate training program has changed their use of technological platforms over a period of three years and how those changes have affected students' online engagement. Instead of going into technical details, she presents the technological choices of the teachers and reflects their choices in relation to the typology of e-learning 1.0, 2.0, and 3.0. Her main argument is that it is important that we as teachers take the time to discuss the use of scenarios of e-learning before a technological platform is used. Had the teachers at the program Camp Future given themselves time to discuss

Chapter 1

the use of scenarios in a pedagogical and technical perspective with former and current students, they most likely would not have changed technological platforms three times in three years. Reading Anne's chapter, you will: 1) get an introduction to a postgraduate training program, which actively links unemployed university graduates with private businesses and leads to the creation of jobs; 2) hear about the experiences with the use of different technological platforms in the attempt to enhance student engagement; and 3) reflect on strengths and weaknesses of using different e-learning technologies seen in the light of the typology of e-learning 1.0, 2.0, and 3.0.

Chapter 6, *Using e-learning to improve the student experience of lectures*, is written by Rhiannon Evans. She focusses on the way automated lecture recording in lecture theatres has affected student attendance and engagement and suggests one possible e-learning solution to this problem. Her main argument is that the 'one-size-fits-all' solution of institutional lecture recording has resulted in low student engagement and that these badly produced recordings are not utilized by the majority of the class. A more customized solution is to abandon live performances and to pre-record video lectures. This also allows for a more segmented presentation of material in shorter 'chunks' (making e-learning 1.0 more attractive). Students are then asked to complete tasks in response to material in the short recordings (e-learning 2.0), and ultimately to construct their own research project and a version of the presentation which has been modelled to them (moving towards e-learning 3.0). The most important lesson in her chapter is that e-learning tools as an add-on to traditional teaching do not automatically improve learning for students. Thought should be given to how best to present material and how much material actually needs to be presented. Her chapter should inspire other teachers by showing them how to make relatively small changes to content delivery, which are appropriate to their own students' context and can transform student engagement and assessment. Reading Rhiannon's chapter, you may gain the following three insights: 1) the potential gains and losses of theatre-recorded lectures; 2) the means to provide successful pre-recorded material for students; 3) the ways in which pre-recording provides a model for student adoption of e-learning technologies and also allows for customisation of the curriculum.

Chapter 7, *The E-CIL Framework: An Instructional Practice for*

Promoting Student Engagement with Content, the Instructor, and Other Learners in Online Courses, is written by Malinda Hoskins Lloyd. She focuses on how the E-CIL Framework can be used to foster higher education students' learning. The instructional framework was designed to create an online learning environment during which higher education students engage with three key components in online courses: the content, the instructor, and co-learners. The main argument of her chapter is that students need to interact with each of these components in courses with the aim of positively affecting students' online experiences and, ultimately, their academic achievement. The most important lesson of the chapter is that e-learning tools such as Nearpod, Flipgrid, and Padlet (or other current tools) can be utilized to foster interactions between students and the content they are learning, the instructor of the course, and with other learners also taking the course. She hopes her chapter is an inspiring read for other educators because the information regarding the E-CIL Framework is applicable to any course and to multiple disciplines. In addition, although this framework was designed for online courses, it may also be implemented as a means of enhancing face-to-face and blended courses. Reading Malinda's chapter, you may learn how: 1) they increase students' engagement with content, with the instructor, and with co-learners; 2) they increase students' sense of belonging to a learning community in an online course; 3) a course can be effectively designed with weekly guidelines of specific components to be included.

Chapter 8, *Experiential Learning in Premedical Education: Enhancing Students' Experience through e-Learning,* is written by Reya Saliba and Rachid Bendriss. They focus on the experience of teachers and learners through the design and implementation of an experiential learning project aimed at introducing students to a community of practice. Immersed in this community, students are inspired to share knowledge. Their main argument is that experiential learning provides a unique opportunity to bridge the gap between theoretical concepts delivered through traditional methods and real-world inspiration facilitated through e-learning and experienced in real-life settings. The most important lesson in their chapter is the vital role experiential learning plays within a blended curriculum to complement e-learning methods with face-to-face application of concepts in the real world. Their chapter is an inspiring read because it shares an innovative andragogic practice with hands-on teaching steps to conceptualize and implement experiential learning in a higher education course curriculum. Using e-learning to facilitate instruction, the chapter provides practical tools that incorporate information literacy in an advanced English communication course while challenging learners to critically reflect on their experiential learning within a community of practice. Reading Reya's and Rachid's chapter you may: 1) learn how to design an Experiential Learning project as an integral component of a university blended course; 2) understand the role of e-learning in facilitating knowledge gain and effective communication between instructors and students; 3) gain insight into the opportunities and challenges that faculty and students encounter while engaging in an e-learning environment.

Chapter 9, *Ten e-learning tools to support students' problem-based collaborative work*, is written by Flemming Meier and Claus Nygaard. They discuss how e-learning may be used to support problem-based collaborative work. By introducing e-learning into the pedagogical debate of problem-based collaborative work, they aim to show what e-learning tools and practices are available to support problem-based collaborative work. Their chapter is meant to raise an awareness of some of the positive consequences of linking together e-learning technology with learning theory. They believe that faculty members and those being responsible for implementing e-learning technologies may use their chapter to frame a wider debate on the choice and use of e-learning technology. They see their chapter as being introductory rather than exhaustive. They cover problem-based collaborative work, learning theory and e-learning technologies, but they do so to raise awareness of the ways in which they are possibly linked, not to mirror a text-book on any of these issues. Reading Flemming's and Claus's chapter you may: 1) gain an understanding of problem-based collaborative work as a pedagogical practice; 2) familiarise yourself with social learning theory and its understanding of ways in which students learn; 3) see examples of how e-learning may support problem-based collaborative work when being based on social learning theory.

Chapter 10, *Using e-learning to supervise students' project work in higher education: some pedagogical requirements*, is written by Flemming Meier. He discusses the pedagogical requirements linked to the selection and application of e-learning. Using e-learning in relation to supervision of students' project work is relevant, Flemming argues, because more and more universities face demands to economise on the critical face-to-face time used by teachers to supervise students. He uses the typology of e-learning 1.0, 2.0, and 3.0 (see Nygaard, in this volume) to apply a specific structure to his reflections about ways in which technologies might help to: mediate distribution of texts and other resources (e-learning 1.0); mediate spaces for conversation and dialogue (e-learning 2.0); and, mediate workspaces in which students produce (construct) parts and pieces that go into projects (e-learning 3.0). Reading Flemming's chapter, you may gain: 1) knowledge of the pedagogy related to project work and supervision, and 2) inspiration as to how digital technologies may be integrated into supervision processes.

About the Authors

Malinda Hoskins Lloyd, Ph.D., is Associate Professor at Tennessee Technological University in the Department of Curriculum & Instruction in Cookeville, Tennessee, USA. She may be contacted at the following e-mail: MLloyd@tntech.edu

Willie McGuire is a Senior Lecturer in the School of Education at the University of Glasgow and a Senior Fellow of the Higher Education Academy; Director of the MEd (Professional Practice) degree and Director of the Scottish Unit for Assessment Literacy Support (SULAS). He can be contacted on this e-mail: william.mcguire@glasgow.ac.uk

Reya Saliba is the Learning and Student Outreach Librarian at Weill Cornell Medicine-Qatar. She can be contacted at this e-mail: res2024@qatar-med.cornell.edu.

Rachid Bendriss is an Associate Professor of English as a Second Language and Assistant Dean for Student Recruitment, Outreach, and Foundation Programs at Weill Cornell Medicine-Qatar. He can be contacted at this e-mail: rab2029@qatar-med.cornell.edu.

Rhiannon Evans is Senior Lecturer in Classics and Ancient History at La Trobe University, Melbourne, Australia. She can be contacted at this e-mail: r.evans@latrobe.edu.au

Flemming Meier is Associate Professor at Aarhus University, Denmark. He can be contacted at this e-mail: meier@edu.au.dk

Professor Dr. Claus Nygaard is Executive Director of the Institute of Learning in Higher Education and Executive Director of cph:learning. He can be contacted at this e-mail: info@lihe.info

Bibliography

Alammary, A., Sheard, J., & Carbone, A. (2014). Blended learning in Higher Education: Three different designs. *Australasian Journal of Educational Technology*, 30(4), 440–454. doi:10.14742/ajet.693

Andrews, A., Jeffries, J., & St. Aubyn, B. (2013). By Appointment to Birmingham City University Students: Promoting Student Engagement through Partnership Working. In Nygaard, C., Brand, S., Bartholomew, P., & Millard, L. (Eds.), *Student Engagement. Identity, Motivation and Community*. Oxfordshire, UK: Libri Publishing Ltd., 199–212.

Carliner, S. (2004). *An overview of online learning*. Amherst, MA: Human Resource Development Press.

Davies, J., & Graff, M. (2005). Performance in e-learning: e-learning participation and student grades. *British Journal of Educational Technology*, 36(4), 657–663.

DePew, D. D., Cornelius, F. H., & Patton, C. (2015). Enhancing Student Learning in Online Nursing Education using ApprenNet Technology. In Branch, J., Bartholomew, P., & Nygaard, C. (Eds.), *Technology-Enhanced Learning in Higher Education*. Oxfordshire, UK: Libri Publishing Ltd., 211–232.

Garrison, D., & Kanuka, H. (2004). Blended Learning: Uncovering Its Transformative Potential in Higher Education. *Internet and Higher Education*, 7(2), 95–105.

Gartmeier, M., Bauer, J., Fischer, M., Hoppe-Seyler, T., Karsten, G., Kiessling, C., Möller, G., Wiesbeck, A., Prenzen, M. (2015). Fostering professional communication skills of future physicians and teachers: effects of e-learning with video cases and role-play. *Instructional Science*. 43(4), 443–462.

Graham, C. R., Woodfield, W., & Harrison, J. B. (2013). A framework for institutional adoption and implementation of blended learning in higher education. *The Internet and Higher Education*, 18, 4–14.

Hager, L. L. (2013). ePortfolios and the Twenty-first Century: Learning in Higher Education. In C. Nygaard, J. Branch, & C. Holtham (Eds.),

Learning in Higher Education – contemporary standpoints. Oxfordshire, UK: Libri Publishing Ltd., 151–166.

Hardy, M. & Totman, S. (2012). From Dictatorship to Democracy: Simulating the Politics of the Middle East. In Nygaard, C., Courtney, N., & Leigh, E (Eds.), *Simulations, Games and Role Play in University Education.* Oxfordshire, UK: Libri Publishing Ltd., 189–206.

Harvey, L. (2000). New realities: the relationship between higher education and employment. *Tertiary Education and Management,* 6(1), 3–17.

Harvey, L., & Knight, P. T. (1996). *Transforming Higher Education.* Bristol: Taylor and Francis for Open University Press.

Helms, S. A. (2012). Blended/hybrid courses: a review of the literature and recommendations for instructional designers and educators. *Interactive Learning Environments,* 22(6), 804–810.

Hiltz, S. R., & Turoff, M. (2005). Education goes digital: The evolution of online learning and the revolution in higher education. *Communications of the ACM,* 48(10), 59–64.

Hrastinski, S. (2008). Asynchronous and synchronous e-learning. *Educause Quarterly,* 4(1), 51–55.

Hugenholtz, N. I. R., de Croon, E. M., Smits, P. B., van Dijk, F. J. H., & Nieuwenhuijsen, K. (2008). Effectiveness of e-learning in continuing medical education for occupational physicians. *Occupational Medicine,* 58(5), 370–372.

Jarvis, P., Holford, J., & Griffin, C. (1998). *The Theory and Practice of Learning.* London: Kogan Page.

Keegan, D. (1996). *Foundations of distance education.* London: Routledge.

Keller, J. M., & Suzuki, K. (2004). Learner motivation and e-learning design: A multinationally validated process. *Journal of Educational Media,* 29(3), 229–239.

Kim K.-J., & Frick, T. W. (2011). Changes in Student Motivation during Online Learning. *Journal of Educational Computing Research,* 44(1), 1–23.

Lenstrup, C. (2013). Social-media Learning Environments. In Nygaard, C., Branch, J., & Holtham, C. (Eds.), *Learning in Higher Education – contemporary standpoints.* Oxfordshire, UK: Libri Publishing Ltd., 29–44.

Löfvall, S., & Nygaard, C. (2012). Interrelationships between student culture, teaching and learning in higher education. In Nygaard, C., Branch, J., & Holtham, C. (Eds.), *Learning in Higher Education – contemporary standpoints.* Oxfordshire, UK: Libri Publishing Ltd., 127–150.

Luo, N., Zhang, M., & Qi, D. (2017). Effects of different interactions on students' sense of community in e-learning environment. *Computers & Education,* 115(1), 153–160.

McConnell, D. (2000). *Implementing computer supported cooperative learning.* London: Kogan Page Limited.

Moore, M. G., & Kearsley, G. (2011). *Distance education: A systems view of online learning.* California: Cengage Learning.

Noesgaard, S. S., & Ørngreen, R. (2015). The Effectiveness of E-Learning: An Explorative and Integrative Review of the Definitions, Methodologies and Factors that Promote e-Learning Effectiveness. *The Electronic Journal of e-Learning,* 14(4), 278–290.

Newton, D. (2015). Using technology-enhanced learning to pave the way to a new performative teaching and learning culture. In Branch, J., Bartholomew, P., & Nygaard, C. (Eds.), *Technology Enhanced Learning in Higher Education.* Oxfordshire, UK: Libri Publishing Ltd., 51–78.

Nygaard, C. (2015). Rudiments of a Strategy for Technology Enhanced University Learning. In Nygaard, C., Branch, J., & Bartholomew, P. (Eds.), *Technology Enhanced Learning in Higher Education.* Oxfordshire, UK: Libri Publishing Ltd., 31–49.

Nygaard, C. (2015). Rudiments of a Strategy for Technology Enhanced University Learning. In Nygaard, C., Branch, J., & Bartholomew, P. (Eds.), *Technology Enhanced Learning in Higher Education.* Oxfordshire, UK: Libri Publishing Ltd., 31–50.

Nygaard, C., Holtham, C., & Courtney, N. (2009). Learning Outcomes – Politics, Religion or Improvement? In Nygaard, C., Holtham, C., & Courtney, N. (Eds.), *Improving Students' Learning Outcomes.* Copenhagen: Copenhagen Business School Press, 17–32.

Nygaard, C., Højlt, T., & Hermansen, M. (2008). Learning-Based Curriculum Development. *Higher Education,* 55(1), 33–50.

Phillips, H., Craig, T., & Phillips, C. (2013). Engaging Students as Practitioners through Experiential Learning. In Nygaard, C., Brand, S., Bartholomew, P., & Millard, L. (Eds.), *Student Engagement. Identity, Motivation and Community.* Oxfordshire, UK: Libri Publishing Ltd., 251–270.

Pilkington, R. M., & Walker, S. A (2003). Facilitating debate in networked learning: Reflecting on online synchronous discussion in higher education, *Instructional Science,* 31(1), 41–63.

Rassow, L. C. (1998). Assessing the Under Graduate International Business Major. *Journal of Studies in International Education,* 2(1), 59–80.

Rhode, J. F. (2009). Interaction equivalency in self-paced online learning environments: an exploration of learner preferences. *The International Review of Research in Open and Distance Learning,* 10(1), 13–24.

Ross B., & Gage, K. (2006). Global Perspectives on Blending Learning: Insight from WebCT and Our Customers in Higher Education. In Bonk, C. J., &

Graham, C. R. (Eds.), *The Handbook of Blended Learning: Global Perspectives, Local Designs*. San Francisco: Wiley, 306–335.

Russell, T. L. (1999). *The No Significant Difference Phenomenon*. Raleigh, NC: North Carolina State University.

Shachar, M., & Neumann, Y. (2010). Twenty years of research on the academic performance differences between traditional and distance learning: Summative meta-analysis and trend examination. *Journal of Online Learning and Teaching*, 6(2), 318–334.

Simonson, M., Smaldino, S., & Zvacek, S. M. (Eds.) (2015). *Teaching and learning at a distance: Foundations of distance education*. North Carolina: IAP.

Warmelink, H., Harteveld, C., Bekebrede, G., & Meijer, S. (2012). Lessons learnt from a decade of game development for higher education in Delft. In Nygaard, C., Courtney, N., & Leigh, E. (Eds.). *Simulations, Games and Role Play in University Education*. Oxfordshire, UK. Libri Publishing Ltd.

Chapter 2
E-learning as a strategy for improving university students' learning outcomes

Claus Nygaard

Introduction

With this chapter, I contribute to the book *E-learning 1.0, 2.0, and 3.0 in Higher Education* as I discuss ways in which e-learning can be used as a strategy for improving university students' learning outcomes. In the chapter, I connect three important aspects of university education: 1) e-learning, 2) learning outcomes, and 3) curriculum design. My aim is to inspire a discussion of ways in which we can use e-learning to improve students' learning outcomes. It is a conceptual chapter. This means that I do not report from a practical curriculum design example, where e-learning technologies were used. Instead, I suggest a typology for e-learning which can be used to reflect on your own curriculum design and e-learning practices. Reading the chapter, you will:

1. be presented with a central typology for e-learning, which distinguishes between e-learning 1.0, 2.0 and 3.0;

2. be introduced to learning theory and discussions of how different approaches to learning may have implications for your understanding of students' learning outcomes.

3. be invited to reflect on your own curriculum design, when using e-learning to improve students' learning outcomes.

The chapter has three sections. In the first section, I present a central typology of e-learning, distinguishing between e-learning 1.0, 2.0, and 3.0. This typology guides my further discussion of both learning outcomes and curriculum design. In the second section, I conceptualise learning and learning outcomes. I do so to present a theoretical terminology, which can guide the discussion of ways in which learning outcomes may be improved. In the third section I present a central model for designing the e-learning curriculum, which may inspire to use e-learning in different ways to improve university students' learning outcomes.

Section 1: A typology for e-learning

The research on e-learning has been extensive over the past 20+ years. One of the common conceptualisations of e-learning has distinguished between synchronous and asynchronous learning activities. Here the idea has been to show how e-learning allows students to use technology to work asynchronously, yet at the same time be devoted to the same learning journey (Hrastinski, 2008). E-learning has also been linked to discussions of blended learning, that is the pedagogical mix between traditional educational settings (classrooms, lecture halls, libraries, etc.) and technological settings (Garrison & Kanuka, 2004; Helms, 2012). In my work (Nygaard 2015) I have conceptualised technology-enhanced learning activities due to the nature of the type of *relational practice* facilitated by the technology itself. By relational practice I mean the practice of students occurring as a consequence of the type of technology chosen. The argument is that the student and the technology forms a relation which feeds a certain type of practice. The relational practice is in other words the practice that occurs as a result of the relation between student and technology. Linking that to e-learning, I will distinguish between three types of relational practice occurring from specific uses of e-learning technology: 1) distribution; 2) dialogue; and 3) construction (Figure 1).

	E-learning typologies		
	1.0: Distribution	**2.0: Dialogue**	**3.0: Construction**
Use of e-learning	E-learning is used to distribute information to students.	E-learning is used to facilitate a dialogue between students (and teachers and other relevant peers).	E-learning is used to enable construction of new knowledge or innovation of new processes/products.
Type of relational practice	Students become users who access information and learning materials.	Students become learning partners who engage in learning dialogues.	Students become learning innovators who constructs new knowledge.

Figure 1: A typology for e-learning.

Under 'Distribution' I refer to situations where a sender sends a message to a recipient. In education, it is typically the teacher or the administrator who distributes information to students. Usually, distribution leads to assimilative learning within existing cognitive structures, because students are provided with information, which is perceived to support their ongoing learning journey. Teachers and administrators choose to distribute content which is perceived as needed by students in the context of their current studies. It may be the distribution of modularised content. Often, when teachers talk about programmed learning, learning progression or/and scaffolded learning, they refer to situations, where the learning content is pre-planned and may be distributed according to a defined schedule. Summing up, the use of technology to distribute information forms a relational practice where students become users who access information and learning materials.

Under 'Dialogue' I refer to situations where two parties actively communicate. In education, it is typically students who engage in learning dialogues with each other, and/or with teachers. Usually, the dialogue is linked to a pre-defined learning objective and thus leads to assimilative learning. This is the case when the dialogue is structured around existing cognitive structures, adding to what is already known as domain knowledge. This is most often the case when teachers wish students to strengthen their domain knowledge and demonstrate theories-in-use. Summing up, the use of technology to facilitate dialogue forms a relational practice where students become learning partners who engage in learning dialogues.

Under 'Construction' I refer to situations where one or more parties construct knowledge together. In education, it is typically students who are given a task by teachers to construct new knowledge. Construction has the built-in requirement that students work to be innovative in the sense that they construct new knowledge. Usually, construction creates accommodative learning, because the requirement for innovation leads students to actively rearrange existing cognitive structures as they challenge their own presuppositions and create new knowledge. Summing up, the use of technology to facilitate construction forms a relational practice where students become learning innovators who construct new knowledge.

Having worked as a learning consultant at Copenhagen Business School and the IT-University in Copenhagen, Denmark over a period of 18 years, I have participated in a large number of technology-enhanced curriculum design projects. I have also supervised teachers who use e-learning as an integrated component in their curriculum. It is my experience that when working with e-learning as a strategy for improving students' learning outcomes, it is beneficial to distinguish between the relational practice stemming from both faculty's and students' understanding of e-learning. This is significant, because it enables a much more concrete dialogue about both learning goals and expected practices. Often, I have experienced that the university LMS (Learning Management System) has been used as a standard CMS (Content Management System), where faculty and admin uploaded reading lists, course descriptions, assignments, and PowerPoint slides for students to download. Although the vision has been to facilitate learning through the use of e-learning, the main result has been distribution of content. This has not been because faculty and students wanted it this way, but because the implicit use of technology didn't facilitate the formation of a non-distributional relational practice. It is my belief that adding the typology of e-learning 1.0 (distribution), 2.0 (dialogue), and 3.0 (construction), encourages a much more tangible and clear discussion of the use of e-learning in university education. It is also possible to link that discussion to learning outcomes and curriculum design.

With that said, let me look further into learning theory and learning outcomes. This is important, because without a clear understanding of the effects of our conceptualisation of learning it becomes unclear at best – and meaningless at worst – to discuss learning outcomes. Because, how can we know which learning outcomes to aspire for, if we don't know what learning is? And how can we design for e-learning if we don't know what learning is?

Section 2: Learning and learning outcomes

Often when working with e-learning we focus mainly on technology – what we could call the "e". This is an obvious choice, because our aim is to design ways in which technology can help improve learning. However, learning itself is a human process. Therefore, to understand the design and effect of the "e", a clear understanding of learning as a human process is needed. It is humans who learn, not machines. And a deeper understanding of human learning allows us to also understand how adding the "e" to learning may affect the process of human learning. In other words, by reflecting on learning theory we become capable of making wiser decisions regarding e-learning. I therefore use this section 2 of the chapter to discuss learning theory in more detail.

Ask the question: *"What is learning?"*, and you may be surprised by the many answers and definitions available. It appears that we lack a common definition of learning. At first it may appear to be a weakness that one cannot get a concrete answer to such a concrete question. Looking further into various definitions of learning and their origins, it appears to be a strength that multiple definitions exist, because it gives us the opportunity to discuss and reflect on learning from different positions. It also becomes apparent that we have multiple definitions of learning because researchers of learning come from different disciplines like biology, psychology, philosophy, and sociology, and they themselves therefore have different foci points and different understandings of human beings and the relation between human beings and their environment.

One stream of thought, which has had an immense effect on curriculum design and education in general is *Behavioural Learning theory (Behaviourism)*. This origins from the late 19th century and has governed the way in which many educationalists have thought about learning. Another stream of thought is *Cognitive Learning theory (Cognitivism)*. This origins from the 1950s and has helped educationalists to add human agency to the theory of learning. In the last half of the 20th Century, it made an impact on ways in which the learner was actively brought into the discussion of learning. A third and more recent stream of thought it *Social Learning theory (Community of Practice)*. Although it has just been around for a little more than 25 years, it has made a strong impact on the way in which education and learning is perceived today. In the next three subsections, I will briefly look into Behavioural Learning theory, Cognitive Learning theory, and Social Learning theory to reflect on their understandings of learning and discuss how they inspire us to work with learning outcomes in different ways. The motivation for this discussion is to give us more food for thought when we then look at ways in which we may design a curriculum using e-learning to improve students' learning outcomes. The subsections do not present a thorough walk-through of the three streams of thought. They are meant to guide the following discussion of curriculum design. I encourage you to dig deeper into the references, should you want to go beyond my short presentation.

Behavioural Learning theory

The stream of thought named Behavioural Learning theory builds on Behaviorism. It is mostly traced back to Thorndike (1898) who published his theory of *Law of Effect* stemming from his studies of cats. His argument was that behaviour which is followed by pleasant consequences is likely to be repeated, whereas behaviour which is followed by unpleasant consequences is likely to be stopped. If we pause here and think of the ways in which educationalists have designed curricula in schools, colleges and universities, where students are honoured with marks and grades, this may be seen as a way to reinforce a certain behaviour by adding pleasant consequences. The cats in Thorndike's studies, were rewarded with a fish, if they solved the puzzles in his puzzle box and then pressed the lever to escape. The students in our institutions are rewarded with high marks and good grades, if they solve the assignments in our courses by giving the correct answers. Building on Thorndike (1898, 1905), Watson (1913) coined the term Behaviorism in his article "Psychology as the behaviorist views it". He later described the purpose of psychology as: *"To predict, given the stimulus, what reaction will take place; or, given the reaction, state what the situation or stimulus is that has caused the reaction"* (Watson, 1930:11). Behaviorists were aware of the existence of cognitions and emotions, but they preferred not to study them, as they argued that only observable (i.e., external) behaviour could be objectively and scientifically measured. In an institutionalised context, we may find teachers arguing that, since students' cognitive processes are not observable, the focus has to be on the visible products of their thought processes, such as written assignments, oral presentations, etc.

Skinner (1936) introduced to Behaviorism the concept of operant conditioning, which he used to stress that the best way to understand behaviour is to look at the causes of an action and its consequences. Where Thorndike had studied cats in his puzzle box, Skinner studied rats in his Skinner Box. The principle was in reality the same. To test the effect of stimuli on the response of the animal. Skinner identified three types of operants (responses) to stimuli. 1) neutral operants, which were responses that neither increased nor decreased the probability of a behaviour being repeated; 2) reinforcing operants, which were responses from the environment which increased the probability of a behaviour being repeated. Such reinforcers could be both positive and negative; and 3) punishing operants, which were responses from the environment that decreased the probability of a behaviour being repeated. As one may have guessed, punishment naturally weakens behaviour. If we link that to our educational setting, we find teachers who reward or punish student behaviour in order to regulate the ways in which students engage and participate, and who also work to motivate students through assessment and evaluation of both processes and outcomes of student learning. Reflecting on the practices in our educational sectors, we find that a lot of what we take for granted about curriculum design and teaching and learning practices in fact builds on Behaviorism with the Law of Effect (Thorndike, 1898) and Stimuli-Response (Skinner, 1936). And we see examples of student assessment where learning is based on objectively observable changes in student behaviour (Crone *et al.*, 2007; Ervin *et al.*, 2001) all leading back to the idea that learning can be assessed by looking at behaviour.

Cognitive Learning theory

In the wake of Behavioural Learning theory came Cognitive Learning theory. It was somewhat natural to introduce cognitive processes and their importance for learning because the behaviouralists has chosen not to focus on the inner mind and feelings of the learner. Cognitive Learning theory was developed by cognitive psychologists who focused on the role of cognitive (mental) processes for learning. They discussed how students observe, categorise and form generalisations to make sense of the information provided. The argument is that the learner holds knowledge, skills and experiences which affect learning. Cognitive Learning theory sets the individual (the subject) in a learning environment (among objects). The main focus is on the capacity of the individual to learn. Thus, learning is principally seen as an individual matter. Piaget (1936) was one of the founding fathers of the movement, and he developed a stage theory of child cognitive development. His main argument was that child cognitive development happens through the use of schemas, where new experiences are related to existing schemas and adjusted to the world through a process of either assimilation or accommodation. Piaget (1936) saw cognitive development as a process occurring due to biological maturation and interaction with the environment. In his view, mind/brain and environment was in a dynamic interrelation. The mind/brain was the subject and the environment was the object. Cognitivists in other words argue that our brain is responsible for processing, organising and interpreting information and therefore is responsible for our learning. That learning results from internal mental activity rather than external stimuli (as was the main argument of Behaviourism).

Subscribing to Cognitive Learning theory, the role of the teacher is to make available to the student the right information within the theoretical domain studied and see to that the learning environment (as an objective realm) enables students to perform (learn). Leaving the responsibility for learning to the student – as long as the information and the learning environment are perceived to be suitable – curriculum design becomes a matter of designing specific ways in which information can be distributed to students (i.e. through lectures, books, or technology-enhanced techniques). Since learning is a cognitive process, and because what is learned is stored in either short-term or long-term memory, it becomes possible to assess students' learning (often measured as well-defined learning outcomes). Students can then be divided into groups of excellent students, good students or poor students. As I shall show later when I present a possible typology for technology-enhanced university learning, the focus on teacher-driven distribution of information to individual students engaged in cognitive learning processes seems to be dominant at universities.

As mentioned above, Piaget (1936) pointed out the processes of assimilation and accommodation. Assimilation is the process of using existing schemas to relate to new situations. It means that the learner understands new situations in the context of what is already known. The leaner tries to fit new situations into existing schemas. In education we encourage assimilation, when we ask students to repeat a certain method over and over again. Or design exercises or assignments where students have to fit empirical data or new observations into existing theories. To order new situations using theory they already know.

Accommodation is the process of changing existing schemas to fit new experiences. This is where new learning occurs in the sense that the learner develops alternative schemas that help them to understand the new situation at hand. In education we encourage accommodation, when we ask students to investigate, analyse, and synthesise in order to come up with new and to them hitherto unknown answers. Problem-based learning, inquiry based learning, and case based learning are some of the pedagogical practices which often leads to accommodation.

Although Piaget focused on child development, and not learning itself, his theory of schemes has been widely used by educationalists to account for learning. He is often referred for arguing that assimilation and accommodation require an active learner, because problem-solving skills must be discovered rather than taught (Piaget, 1958). This means that educationalists who support Piaget's views would argue for pedagogical practices that challenge students to work with active discovery. Because cognitive theory argues that humans process the information they receive, rather than responding to stimuli only, changes in behaviour are only an indicator of what goes on in the mind of the learner. Therefore, active discovery, problem solving, engaged learning, and the like, are fruitful techniques in education, as they become a mirror of students' actions, reflections, and thus learning. Bloom *et al.* (1956) came up with three taxonomies which enabled teachers to distinguish between different levels of student learning so-called classifications of learning objectives. One taxonomy for the cognitive domain, a second for the affective domain, and a third for the psychomotor domain. The taxonomy covering the cognitive domain differentiated between: 1) remembering, 2) comprehending, 3) applying, 4) analysing, 5) synthesising, and 6) evaluating. This taxonomy helps educators and students to formulate learning goals and assess learning.

As a consequence of the cognitivist movement the role of the teacher changed from that of direct tuition to the facilitation of learning. And it also became the teachers' role to help students plan and govern their own learning process. Where Behaviourism is an objectivist theory, Cognitivism is a constructivist theory meaning that there is no objective measurement of learning and that not all learners will learn the same although being present at the same possible learning situation. If we look at university curricula and the learning goals defined there, it is rather common to find the cognitive domain taxonomy from Bloom *et al.* (1956) as the key descriptor of learning outcomes.

Chapter 2

Social Learning theory

The stream of thought we call Social Learning theory is the most recent of the three perspectives. Social Learning theory studies how social relationships (social embeddedness) and communication (discourse) both contribute to peoples' understanding of situations (contexts/learning environments). This is slightly different from Cognitivism, where the argument was that people (the subject) are placed in a learning environment (the object). In Social Learning theory, people are not placed in an environment per se, they construct their environment. Therefore, there is not one such thing as a designed learning environment. Here the learning process is situated in an ever-changing context (they are embedded in ongoing social relations). McDermott (1999:15) wrote about context that: *"...context is not so much something into which someone is put, but an order of behavior of which one is a part"*. Seeing the learning context as an order of behaviour, rather than a fixed structure of objects, shifts the focus from the design or layout of the classroom or the design of the online platform to the ongoing relational processes between students and their peers, teachers and other key stakeholders in students' learning process. This is not to say that it is not the individual student who learns. Of course it is. But learning is to be perceived as a socially embedded process influenced by the individuals' position in what Granovetter (1992) called "ongoing systems of social relations". He defined embeddedness as: *"...the argument that the behaviour and institutions to be analyzed are so constrained by ongoing social relations that to construe them as independent is a grievous misunderstanding... Actors do not behave or decide as atoms outside a social context, nor do they adhere slavishly to a script written for them by the particular intersection of social categories that they happen to occupy. Their attempts at purposive action are instead embedded in concrete, ongoing systems of social relations."* (Granovetter, 1992:53–58). Social Learning theory is closely linked to the theory of Communities of Practice as it was presented by Lave and Wenger (1991). In their theory, they point out the relationship between practice, identity and learning. They see our behaviour as a product of the practices of the community in which we are legitimate members (embedded as Granovetter (1992) would have put it). This means that our learning goes hand in hand with our socially constructed identity as human beings. The idea that learning occurs as we reflect our own practices in the practices of others is not entirely new. Vygotsky (1978) had argued that learning of the child occurs through social interaction with a skilful teacher. And he came up with the term *More Knowledgeable Other* to explain the role of the teacher who guides the child through collaborative dialogue. With collaborative dialogue, he stressed the importance of seeing learning as an interrelated process during which both child and teacher have to engage. Following his theory, the teacher changes role from being instructor to become a role model. If we add the theory of Lave and Wenger (1991) to Vygotsky (1978), we can conclude that learners look for role models in the communities in which they are embedded. What drive human beings to learn are their urge to develop their own identity and belong to a community. Like Cognitivism, Social Learning theory is a constructivist theory seeing learning as a process where individuals construct new knowledge based on prior knowledge and past experience. Learning is embedded in a unique order of behaviour as each social situation in which the student takes part is new. Because the order of behaviour of students in higher education is regulated by as varied contextual elements (social situations) as curriculum, classrooms, online platforms, rules, norms, values, structures, etc. there is no best way to learn. Therefore, the learning environment is perceived in different way by different students (and teachers). Consequently, distribution of information or the design of learning environments will not lead to a particular type or level of learning.

Arguing within the realm of Social Learning theory the role of the teacher is to facilitate, so that students are encouraged to take part in ongoing systems of social relations of the education. Curriculum design then becomes a matter of designing a learning environment (a community of practice) where students can identify themselves with *More Knowledgeable Others* (may it be fellow students, teachers, or others) and thereby engage in their own identity projects (trying to become whom they dream of becoming). Because learning is a social process, it is not a good idea to assess students on their response to stimuli (how they solve fixed assignments). Assessment should assess how students engage in ongoing social relations, the methods they use to direct themselves, and their reflections of how they become whom they dream of becoming and how what they learn in the context of the university may be transferred to other contexts.

Chapter 2

The three learning theories in summary

Behavioral Learning theorists would argue that students learn (response) from listening to the teacher (stimuli). And they would also believe that all students would potentially learn the same from, say, the teacher lecturing. Most probably they would design the curriculum with a mix of lectures and exercises. It would be teacher-driven in the sense that the teacher was responsible for the inputs given to students, and also responsible for planning the work of the students. When students work, they would be perceived to learn what was expected of them (expected by teachers), which could then be assessed by teachers. All students' get the same stimuli. They respond in pre-programmed ways by solving a pre-designed assignment. They are assessed using a unified assessment method suitable for the exercise in question. And they are graded using a unified grading system.

Cognitive Learning theorists would argue that students learn based on their cognitive abilities (the mind/brain of the subject) and as a consequence of the learning environment in which they are placed (the object). And they believe that students would potentially learn the same if they had the same cognitive abilities. Most probably they too would design the curriculum with a mix of lectures and exercises. But they would be aware that one type of learning environment would appeal to students with certain cognitive abilities, whereas another type of learning environment would appeal to students with other cognitive abilities. Some students would prefer a teacher-driven learning environment, whereas other students would prefer a student-driven learning environment. Some students would prefer to work online, while other students would prefer to work face-to-face. So on and so forth. Students take part in pre-designed learning situations, which is expected to enhance their learning (or the learning of the good students, meaning the students with the right cognitive abilities). They respond in pre-programmed ways by solving a pre-designed assignment. They too are assessed using a unified assessment method suitable for the exercise in question. And they too are graded using a unified grading system.

Social Learning theorists would argue that students learn based on the ways in which they fit their own identity projects (whom they dream of becoming) to the order of behaviour in which they are embedded. And they believe that students would all learn something different from their studies even if they were exposed to exactly the same input (be it from a teacher lecturing, a film, a book, an e-learning portal, etc.). Most probably they would design the curriculum with a mix of lectures and exercises but add to that student-driven activities, which could be problem-oriented project work (Meier & Nygaard, 2009). Students take part in iterative learning situations, where they interpolate between what they do know and what they don't know in an ongoing social relationship with *More Knowledgeable Others*. The ways in which students direct themselves in this process is what affects their learning. They respond in thousands of different ways. Teachers would not know, and nor would students. They only know it when they see it. Therefore, students are assessed using mixed assessment methods. Such assessment methods have to be capable of assessing how students engage in ongoing social relations. They also have to assess the methods students use to direct themselves. Assessment has to also look at students own reflections of how they become whom they dream of becoming, and how what they learn, in the context of the university, may be transferred to other contexts. All that may well be graded using a unified grading system.

To sum up the key aspects of the three learning theories are presented in figure 2.

	Behavioural Learning theory	Cognitive Learning theory	Social Learning Theory
The key argument about learning	Learning is a consequence of stimulus-response.	Learning is a consequence of cognitive abilities and a process of adaptation to the environment.	Learning is a consequence of fitting ones' identity project to the order of behaviour in which one is embedded.
The key mechanism of learning	Learning occurs due to operant conditioning.	Learning occurs due to discovery (doing and actively exploring).	Learning occurs due to social construction of meaning in a given situation.

	Behavioural Learning theory	Cognitive Learning theory	Social Learning Theory
Consequences for educational design	Input oriented and teacher driven education, where students are given tasks and challenges and assessed and evaluated on their performance.	Process oriented and teacher inspired, where students are challenged with active methods that requires reconstruction of known schemes.	Process oriented and mainly student-driven, where students are given the responsibility for their own learning process.
Key thinkers	Thorndike (1898, 1905); Watson (1913); Skinner (1936).	Piaget (1936); Bloom et al. (1956); Piaget (1970); Bruner (1966); Freeman (1999).	Bandura (1975); Vygotsky (1978); Lave & Wenger (1991).

Figure 2: Key aspects of three different learning theories.

So far, I have presented a typology for e-learning where I stress the differences between e-learning 1.0 (distribution), 2.0 (dialogue), and 3.0 (construction). I have also presented three learning theories (Behavioural Learning theory, Cognitive Learning theory, and Social Learning theory). In the third section I will present a central model for designing the e-learning curriculum, where I draw on my typology of e-learning and the insights from the three learning theories. I do so to hopefully inspire to a fruitful discussion of how to use e-learning to improve students' learning outcomes.

Section 3: Curriculum design to improve students' learning outcomes using e-learning

Now, if we look at curriculum design principles and ask ourselves how we should design a curriculum using e-learning if we were to improve students' learning outcomes, we could draw on the reflections presented in sections 1 and 2 of this chapter. First, we could use the typology for e-learning, which distinguishes between e-learning 1.0, 2.0, and 3.0. That would be helpful for us, because it would give us a typology for distinguishing between different practical uses of e-learning. Second, we could also look at learning theory to help us understand the role of the learner (and thus the role of the teacher). This is exactly what I wish to do in this third section of the chapter. I shall combine the proposed e-learning typology with the sketched-out learning theories, in order to see what it tells us about how we can design the e-learning curriculum to improve students' learning outcomes. In this chapter I have also used the terms teacher-driven and student-driven to reflect on the responsibilities and roles of both teachers and students. This distinction also becomes an important one in the curriculum design model I am to present here.

Figure 3 is the central curriculum design model, which I suggest is used when designing a curriculum using e-learning. The curriculum design model is based on three important questions, which should always be asked, when we work with e-learning. The three questions are: 1) how do we perceive learning?; 2) how do we perceive e-learning?; and 3) how do we perceive curriculum?

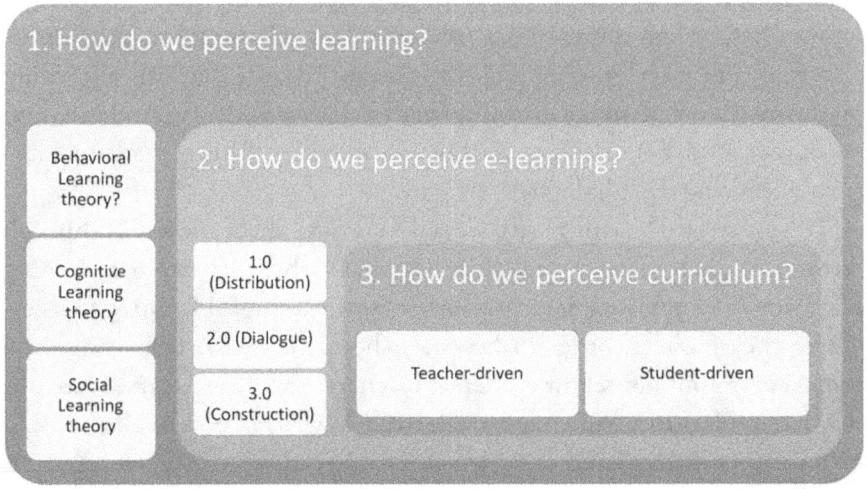

Figure 3: the curriculum design model.

Chapter 2

"How do we perceive learning?"

"How do we perceive learning?" is the first important question we as curriculum designers have to ask ourselves, because it has implications for our understandings of the basic needs of our e-learning platform.

If we perceive learning with Behavioural Learning theory, we will think in terms of stimuli-response. Here our e-learning platform will contain a variety of relevant learning resources (stimuli). Articles, videos, cases, podcasts, drawings, etc. And we will measure student learning (response) with online quizzes, online surveys, and online tests. In other words, we need an e-learning platform that can make learning materials available to students and test their learning. This is made possible with e-learning 1.0 (distribution).

If we perceive learning with Cognitive Learning theory, we will think in terms of active discovery, problem solving, and engaged learning. Here our e-learning platform will contain a variety of relevant learning resources to stimulate the cognition of the student, but more importantly it will invite students to engage through dialogue. This could be through online chat, online conferences, online student presentation, online peer review, online peer grading, etc. In other words, we need an e-learning platform that can make learning materials available to students and encourage students to engage in learning activities. This is made possible with e-learning 2.0 (dialogue).

If we perceive learning with Social Learning theory, we will think in terms of student identity and Most Relevant Others. Here our e-learning platform will enable students to construct a meaningful learning journey, where they learn in order to become whom they wish to become in a social community of fellow students, teachers, and other peers. Here our e-learning platform will support ePortfolios, writing of e-books, writing of wiki's, online collaborative work, etc. In other words, we need an e-learning platform that can govern student self-development and collaborative work with significant others. This is made possible with e-learning 3.0 (construction).

"How do we perceive e-learning?"

"How do we perceive e-learning?" is the second important question we as curriculum designers have to ask ourselves, because it has implications for our design of the e-learning platform.

If we perceive e-learning as a technological extension of traditional face-to-face teaching/activities, we will design our e-learning platform so that it supports students in their everyday studies. We will most probably use a CMS (content management system) or LMS (learning management system) where administrators upload program/course descriptions and similar study relevant materials; and where teachers upload learning resources such as presentations given at lectures, assignments, quizzes, background articles, links to relevant websites, etc. This is made possible with e-learning 1.0 (distribution).

If we perceive e-learning as a technological support of student engagement, we will design our e-learning platform so it invites students to become active in the online realm. It may be by having students design a personal avatar, make them engage in online discussion forums, arrange online conferences, etc. We will most probably use an LMS where teachers guide students through relevant online exercises and facilitate online dialogues; and also upload assignments which call for further student online engagement. This is made possible with e-learning 2.0 (dialogue).

If we perceive e-learning as a technological facilitation of students creating a meaningful learning journey, we will design our e-learning platform so that it enables students to create their own identity projects as students, as they learn how to become a future professional. We will most probably use a LMS and/or programs/Apps, which allow for students to document their own learning and personal development. This could be ePortfolios, personal wiki's, academic blog's, online collaborative tools, role play games, etc. This is made possible with e-learning 3.0 (construction).

Chapter 2

"How do we perceive curriculum?"

"How do we perceive curriculum?" is the third important question we as curriculum designers have to ask ourselves, because it has implications for the role of teachers and students on our e-learning platform. I distinguish between the teacher-driven paradigm, in which the teacher plans activities and decides what information is distributed to students, and the student-driven paradigm, in which students are responsible for planning their learning activities and find the information needed for their own learning process.

If we are in favour of the teacher-driven paradigm, we will make teachers responsible for designing the student online experience. We will argue that teachers are experts who know best, and we will therefore make teachers responsible for designing a scaffolded journey for students as they progress through the program/course/module. This would probably be done by drip-feeding literature, exercises, videos, podcasts, etc. to students on the online platform, so they could access the material considered to be relevant for the course. Teacher-driven activities will often focus on the course literature and be based on the theory and methodology taught, which will enable students to mirror the role of an academic scholar.

If we are in favour of the student-driven paradigm, we will on the other hand make students responsible for their own learning process. Although teachers are experts in their academic field, we will ask teachers to take upon themselves a more facilitating role, guiding students towards problem-solving activities and identity creating activities. Student-driven activities will often take their outset in identified problems, challenges or real-life cases, which will enable students to mirror the role of a future professional.

Having reflected on the three important questions in the online curriculum design model I propose, I will end this section by presenting Figure 4 in which I present examples of e-learning activities in the light of learning theory, e-learning typology, and the role of teachers/students. With Figure 4 I also ends this final section of the chapter and leads to the conclusion.

	E-learning 1.0 (Distribution)	E-learning 2.0 (Dialogue)	E-learning 3.0 (Construction)
Teacher-driven (subject and format decided by teacher)	course website podcast video broadcast online test online quiz online surveys	blogging session chat online conference	online review online assignments online case challenge online collaborative role play games
Student-driven (subject and/or format decided by student)	online presentation	blogging session chat online conference online discussion forum Facebook Groups Facebook Pages Google Hangouts Skype	ePortfolio personal wiki e-book / iBook academic blog online research tools online review / opponent creation of academic database online collaborative tools role play games
	E-learning based on Behavioural Learning theory	E-learning based on Cognitive Learning theory	E-learning based on Social Learning theory

Figure 4: Examples of teacher-driven and student-driven e-learning 1.0, 2.0, and 3.0 activities with reference to Behavioural Learning theory, Cognitive Learning theory and Social Learning theory.

Conclusion

In this chapter I have discussed e-learning solutions in relation to learning theory. I have done so, because I found from my own practical examples of using e-learning and from being involved in e-learning projects, that e-learning decisions are often taken with focus on technology rather than learning. This has in many cases led to implementation of unitary stand-alone e-learning systems (CMS and LMS) which at the end of the day have been used as repositories for learning material only. It is my argument that e-learning in Higher Education had been skewed towards e-learning 1.0 (distribution) with a little bit of e-learning 2.0 (dialogue). This is, I have argued, due to the majority of curriculum design being based on Behavioural Learning theory and to a lesser degree Cognitive Learning theory. It will come as no surprise that my own ideal for designing e-learning is the use of e-learning 3.0 (construction) based on Social Learning theory. It is my belief that by asking the three central questions in the curriculum design process, as I proposed in the curriculum design model, e-learning decisions will be more reflected and hence more tailored to engage students in self-directed learning activities and thereby improve students' learning outcomes.

About the Author

Professor Dr. Claus Nygaard is Executive Director of Institute for Learning in Higher Education and Executive Director of cph:learning. He can be contacted at this e-mail: info@lihe.info

Bibliography

Bandura, A. (1975). *Social Learning & Personality Development*. New Jersey: Holt, Rinehart & Winston.

Bloom, B. S., Engelhart, M. D., Furst, E. J., Hill, W. H., & Krathwohl, D. R. (1956). *Taxonomy of educational objectives: The classification of educational goals. Handbook I: Cognitive domain*. New York: David McKay Company.

Bruner, J. S. (1966). *Toward a theory of instruction*. Cambridge, Mass.: Belkapp Press.

Crone, D. A., Hawken, L. S., & Bergstrom, M. K. (2007). A demonstration of training, implementing, and using functional behavioral assessment in 10 elementary and middle school settings. *Journal of Positive Behavior Interventions*, 9(1), 15–29.

Ervin, R. A., Radford, P. M., Bertsch, K., & Piper, A. L. (2001). A descriptive analysis and critique of the empirical literature on school-based functional assessment. *School Psychology Review*, 30(2), 193–210.

Freeman, W. J. (1999). *How brains make up their minds*. Phoenix: Orion Books.

Garrison, D., & Kanuka, H. (2004). Blended Learning: Uncovering Its Transformative Potential in Higher Education. *Internet and Higher Education*, 7(2), 95–105.

Granovetter, M. (1992). *The sociology of economic life*. Boulder: Westview Press.

Helms, S. A. (2012). Blended/hybrid courses: a review of the literature and recommendations for instructional designers and educators. *Interactive Learning Environments*, 22(6), 804–810.

Hrastinski, S. (2008). Asynchronous and synchronous e-learning. *Educause Quarterly*, 4(1), 51–55.

Lave, J., & Wenger, E. (1991). *Situated Learning: Legitimate peripheral participation*. Cambridge: Cambridge University Press.

McDermott, R. P. (1999). On Becoming Labelled – the Story of Adam. In Murphy, P. (Ed.), *Learners, Learning & Assessment*. London: Paul Chapman Publishing, Ltd., 1–21.

Meier, F., & Nygaard, C. (2009). Problem Oriented Project Work in Higher Education. In Nygaard, C., & Holtham, C. (Eds.), *Understanding Learning-Centred Higher Education*. Frederiksberg: Copenhagen Business School Press, 131–144.

Nygaard, C. (2015). Rudiments of a Strategy for Technology Enhanced University Learning. In Nygaard, C., Branch, J., & Bartholomew, P. (Eds.), *Technology Enhanced Learning in Higher Education*. Oxfordshire, UK: Libri Publishing Ltd., 31–50.

Piaget, J. (1936). *Origins of intelligence in the child*. London: Routledge & Kegan Paul.

Piaget, J. (1958). The growth of logical thinking from childhood to adolescence. *AMC*, 10(12).

Piaget, J. (1970). *Main trends in psychology*. London: George Allen & Unwin.

Skinner, B. F. (1936). *The Behavior of organisms: An experimental analysis*. New York: Appleton-Century.

Thorndike, E. L. (1898). Animal intelligence: An experimental study of the associative processes in animals. *Psychological Monographs: General and Applied*, 2(4), i-109.

Thorndike, E. L. (1905). *The elements of psychology*. New York: A. G. Seiler.

Vygotsky, L. S. (1978). *Mind in society: The development of higher psychological processes*. Cambridge, MA: Harvard University Press.

Watson, J. B. (1913). Psychology as the behaviorist views it. *Psychological Review*, 20, 158–178.

Watson, J. B. (1930). *Behaviorism*. Chicago: University of Chicago Press.

Wenger, E. (1998). *Communities of Practice. Learning, Meaning and Identity*. Cambridge, UK: Cambridge University Press.

Chapter 3

Using a peer-centred online learning platform to support students' academic-professional transition

Willie McGuire and Olan Harrington

Introduction

With our chapter, we contribute to the book *E-learning 1.0, 2.0, and 3.0 in Higher Education* as we show how we have designed a peer-centred online learning platform to support the academic-professional transition of our teacher students at Glasgow University in Scotland. Our peer-centred online learning platform is named TeachingJobs to indicate that it is designed to teach our alumni how to get jobs – how to make the transition from academia to professional practice. We found that supporting our students' transition from academia to professional practice is important for several reasons. Firstly, often university education focusses more on academic content and less on professional practice. We wanted to put equal focus on professional practice. Secondly, the job market is beyond the traditional scope of universities, often leaving alumni "on their own" once they have graduated. We wanted to change that by developing a supportive university-alumni relationship. Thirdly, the job market is constantly changing – in the school sector it is dependent on the changing recruitment strategies of local councils. We wanted to make a peer-centred online learning platform, where alumni could share knowledge of specific, and varied, recruitment strategies of local councils. Fourth, academia and professional practice ought to be much more integrated, because they can inform and support each other. We wanted to support that integration by providing a university-driven online learning platform where alumni can share knowledge of professional practice and reflect on their successes.

Furthermore, we wanted to support the academic-professional

transition by facilitating the development of specific skills in students: knowledge, critical thinking, and adaptation.

As much as we would like to take upon ourselves the main responsibility for students' academic-professional transition, it is to a large degree beyond the control of universities. In relation to the Scottish school-sector knowledge of specific, and varied, recruitment strategies of the local councils can only come from alumni who have familiarised themselves with the local recruitment strategies, who have participated in job interviews, and who are now employed as teachers in local councils. Therefore, Scottish universities face two challenges in relation to academic-professional transition:

1. How can universities deliver knowledge of school-specific recruitment strategies when this knowledge is largely outside of the public domain?

2. How can universities develop critical thinking and self-analysis skills in their students for them to adapt successfully to these recruitment strategies?

In our chapter, we seek to show how our peer-centred online learning platform, TeachingJobs, is a response to these challenges. We describe the design of Teachingjobs and the way it is used. We also evaluate whether the site supports student transition from academia into the professional environment.

When reading this chapter, you will take away three insights in relation to supporting academic-professional transition:

1. The reasons why we created the peer-centred online learning platform to support students' academic-professional transition;

2. Two key modes of support: dialogue with peers and access to the online support materials;

3. Our attempts to create a self-perpetuating system, by which we mean a resource, which once established, would then be controlled exclusively by alumni for alumni.

The chapter has three main sections. In section one, we briefly introduce TeachingJobs as a peer-centred online learning platform and explain the background for our development. Here we refer to two case studies and to the literature in the field of online learning in relation to academic-professional transition. We do so to further explore the current discourse on the topic. In section two, we elaborate on the solutions we deployed to address the challenges of students' academic-professional transition. Here we also outline our methodology and then we analyse the data to determine the strengths and weaknesses of the resource. Thereafter, we attempt to deconstruct its main usage, which we define as broadly monologic or broadly dialogic. We then draw out key points for our own resource architecture from the literature and summarise the key findings. Following this, in section three, we describe the outcomes of the first iteration of the TeachingJobs resource and consider its strengths and development needs.

Section 1: Our development of the online learning platform

When we first began our work on designing the online learning platform, we were driven by the aim to improve the job attainment rate for our graduates. From our practice and experience, we had identified peer-to-peer learning as integral to their success. Improving knowledge, critical thinking, and adaptation was for us one solution to closing the knowledge gap that universities aim to close between academia and professional practice. In its original form, we wanted our online platform to collect feedback and guidance from alumni who had successfully applied for jobs in specific local councils. This process feeds back into supporting our peer-to-peer development goals. We therefore aimed to design an online learning platform, which would contain a collection of material and experiences provided by candidates and former candidates in employment. Furthermore, it should provide critical feedback facilities and peer-to-peer engagement opportunities for alumni. We aimed at this self-perpetuating peer-centred online learning system, because the varied recruitment landscape requires new graduates to be adaptable and adept problem-solvers. Imagine a scenario in which a student has gained knowledge from our learning platform that a local council values extra-curricular activities. This student is, therefore, required to produce a cover letter for a position which draws attention to, say, their musical talents rather than their academic background. The student is then required to critically assess their own work. These assessment skills are developed by virtue of engaging in comparison, feedback, and analysis activities on our online learning platform, and developing these specific skills is where peer-to-peer critical analysis becomes important. Given the wide range of experiences that graduates have with different kinds of recruitment processes, it is important to develop a method of communication to facilitate knowledge exchange and adaptability on these recruitment processes. TeachingJobs was seen as a possible way to use e-learning as a method for supporting students' academic-professional transition.

As we set out to design TeachingJobs, we aimed to develop our understanding of how to best support student transition to the professional environment. We then reviewed current research in blended learning strategies as a way to address this. Blended/Online Learning strategies combine face-to-face and distance learning methods to develop a community of inquiry and offer a virtual environment in which students can interact with each other in real time synchronously, or through discussion boards asynchronously (Volery & Lord, 2000). We, therefore, had two main objectives with our review.

1. To develop an evidence-based rationale for a Blended/Online Learning model with a constructivist pedagogy that supports the academic-professional transition by facilitating the development of specific skills in students: knowledge, critical thinking, and adaptation.

2. To introduce a Blended/Online Learning model at The University of Glasgow to enhance knowledge, critical thinking, and adaptability skills in our graduate students designed to aid student transition to the professional environment.

As classroom sizes increase and university funding declines there has been a move towards online and blended forms of learning. This has been to maximise the use of facilities within universities. Subsequently it is being used in schools, colleges, and universities across the globe (Cheung & Hew, 2011; Hadjerrouit, 2008). In-class learning experiences can be replaced or supplemented with an online learning environment, such as 'Moodle,' or 'Blackboard,' with students independently working on coursework outside of the physical classroom. Key components of the blended-learning strategy are to develop a community of inquiry and to develop the skills necessary to maintain engagement with students. The main goal of blended learning is for online and in-person learning to interact in such a way that they provide some parallel to, or complement, traditional methods of education. At the same time, they provide flexibility and convenience for the course coordinators, teachers, and students. This is especially true where the appetite to learn as an adult has been increasing but comes into conflict with work or family commitments (McCray, 2000; Strambi & Bouvet, 2003; Wingard, 2004). And it is in addition to other aspects such as strain within institutions and increasing teacher:student ratios. Blended learning models also allow universities to increase student to employment ratios at a lower cost overall (Battaglino et al., 2012).

There are other benefits to blended learning aside from the obvious financial and pragmatic reasons. Some practical advantages include increased student satisfaction (Green et al., 2006), increased knowledge (Campbell et al., 2008) and, arguably, a reduced staff workload (Dorrian & Wache, 2009). Cheung and Hew (2014:4–5) have argued that there are four main benefits to blended learning in higher education: *"an ability to meet students' educational needs, improving student-to-student communication, reducing the average overall per-student cost, and improving student learning outcomes as well as lowering attrition rates."* In an age where technological reform has been slow to take hold, these benefits can act as solutions to some of the transition challenges facing The University of Glasgow that we discussed above.

Since blended learning has been increasingly characterised as the 'new norm' for course delivery worldwide (Norberg et al., 2011) we evaluated the use of online learning in developing transferrable skills and knowledge through a constructivist pedagogy. Therefore, we investigated how:

+ peer-to-peer knowledge creation; and
+ peer-to-peer critical thinking and adaptability

in an online, moderated environment can help to develop the knowledge and skill-set necessary for graduates to successfully transition to the professional environment.

Chapter 3

Peer-to-peer knowledge creation

Blended learning can offer a more balanced approach to learning by removing the instructor-facing position. In its initial form, Teaching-Jobs should contain content from former students who have provided some material or experiences on local council recruitment processes. We envisage that subsequent students will add to this platform. This answers one of our questions from above: How should universities aid the facilitation of knowledge generation to assist students in transition? We believe this can be done *via* an online Moodle platform. Handing (initially) some (and later all) of the course direction and content creation to the students can offer more interaction than a face-to-face course (Dziuban *et al.*, 2004; Wingard, 2004). When students have more control over the direction of their own learning they are allowed to have more control over their discussion and knowledge creation (Salmon, 2003). Peer to peer learning is also facilitated and grown where communication is facilitated *via* technology and access to material that may otherwise be unavailable is available on the platform (Dziuban *et al.*, 2004). Our model builds on previous work, and on a constructivist pedagogy guided by Piaget and Vygotsky (Woo & Reeves, 2007). In constructivist learning, students build up their own knowledge (from our proposed Moodle content, which is self-generated) and then apply the knowledge to their real-world scenarios. Students apply these directly to recruitment processes. It is noted, however, that this model depends on altruistic principles where students are willing to 'give back'. This, and other challenges to knowledge and content creation, will be discussed further in the discussion section.

Peer-to-peer critical thinking and adaptability

There are strong reasons to believe that blended learning produces the same learning outcomes for student learning, and in some cases, in comparison to face-to-face contact alone, have even greater impact (Means *et al.*, 2010). Further, it enhances the value that peers place on the opinion of others. This stimulates critical and creative thinking and enhances critical skills development, which then gives support to using online learning as a scaffolding tool to assist graduates into specific employment sectors either in addition to or in place of, face-to-face workshops on CV building and cover letter writing. The opportunities for self-reflection and consideration of other students' work allows for the development of critical skills. It also allows students to get a sense of how others are adapting to recruitment processes. Overall, critical thinking and the ability to be adaptable are essential skills when students have to navigate often-unknowable recruitment strategies and therefore have to become adaptable.

Insight from two case studies

Following our review of research, we also looked at case studies of how other universities have adapted a sequential blended learning, and online learning strategy. Focusing on the benefits to the students and the online aspect of these models, we came to present evidence that suggests that TeachingJobs could play a role in supporting the transition to the professional environment. TeachingJobs provides no face-to-face structural environment. However, it can be very useful in developing the kind of peer-to-peer skill set that our graduates require to achieve higher levels of adaptability and critical thinking. Given that many of the students that this project aims to support will be in their placement year at university – and will be working at a second level school – it is expected that their face-to-face interactions will be limited.

Previous studies have shown that students who are engaged with blended learning programs appreciate the flexibility and convenience of being able to study in their own time and at their own pace (Ireland *et al.*, 2009; Welker & Berardino, 2005; Song *et al.*, 2004; King, 2002). This proposed research would expand on the body of literature that supports online learning where face-to-face contact is not convenient or where the benefits of peer-to-peer content creation are stronger and develop a specific skill-set.

An Australian postgraduate nursing program uses a blended learning strategy to aid transition to the nurse practitioner (NP) role. Presented with their current knowledge, graduates were then provided with an online programme that aided the development of practical skills. These skills were deemed necessary to assist the successful transition to the nurse practitioner role, which has grown since the first two NPs programmes were endorsed in 2000. Since then Australia has seen a steady increase in the number of registered NPs. With growing diversity in roles, areas of specialization, and day-to-day experience, a knowledge gap opened up between students' learning and the realities of working as an NP. This necessitated a way to build specific skills that could be applied in the professional world. This blended learning model offered engagement on campus while also offering complete online delivery for remote students. This approach reflects the current fiscal constraints and student demand for flexibility. As such, there is increasing demand for online learning management systems (Blackboard, Moodle, etc.) to provide platforms to support student education. Care was taken to ensure engagement, by acknowledging the complex and multifaceted reality of adult learning while also ensuring that, "…*principles of effective adult learning practice were embodied throughout; specifically, that adult learner engagement needs to be voluntary…learning is a co-operative experience with praxis at its heart, and facilitation aims to foster critical reflection and nurture self-direction.*" (Brookfield, 1986:9–11). Although this case study included more than just online learning, such as: orientation workshops, the development of a clinical portfolio, a residential workshop, and a post-residential online reflection, the collaborative experiences of working online developed critical thinking and evaluative skills in the students. These activities, along with a self-directed learning plan, developed responsibility, self-leadership and also promoted active learning (Lowenstein, 2011). This andragogic model, which differs from our constructivist model, can provide some knowledge of how the online delivery of learning can have an impact on the skills of students.

The challenge for our model is, with limited engagement, how do we ensure that collaborative activities develop a sense of community?

The sequential approach, where students were engaged in developing a practical reality of their role was shown to assist student transition to the NP role. This is something that we should adopt in our own model, where students are more aware of the realities of the required skill set and ensure there are opportunities to develop this adaptability prior to entering the job market. This study concluded that access to a blended learning environment early in their postgraduate degree allowed students to "*more clearly envision the gap between their current level of competence and that of the Australian NP role*" (Day & Rossiter, 2015:164).

Therefore, this suggests that an online platform that contains content relevant to gaining employment in education would be hugely beneficial for the students early in their education placements.

A similar study from the National University of Ireland Galway (NUIG) found similar positive outcomes to the development of soft skills and career transitions in the field of nursing. For our own research, their findings suggest that skills such as self-reflection, peer-to-peer support to develop personal leadership skills and confidence, and adaptability are essential features to successfully transition to the professional environment. This, in parallel with an online platform with specific local knowledge of recruitment processes in local councils provided by a university, could strongly support student transition. This study, in comparison to the previous one discussed, offered specific complete online learning. They draw on previous research from Garrison and Kanuka (2004) and Volery and Lord, (2000) to put forward a description of what online learning involves. They say that, *"on-line learning involves providing students with access to learning resources, facilitating communication, and collaborative working among and between students and academic staff."* (Smyth et al., 2001:464). This course was offered *via* an online learning platform. Students reported that this approach enabled problem solving. It also aided the students in being more active in their practice. This practice could be compatible to activity with the jobs market, or in developing new skills to meet the specific requirements of schools. As with the last study, the flexibility offered fostered a sense of autonomy and assisted in allowing students to plan their own learning.

This online model supports our own constructivist model of knowledge development and learning. Given these benefits, we can provide a rationale for the development of our own model. To further this aim we will provide evidence that our proposed model can support graduates in the development of two critical skill-sets. We assert that these provide graduates with the skills necessary to improve their chances of finding gainful employment.

Some challenges should also be considered. Students at the NUI Galway felt that often the online driver model was intrusive. Many reported that they felt like they had a very weak separation between their home life and university work. This influenced both their wellbeing and home life. Others suggested that it was sometimes hard to maintain that sense of community. That along with blogging credits, there should be more aspects of the online driver model that develop a better community spirit.

Given all of this, some questions we considered for our own design proposed model are:

1. How should the platform develop a sense of community and maintain peer-to-peer communication in the students/graduates? Should this be with blogs, discussion boards, or external platforms such as Facebook?

2. How can the platform foster content creation from those who successfully gain employment?

3. What moderation roles will university staff play in maintaining community and supporting peer-to-peer communication? Who will work with former students to add content to the platform?

From a purely competitive angle, should we also consider how competition would affect the level of interaction and support between students? We should also consider whether face-to-face interactions are necessary, and if so then what level of interaction is necessary? Given these issues, it is important that the proposed platform mitigate some of the negative aspects of online learning.

TeachingJobs as our platform for academic-professional support

After our review of current research and the insight from the two case studies, we came to design TeachingJobs. Figure 1 shows a screenshot representing a student view of the online landing page of TeachingJobs. The platform is straightforward, user-friendly and uncluttered. How though, did we arrive at this design? First, we examined the literature on online learning in relation to transition, which is described above, and we then attempted to configure a structure that met the recommendations described in the extant research within the parameters of the online platform. We required a meeting space for: online dialogue with peers and/or mentors. We also required both contributions and contributors. We designed the platform to be self-perpetuating. By this, we mean that control of the resource was designed, from the outset, to pass from

Using a peer-centred online learning platform

teacher control to student control. Mirroring Nygaard's (in this volume) relational model of online learning typologies it deploys distribution (e-learning 1.0) as well as dialogue (e-learning 2.0), but it is also in the process of transforming into construction (e-learning 3.0) as students become the curriculum architects of the future iterations of the alumni site. This is so as the online learning platform collects feedback and guidance from the alumni who have successfully applied to jobs in specific local councils. This process feeds back into supporting our peer-to-peer development goals and maintains the construction of new and relevant information for alumni.

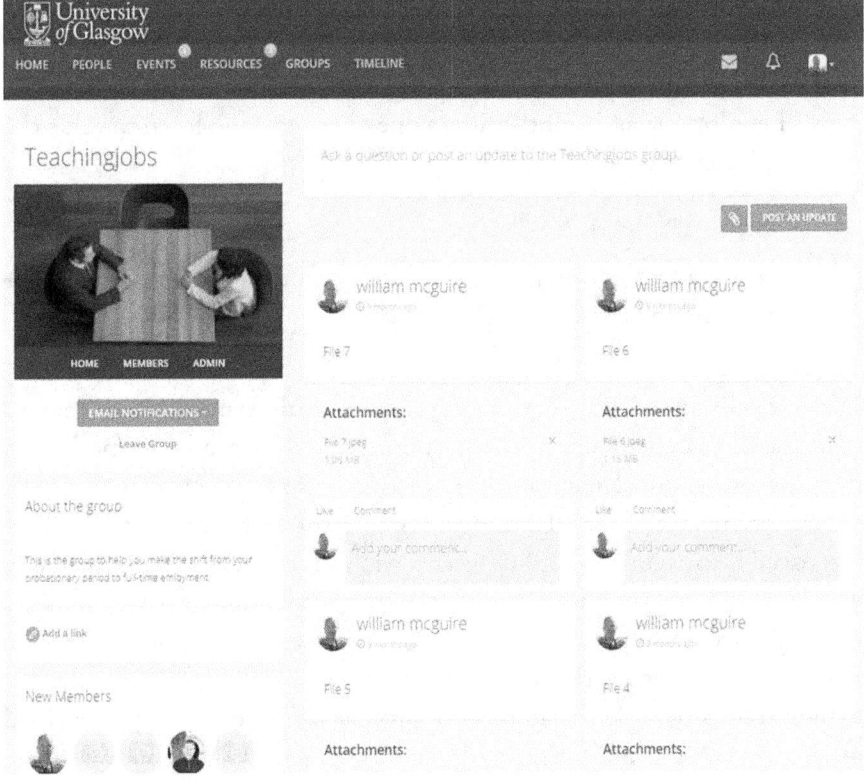

Figure 1: *The TeachingJobs online learning platform.*

Another advantage of TeachingJobs as a platform is that it allows students to keep access to their course materials after graduation. Usually, students at Glasgow University lose access to their course materials within six months of course completion and so the online platform for TeachingJobs was highly attractive as a means of solving this key problem.

From case studies and theoretical research, we can see how the online driver model may be able to support the kind of skills development that we aim to improve in students. This model can support students in the following ways:

- Provide flexibility and freedom to learn and develop at their own pace;
- Deliver access to material that would otherwise be unavailable;
- Enable a space to engage in peer-to-peer learning;
- Develop a sense of authority in one's opinion, and learn to value the opinion of others;
- Foster leadership skills;
- Create adaptability and flexibility in students by developing their critical self-assessment skills.

We have discussed the role of universities to determine the extent to which they can support student transition from academia/probation into the professional environment. In this review, we presented a brief introduction into online learning to support our framework. We also discussed the rational for online learning in the context for The University of Glasgow along with two case studies that use online learning models. Having discussed these, we identified two key areas that students require to develop in order for the university to provide support for student transition. Following a discussion of the proposed framework, we identified model weaknesses and committed to addressing these with our platform. Finally, we listed the main benefits to students in supporting their transition. Now we move from theory to practice.

Section 2: Using TeachingJobs to support academic-professional transition

Communication with former students can be complicated, as electronic conduits such as email and online links tend to be rescinded soon after graduation, effectively severing links. Contact by private email is only possible in the circumstance where these have been obtained prior to graduation and with permission given for later contact. In the first iteration of TeachingJobs, this was not obtained. As such, this presented a significant problem in sourcing an appropriate platform through which we could communicate with alumni. In its second iteration, on which this chapter reports, we secured fifty email addresses from a (reduced) cohort of under two hundred as we had approached students at their final lecture at which attendance was lower than normal. Additionally, we suspected that it would be difficult for students who had just completed an arduous course, to focus their attentions, a full year forward in time, to consider their job chances one year after graduation. This is because students are offered a place on the Probationer teacher scheme under which every successful Postgraduate Diploma in Education student (PGDE) is offered a 0.8 FTE (full-time equivalent) contract in a school, with the other 0.2 FTE forming part of a probationer induction scheme to support the transition from provisional to full status.

The Solution

Modelled loosely on the ancient Greek concept of civic debate, the *agora*, the medium used to gather together interested parties had to be capable of some flexibility: the provision of an online forum within which participants might engage in supportive debate based on mentoring, again a Greek concept based on the role of Mentor, adviser to Odysseus and counsellor/coach to his son Telemachus. This was a project with limited funding that was likely not to be repeated, therefore if it were to continue to function, it had to be self-sustaining and participant-driven – a key element of its originality and innovation. This was based on the utilitarian premise that those who had been helped in the past would go on to become mentors for those currently seeking support. Ironically, the original concept was for university-based staff to function as mentors. It soon became apparent, however, that the tutor demographic was unsuited to this role as many had not had involvement in supporting new teachers in many years and lacked the confidence and up-to-the minute knowledge of how interviews are conducted and the type of questions asked in recent interviews.

Mentoring and Transitioning

The Network platform allows alumni with shared study histories to communicate both formally and informally. While those study patterns might be similar, online users might be of very different ages. The aspiration is that older alumni would mentor the younger cohorts in their continuing disciplinary learning journey. With advantage, however, comes disadvantage. The TeachingJobs site was constructed along connectivist/constructivist principles, but its key aim was to provide mentorship of a very specific form-job seeking skills within the teaching profession. As such, the dialogic elements of the platform were supportive of participants, but the focus on the dialogic element made it unhelpful in terms of storing and accessing materials that participants required to develop their interview skills such as question types and modelled responses to those questions, which were required prior to a more in-depth discussion of the appropriacy of specific responses to key questions. Nor did the platform allow for synchronous communication, which left a reliance on the asynchronous model, and this often resulted in a considerable time-lag between questions being posed and responses being provided often resulting in participant frustration.

Methodology

The review of research in section one highlighted three areas of enquiry which were to be as follows:
1. How could the platform develop a sense of community and maintain peer-to-peer communication in the students/graduates?
2. How could the platform foster content creation from those who successfully gain employment?
3. What moderation roles should university staff play in maintaining community and supporting peer-to-peer communication?

Because of the small numbers involved, the methodology deployed was straightforward and qualitative, although we would propose the use of a quantitative element in a second review of the scaled-up project planned for next session. We are attempting to answer two broad questions:

1. In what ways(s) was the TeachingJobs resource helpful?

2. In what way(s) could it be improved?

A single data collection method was used to answer these questions: the focus group lasting 45 minutes *via* Zoom to minimise disruption and because this platform offered the option of audio recording of the discussion, which obviated the need for a physical meeting with audio recording.

Sampling

Participants onto the project volunteered at the stage where they were still PGDE students last session, which was problematic in that their minds were, perhaps, focused on their recent successes, their impending vacations and their new careers, which may have distracted them from thoughts which they may have felt to have little relevance for them a year hence. 38 responded to the initial call in August 2017. On follow up on current interest levels in February 2018, 13 respondents registered interest in joining the TeachingJobs group. This evaluative study used 4 participants to take part in a (Zoom) focus group. It should be noted that, while we are dealing with very small numbers, this still represents 33% of those who took part in the project.

Data Analysis

An adapted form of the six-phase guide to thematic analysis by Braun and Clarke (2013) was deployed, which can be categorised as either realist or constructivist methods used to explore the experiences of the participants.

1. Familiarisation with the data;

2. Transcription of verbal data;

3. Generating initial codes;

4. Identifying themes;

5. Reviewing themes;

6. Defining and naming themes.

Because of the sample size, it was felt to be unnecessary to deploy each stage of the above guide; instead it was refined to three sub-stages:

- Data (and concept) immersion;
- Generating themes;
- Finalising themes.

The Sub Stages Deconstructed

The focus group transcript was reviewed on three occasions to provide a wide range of potential topics for further enquiry. Additionally, the concept of the support model provided and its requirements were also considered as part of this initial process of immersion. These were then taken individually to generate 'potential' themes for the final stage of the process in which themes were finalised following return to the participants for verification.

Benefits	Challenges
1. Variety of forms of interview and selection processes as well as types of support.	1. The paradox of support; it activates the need for more (detailed/refined) support.
2. Peer mentoring v tutor mentoring.	2. Timing and the issue of utilitarianism v pressing need-the day job.
3. Alerts.	3. In house or Dropbox?
4. Notes taken by job applicants.	4. Digital Landscape/Topography.
5. Modelled responses.	5. Dialogue tended to happen beyond the medium.
6. Contributions/support from peers.	6. Two dimensional v three dimensional.
	7. Self-sustaining due to time lapse.
	8. The paradox of the preference for peer v tutor support.
	9. Trouble of access to private emails.

Figure 2: Perceived benefits and challenges of the platform.

We also sub-divided the core elements of the structural design of the medium into two broad areas: the dialogic elements refer to support given *via* constructivist principles, while the second monologic elements relate to support mechanisms that were accessed without the use of later, intermediate, or prior challenge from a peer.

Dialogic (e-learning 2.0)	Monologic (e-learning 1.0)
A priori	*Strategic*
Use of peer support prior to accessing the online support materials.	Access to specific online materials, without peer support.
A posteriori	*Generic*
Use of peer support materials following access to the online support materials.	Access to all online materials, without peer support.
Meso	
Level use of the peer support.	

Figure 3: The characteristics of dialogic and monologic e-learning.

Respondents praised the efforts of the research team to provide a practical tool to support transition through the portal from academia to professional status and highlighted the varying degrees of support that were available within different local authorities to support this transition and which were then stored, within one locus and within one medium. The Network, was designed on constructivist/connectivist principles to encourage peer mentoring *via* online fora, which was ideal for one of our purposes – online dialogic support, but it proved to be less useful as a receptacle for the sharing of materials related to job interview formats, question types and modelled responses to questions asked at interview as a key issue concerns the functionality of the file attachments. As can be seen from the diagram, there is no search facility and users can only see the files physically displayed onscreen, which engenders constant vertical navigation which then leads to users being unable to remember the available support resources. There are, as always, advantages and drawbacks to any online platform.

Chapter 3

Benefits, paradoxes and discussion

While none of the respondents made use of the dialogic support, paradoxically, they all valued its availability and felt that others might benefit from such support. All were also agreed upon the benefits of the variety of monologic support materials available to them such as recent interview questions as well as modelled responses to those questions and even the notes taken by those who were attempting to respond to interview questions during the preparation phase. Perhaps this formed a kind of unintended dialogic element to the process within which they could challenge, add to, clarify or even remove ideas they may have held about the appropriacy of certain interview responses. Yet another unexpected outcome was the preference for peer *versus* tutor mentoring. In our conception of the first iteration, it was hoped that we could provide one-to-one tutor mentors and, when it became apparent that workload constraints would not permit such availability, it was decided to opt for peer mentors instead, yet when we tested the idea of tutor mentors, some respondents did not feel that this would have been beneficial:

- *"Some of the tutors haven't taught in schools for a very long time and might not be, kind of, up-to-speed with the latest developments."* (Respondent 2).

- *"My school experience tutor, during the PGDE year, mentioned having no idea of how probationers are recruited into permanent jobs these days."* (Respondent 4).

On the theme of receiving an alert when interview processes were imminent, respondents unanimously declared that they would not have accessed the medium. Upon further analysis, it would appear that the combination of the pressing demands of the probationary year, the timing of the selection process (which was much earlier than they had expected), and the priorities of daily life conspired to mitigate against use of the resource. When asked about the helpfulness of having access to notes taken by their peers prior to interview, there was a difference of opinion among respondents. Most (R1,2,3) were in favour of such access, arguing that this allowed insight into the thought processes of other applicants and therefore expanded/embellished the way in which they thought about answering such a question:

- "It gives you new ideas." (Respondent 1).
- "You might not have thought of that particular approach." (Respondent 2).
- "Sort of let's you see how others' think." (Respondent 3).
- Respondent 4 however, stated that first you had read through 'scribbles...incomplete thoughts... and incomplete sentences' in order to make sense of the information before the deciding on the efficacy of the information." (Respondent 4).

There was also an implication with time in deciding if this resource were to be used as it is possible that some users might find the latter difficulty off-putting.

Modelled responses were very highly praised by all participants:
- "Really helpful. A terrific idea. Made me really think." (Respondent 1).
- "Yes, that was a good idea. Showed you what not to do. Gave you ideas about how to answer these questions in a real interview." (Respondent 2).
- "Great, but I was a bit lazy with it; I just read the three options, noted the ideas and didn't really think about which was the best of the three options...but it still helped!" (Respondent 3).

While irrelevant to the thematic analysis, it should be noted that all respondents were visibly excited when discussing this aspect of the resource. Broadly, they appreciated the insight provided by the models; the variety of responses; the varying depths of those responses and the confidence which derived from this form of preparation. One of the key insights provided was provided by R3 who noted that:
- "It made me think about how the responses would be received by a potential employer and this kind of ...you know...heightened my awareness of what an employer might prefer." (Respondent 3).

Chapter 3

Challenges, paradoxes and discussion

A number of challenges emerged which may be separated into two broad categories: respondent-centred and system-centred, although it is also recognised that these can also interrelate.

Respondent – Centred

One of the key issues recorded by all respondents was the felt need for yet more support. Accessing the online materials appeared to have paradoxical effects: it helped to build a knowledge-base on how to answer interview questions, but it also activated the need for more (detailed or refined) support, which also led to angst about the state of preparedness, which in turn led to more access to the resource creating a form of cyclical dependency. One alumnus summarises this very succinctly:

- *"I thought I was fairly well prepared, but when I saw the detail in some of these responses, I sort of panicked. Really panicked. It was as if when I didn't know what I didn't know I was ok, happy, but when I found out what I had to know... Oh my!"* (Respondent 3).

Respondents all acknowledged the value of the resource, were aware of the need to contribute themselves in order to create a self-perpetuating system, but a conflict appeared to ensue between the pressing needs of the day job and the more elevated concept of utilitarianism required to drive the resource forward:

- *"It was a big, big help to me, but I just couldn't find the time to add to it. I kept making notes in my diary to do it, but didn't get around to it."* (Respondent 2).
- *"When you need to use the resource, it's at a frantic time of the year... around February...when you just don't stop in work and you're really struggling to gather together pupil work to be sent to the SQA (Scottish Qualifications Authority) in March and it's just crazy. Maybe a reminder to people after that?"* (Respondent 3).
- *"I was selfish. And exhausted. I wanted to help, but just couldn't find the time."* (Respondent 1).

Another interesting (and perhaps contradictory) aspect of the human-machine interface was the difficulty experienced by respondents in navigating the digital topography. The two dimensional page layout, without nested thematic hyperlinks and the absence of an internal search facility combined to make the process of searching for specific questions and responses laborious, especially given the time-constraints referred to earlier in the Benefits section:

- *"It became annoying very quickly because you couldn't search for specifics."* (Respondent 1).

- *"The layout really slowed things down. The visible stuff on the page was very interesting so it sort of slowed you down because it was hard not to look at it...then you forgot what you were looking for originally."* (Respondent 3).

- *"It put me off...the fact that there was all of this information...and it wasn't organised in any particular way."* (Respondent 2).

Again, the paradox of support referred to in the Benefits section appeared to be significant.

System-Centred

Systemic issues also emerged from the actual process of creating the resource in the first instance. As the resource users were *alumni*, they had to be contacted while still students to determine their interest levels and to secure permission to contact them after they had left as well as to obtain their private email addresses. Because of their familiarity with social media external to the resource medium – The Network – respondents found that dialogue was easier beyond this medium. Additionally, they also tended to move beyond the medium to post support materials of their own *via* Dropbox, for example:

- *"It was easier just to text someone and once you had done that, it was easier to work without beyond the TeachingJobs webpage."* (Respondent 2).

Chapter 3

A final paradox relates to respondent preference for peer tutors as opposed to academic tutor support as it was viewed by all of them that peer supporter had more recent and pertinent experience of the interview processes as well as more current subject credibility:

- *"It's ideally better to have both, but there's a time cost in that, so I'd opt for a peer tutor-someone who had just been through the process... and had got a job!"* (Respondent 1).

- *"My PGDE tutor admitted that he had no idea of what kind of questions were asked at interviews these days."* (Respondent 2).

- *"Peers are always preferable to tutors when it comes to this kind of thing!"* (Respondent 3).

Dialogic or Monologic Usage?

One of the key purposes of The Network was to open lines of communication between current students and alumni as a dialogic support mechanism, i.e, to provide them with a mentor, a more knowledgeable other in Vygotskian terms, to scaffold their progress from academia into professional work. The use of the medium then is interesting in terms of the extent to which it was used either dialogically to discuss, exchange ideas, develop opportunities, clarify points as we identified in our literature review at the outset or whether it was used predominantly as a monologic scaffold used without dialogue with tutors. While all of the respondents had made use of dialogic support, all agreed that its use had been minimal and that their primary use of the resource had been monologic. R1 used the resource in *a priori* fashion, while R2 used it in *meso* mode, and finally, R3 used it in an *a posteriori* manner. Additionally, all respondents made use of the resource as strategically as possible and were therefore strategic monologic users, while none of them made use of all of the resources, as despite the difficulty of using the platform strategically, they tended to speed read the skim and scan the titles and texts to assist with the efficiency of their searches making them generic monologic users.

Section 3: (Unexpected) Outcomes

The highlighted aims of this study were as follows:
1. To develop an evidence – based rationale for a Blended/Online Learning model with a constructivist pedagogy that supports the transition from student to the professional environment by facilitating the development of specific, knowledge, critical thinking, and adaptation skills in students.

2. To introduce a Blended/Online Learning model at The University of Glasgow to enhance critical thinking, knowledge and adaptability skills in our graduate students designed to aid student transition to the professional environment.

Moreover, the conclusion drawn from the extant literature in the field suggested that the following desirable outcomes from the online resource:

- Provide flexibility and freedom to learn and develop at their own pace;
- Deliver access to material that would otherwise be unavailable;
- Enable a space to engage in peer-to-peer learning;
- Develop a sense of authority in one's opinion, and learn to value the opinion of others;
- Foster leadership skills in the more interactive students;
- Create adaptability and flexibility in students by developing their critical self-assessment skills.

From Section 2 it is clear that each success criterion was met with varying degrees of success.

Strength	Development Need
Provide flexibility and freedom to learn and develop at their own pace.	Enable a space to engage in peer-to-peer work.
Deliver access to material that would otherwise be unavailable.	Develop a sense of authority in one's opinion, and learn to value the opinion of others.
Create adaptability and flexibility in students by developing their critical self-assessment skills.	Foster leadership skills in the more interactive students.

Figure 4: Strengths and further developments of the platform.

As in most human endeavours, this project can only claim to be partially successful as is clear from the relatively low number of respondents and also from the range of development needs highlighted above from which a number of conclusions might be drawn. The resource tended to be used monologically, within the small group of respondents. It would also appear that this strategic use was conditioned, at least partly, by the particular demands of this group who were all new teachers and, arguably, at their most vulnerable in terms of honing their craft and in their awareness of what pressures were likely to come next in the academic year. This then, perhaps ironically, may provide a reason for their success in refining their self-assessment skills, especially through the use of the modelled responses which were designed to address this area specifically as respondents tended to spend more time focused on this monologic aspect of the resource. There was, however, a reticence to use the resource extensively as a dialogic tool and so, while there was certainly the provision of a space to engage in peer-to-peer work, this tended not to happen and will feature in the following section on Moving Forward. Again, with the relative paucity of dialogic use, it is difficult to argue that the criterion designed to 'develop a sense of authority in one's opinion, and learn to value the opinion of others' was met and this would also need further consideration. It is also difficult to support the idea that the process, 'foster[ed] leadership skills' simply because of the low number of respondents, but again, this is an area of vital importance for the next iteration of the resource.

It is clear that a number of key areas require to be addressed in the next iteration of TeachingJobs:
1. Participant numbers need to be increased;
2. The dialogic aspects require highlighting in terms of *meso*, *a priori* and *a posteriori* use;
3. The self-perpetuating aim, while noble and utilitarian, requires development;
4. More contributions are necessary to expand the resource and to maintain its currency;
5. The strategic monologic use of the resource needs to be offset.

Conclusion

The opening section of this chapter promised insights into the following:
1. The reasons why we created the resource to support and why it was felt to be necessary;
2. Two key modes of support: dialogue with peers and access to the online support materials;
3. Our attempts to create a self-perpetuating system, by which we mean a resource, which once established, would then be controlled exclusively by *alumni* for *alumni*.

There is a variety of options available to participants in terms of how they interact with the resource dialogically, either on the *meso*, *a priori* or *a posteriori* levels. Each of these modes, however, is also calibrated against the monologic use of the resource itself and within that mode of use there are also several options: to use all of the materials or to access them strategically. The final insight is, perhaps, the most necessary for the continuation of the resource as funding becomes more of a challenge and we are hopeful that the developments we will enact in the next phase of the resource will solve the Aristotelian dream of perpetual motion.

Chapter 3

About the Authors

Willie McGuire is a Senior Lecturer in the School of Education at the University of Glasgow and a Senior Fellow of the Higher Education Academy. He can be contacted on this e-mail: william.mcguire@glasgow.ac.uk

Olan Harrington is a PhD student in Philosophy and a Research Assistant at the School of Education at the University of Glasgow. He can be contacted on this e-mail: o.harrington.1@research.gla.ac.uk

Bibliography

Battaglino, T. B., Haldeman, M., & Laurans, E. (2012). Review of The Costs of Online Learning. *National Education Policy Center.*

Braun, V., & Clarke, V. (2006). Using thematic analysis in psychology. Qualitative Research in Psychology, 3(2), 77–101.

Brookfield, S. (1986). *Understanding and Facilitating Adult Learning: a Comprehensive Analysis of Principles and Effective Practices.* San Francisco, Jossey-Bass.

Campbell, M., Gibson, W., Hall, A., Richards D., & Callery, P. (2008). Online vs. Face-to-Face Discussion in a Web-Based Research Methods Course for Postgraduate Nursing Students: A Quasi-Experimental Study. *International Journal of Nursing Studies,* 45(5), 750–759.

Dorrian, J., & Wache, D. (2009) Introduction of an Online Approach to Flexible Learning for on-Campus and Distance Education Students: Lessons Learned and Ways Forward. *Nurse Education Today,* 20(2), 157–167.

Dziuban, C. D., Hartman, J., & Moskal, P. (2004). *Blended Learning.* London: Springer Verlag.

Garrison, D. R., & Vaughan, N. D. (2008). *Blended learning in higher education: Framework principles and guidelines.* San Francisco: Jossey-Bass.

Garrison, D. R., & Kanuka, H. (2004). Blended Learning: Uncovering Its Transformative Potential in Higher Education. *The Internet and Higher Education,* 7(2), 95–105.

Green, T., Alejandro, J., & Brown, A. H. (2008). The retention of experienced faculty in online distance education programs: understanding factors that impact their involvement. *The International Review of Research in Open and Distance Learning,* 10(3), 1–8.

Hadjerrouit, S. (2008). Towards a blended learning model for teaching and learning computer programming: A case study. *Informatics in Education-An International Journal*, 7(2), 181–210.

Hew, K. F., & Wing, S. C. (2013). Use of Web 2.0 Technologies in K-12 and Higher Education: The Search for Evidence-Based Practice. *Educational Research Review*, 9, 47–64.

Hew, K. F., & Wing, S. C. (2014). *Using Blended Learning Evidence Based Practices*. Singapore: Springer Singapore.

Ireland, J., Martindale, S., Johnson, N., Adams, D., Eboh W., & Mowatt, E. (2009). Blended learning in education: effects on knowledge and attitude. *British Journal of Nursing*, 18(2), 124–130.

King, K. P. (2002). Identifying success in online teacher education and professional development. *The Internet and Higher Education*, 5(3), 231–246.

Lowenstein, A. J. (2011). Blended learning. In Bradshaw, M. J., & Lowenstein, A. J. (Eds.), *Innovative teaching strategies in nursing and related health professions*. London: Jones-Bartlett Learning.

Means, B., Toyama, Y., Murphy, R., Bakia, M., & Jones, K. (2010). *Evaluation of Evidence-Based Practices in Online Learning: A Meta-Analysis and Review of Online Learning Studies*. London: Monograph.

Mccray, G. E. (2000). Information Technology and Management. *Information Technology and Management*, 1(4), 307–327.

Norberg, A., Moskal, P. D., & Dziuban, C. D. (2011). A Time Based Blended Learning Model. *On the Horizon*, 19(3), 207–216.

Rossiter, R., & Day, J. (2016). Cycles of Reflection and Challenge: Using Sequential Blended Learning Strategies to Enhance Student Understanding of, and Transition to, the Nurse Practitioner Role in Australia. *Collegian*, 23(2), 159–166.

Salmon, G. (2003). *E-Moderating: The Key to Teaching and Learning Online*. London, RoutledgeFalmer.

Song, L., Singleton, E. S., Hill, J. R., & Koh, M. H. (2004). Improving online learning: student perceptions of useful and challenging characteristics. *The Internet and Higher Education*, 7(1), 59–70.

Strambi, A., & Bouvet, E. (2003). Flexibility and interaction at a distance: A mixed-mode environment for language learning. *Language Learning and Technology*, 7(3), 81–102.

Volery, T., & Lord, D. (2000). Critical Success Factors in Online Education. *International Journal of Educational Management*, 14(5), 216–223.

Welker, J., & Berardino, L. (2005). Blended learning: understanding the middle ground between traditional classroom and fully online instruction. *Journal of Educational Technology Systems*, 34(1), 33–55.

Wingard, R. G. (2004). Classroom teaching in web-enhanced courses: A multi-institutional study. *EDUCAUSE Quarterly*, 1, 26–35.

Woo, Y., & Reeves, T. C. (2007). Meaningful Interaction in Web-Based Learning: A Social Constructivist Interpretation. *The Internet and Higher Education*, 10(1), 15–25.

Chapter 4

The effectiveness of e-learning in Business Communication at the University of Johannesburg? What students say!

Magas R. Pather

Introduction

With my chapter, I contribute to the book *E-learning 1.0, 2.0, and 3.0 in Higher Education* as I discuss the effectiveness of e-learning from an African perspective. The case reported is from a course in Business Communication given at the University of Johannesburg in South Africa. In the chapter, I let my students have their say as they offer their perceptions of the effectiveness of our use of e-learning in said Business Communication course. Although African countries experience constricting factors with the use of technology in education (which I will explore in section 1 below), e-learning is not new to us. It is common knowledge that we are living in an information and technological era due to sophisticated developments in electronic devices like computers, mobile phones, and tablets. These developments influence almost every aspect of our daily lives. We use technologies at our workplaces, in our learning environments, for entertainment, etc.

At the University of Johannesburg, although e-learning has been welcomed in our learning space, there is insufficient information on its effectiveness. A central question for us to ask is: "*Do students learn more when using e-learning compared to face-to-face learning?*".

Studying the effectiveness of e-learning is not new. Several academics have compared the effectiveness of e-learning to face-to-face learning. Clark (1983) argued that the medium of delivery hardly contributes to the planned outcomes of our education, and concluded from his studies that there is no advantage in favour of technology. He followed this up in his 1994–article, *Media will never influence learning* (Clark, 1994).

Russell (1999) did a comparison of 355 studies of e-learning, which is best known as the "no significant difference" studies. He came to the conclusion that e-learning does not outperform face-to-face learning. McConnell (2000) provided a comprehensive comparison of the differences between e-learning and face-to-face learning. He too came to the conclusion that learning is not necessarily improved using e-learning. Davies & Graff (2005) identified the link between e-learning interaction and student performance. They found that more e-learning interaction was not significantly associated with higher grades; however, students who did fail their e-learning classes tended to interact less frequently with their peers. Hugenholtz et al. (2008) did a study within two groups (e-learning and face-to-face), and found that although both groups of students experienced a significant gain in knowledge, there was no significant difference in effect between the educational approaches.

If that was the whole story, it would leave those of us working with e-learning on a rather pessimistic note. Looking further into the research of the effectiveness of e-learning in comparison with face-to-face learning, it is possible to find just as many studies in favour of e-learning. Keller & Suzuki (2004) studied learner motivation and e-learning design and came to the conclusion that not only did e-learning show a positive change in students' motivation it also diminished drop-out rates. Kim & Frick (2011) showed a positive change in motivation of students engaged in self-directed e-learning. Rowley (2011) argued that the use of e-Portfolios as an integrated part of e-learning increased both student innovation and student learning. McGuigan (2011) showed how e-learning improved students' self-directed learning. Raiker (2013) accounted for the enhancement of teacher students' professional development through computer supported collaborative learning. Ludewig-Rohwer (2017) showed how students' language learning increased through the use of online role play.

Having consulted research on the effectiveness of e-learning one may, therefore, have a split mind. What works? What doesn't work? And why? As I seek to answer the central question: *"Do students learn more when using e-learning compared to face-to-face learning?"* I will consult my students and let them have their say. I use a qualitative research method for my investigation, and I use both questionnaires and one-on-one interviews to ascertain the students' views. I will come back to the research methodology in more detail in section three.

Reading my chapter, I hope you will gain awareness about:

1. e-learning for Business Communication from an African perspective;

2. e-learning as a pedagogical and practical tool for Business Communication;

3. my students' perceptions of the effectiveness of e-learning for the Business Communication course.

The chapter is divided into three main sections. In section one, I briefly introduce some of the major challenges to e-learning in Africa. I do so to set the scene and show that those of us working with online higher education on the African Continent face a different reality to our colleagues in North America, Europe and Australasia. This section allows me also to present the South African context affecting the University of Johannesburg and our course on Business Communication. In section two, I discuss some of the pedagogical and practical aspects surrounding e-learning. My intention with this section is to frame e-learning as a pedagogical and practical tool. In section three, I turn to my own students and let them comment on the perceived effectiveness of e-learning in the Business Communication course. This is the main section of my chapter, and the section in which I report my own research contribution. The results of this qualitative research also lead to my conclusion of the chapter. I hope that reading my chapter will inspire you to not only reflect on your choice of an e-learning tool, but also on the pedagogy behind choosing and practicing e-learning activities.

Section I: Challenges to e-learning in Africa

In this first section, I set the scene by briefly discussing some of the challenges to e-learning in an African context. e-learning and the availability of technology is changing the face of education across the African continent, but, although more and more universities experience successes with e-learning, African countries still experience impediments to implementation and access to technology. Major constraints such as poor infrastructure and availability of resources make e-learning unfeasible. Some of the most common and key constraints to e-learning which are present at the national level in Africa are listed in the table below.

Rank	Constricting factor	Percen-tage	The country most likely to be constrained	The country least likely to be constrained
1	Bandwidth is limited	17	Zambia	Kenya
2	Financial resources are lacking	11	Zambia	Nigeria
2	Human resource capacity is inadequate	11	South Africa	Tanzania
2	Electricity is limited	11	Nigeria	South Africa
5	Appropriate training is lacking	8	Kenya	Uganda
6	Appropriate hardware is lacking	7	Tanzania	Ghana
7	Insufficient resources	6	South Africa	Nigeria
8	Appropriate software is lacking	6	Tanzania	Ghana
8	Political will is lacking	4	Nigeria	Uganda
8	Corruption and theft of resources	4	Uganda	Zambia
11	Adequate content based on e-learning	3	Tanzania	Nigeria South Africa
12	Pressure of poverty	3	Kenya South Africa	Uganda
12	Sustainability is not prioritised	3	Kenya	Tanzania
12	Leadership is lacking	3	Nigeria	Uganda
15	Instability and lack of security	1	South Africa	Zambia

Table 1: *Major restrictions to e-learning in Africa.*

Table 1 demonstrates that some countries in Africa may be facing multiple restrictions in their ability to provide e-learning solutions to educational needs in the Higher Education sector. The most common problem is the limitation of bandwidth which reduces internet capability and stability (Ekundayo & Ekundayo, 2009). Additionally, Ekundayo & Ekundayo (2009) mentioned other limitations with the availability of technology such as access in rural areas and the capacity of the technology owned by many people to support new learning techniques. Furthermore, an example of this is seen in research conducted in Kenya using Graphogame, a game serving as a research tool to study reading acquisition, which requires the use of a smartphone. Researchers found that most families in rural areas, even those with mobile phones, did not have mobiles with the capability to use the game's technology (Ekundayo & Ekundayo, 2009). More protracted and acute restrictions that may limit access to e-learning platforms generally include political instability. We see this in many places in Africa. My case is based in the University of Johannesburg, and therefore set in a South African context. Specific to the South African context, as seen in Table 1, are: a) human resource capacity is inadequate; b) insufficient resources; c) pressure of poverty, d) instability and e) lack of security.

a) human resource capacity is inadequate

We experience human resource capacity as inadequate when my cohort of five hundred undergraduate students is required to research an assignment online. The computer laboratories on the UJ's Soweto campus cannot cater for this large number of students at one sitting; and furthermore, there are not enough technical support personnel to assist first year diploma students who do not possess the requisite computer skills.

b) insufficient resources

We also experience insufficient resources as another stumbling block. There are insufficient computers and also intermittent power outages, which results in internet connectivity being lost. On the SWC-UJ it is often the case that power is lost, and, because electricity consumption is so large, certain areas remain without power, and concomitantly internet connectivity, for long periods. Students who rely on public transport (the majority) are forced to leave the campus and make their way home. This scenario can occur for a week or intermittently throughout a month.

c) pressure of poverty

The pressure of poverty is exemplified in the following example: twenty percent of Business Communication students rely on the feeding scheme for meals, sponsored by "Gift of the Givers". This further necessitates that these students are physically on campus. Another resultant problem, which is the product of poverty, is the theft of mobile phones and other electronic devices. These underprivileged students have no means of replacing their lost items since they are students who receive external funding.

d) instability and e) lack of security

We also experience instability and lack of security in South Africa. One example is that of student protests in 2015, where we experienced students destroying Computer laboratories through arson. Under such conditions, where we suddenly lacked technological infrastructure and capacity building, students are hamstrung. A private security company had to be brought on-board to provide security for staff, students and UJ property. In sum, these constricting factors represent significant obstacles, and they impinge upon students and academic communities in South Africa relying on e-learning. As Table 1 shows, however, South Africa also has some advantages over other African countries when it comes to e-learning. The lack of electricity is not as severe there as elsewhere, although electricity will be disrupted irregularly. Academically, we are also considered to have adequate content and technological acumen to present courses online.

Overall, this short introduction to the African and South African educational context should make you aware that it is different from educational contexts experienced in other parts of the world. It means that designing e-learning activities and assessments has to be contextualized in light of the particular technological, political, financial and social situations. Please bear that in mind, when you read about our experiences in the Business Communication course at the University of Johannesburg in South Africa. Before I go into detail with the e-learning activities at University of Johannesburg, though, I will touch upon some more general pedagogical and practical reflections on e-learning. I do so in section 2, with the intention of framing e-learning as a pedagogical and practical tool.

Section 2: Pedagogical and practical reflections on e-learning

The impact of a learning environment in relation to learning outcomes has constantly been explored by researchers (Hara & Kling, 2000). Whether e-learning platforms have distinctively impacted the teaching and learning environment, has become a source for vigorous debate. Researchers such as Ramsden & Entwistle (1981) empirically discovered a relationship between learning methodologies and perceived characteristics of the academic environment. Haertela *et al.* (1981) found correlations between student perceptions of the social-psychological learning environments and the impact this has on student achievement. Advocates of e-learning argued that it can be effective in potentially eliminating barriers while providing increased convenience, flexibility, currency of material, tailored learning, and feedback over a traditional face-to-face experience (Hackbarth, 1996; Harasim, 1990; Kiser, 1999; Matthews, 1999; Swan *et al.*, 2000). Opponents, however, are concerned that students in an e-learning environment may feel isolated, confused, frustrated, which will result in disinterest in the subject (Maki *et al.*, 2000). In the following section I examine some of the key differences of learning efficacy focusing on interaction as a key component according to Business Communication students' perceptions about e-learning and face-to-face learning.

Interaction as pedagogy and practice

An important element of classroom learning is the social and communicative interactions between student and lecturer or student and student. A student's ability to ask a question, to share an opinion, or to disagree with a point of view are fundamental learning activities. It is often through conversation, discourse, discussion, and debate among students and between instructors and students that a new concept is clarified, an old assumption is challenged, a skill is practiced, an original idea is formed and encouraged, and ultimately, a learning objective is achieved (Przybylski & Weinstein, 2012). e-learning requires adjustments by instructors as well as students for successful interactions to occur. e-learning courses often substitute classroom interaction with discussion boards, blogs, synchronous chat rooms, electronic bulletin boards and e-mails (Przybylski & Weinstein, 2012). The usefulness of such a virtual interactive environment has not been adequately evaluated.

Student-to-instructor and student-to-student interactions are important elements in the design of an e-learning course because students can experience a "sense of community," enjoy mutual interdependence, build a "sense of trust," and have shared goals and values (Fulford & Zhang, 1993; Kumari, 2001; Sherry, 1996; Davies & Graff, 2005; Rovai, 2002). Interaction in an e-learning environment is less intimidating since there is less pressure on students to respond, than interaction in a face-to-face setting (Warschauer, 1997). e-learning discussions can also encourage more reserved students to participate to a greater extent (Citera, 1988). However, the advantage of e-learning interaction may not be realized if a close connection among the students is absent. Haythornthwaite *et al.* (2000) found that students who failed to make connections with other members in their group reported feeling isolated and more stressed. While this narrative has political and economic significance, we have to be cognizant that if any modicum of success is to be achieved, it is imperative that students air their views. Important differences related to interaction in the two methods of instruction are adapted (Table 2).

	e-learning	face-to-face learning
Mode	Discussions through text only; Can be structured; dense; permanent; limited; stark.	Verbal discussions complemented by non-verbal approaches. Interactive reprographics assist in the delivery.
Sense of Instructor Control	Reduced sense of instructor control; Easier for students to ignore instructor.	More sense of leadership from lecturer; Students are generally wary to ignore the lecturer.
Discussion	Group contact frequently continued; Depth of analysis often increased in science-based courses; Discussion often stops for periods of time, then is restarted; Level of reflection can be high depending on student and instructor interest; Instructor can sway conversations on the basis of curriculum knowledge and designer.	Students develop a sense of belonging; Analysis varies, dependent on time available; Discussions occur within a timeframe; Limited time for reflection during lectures; Conversations are less likely to be shaped by lecturer without retorts by students particularly the high-flyers.
Group Dynamics	Less sense of anxiety; Participation is voluntary; Dynamics are 'hidden' but noticeable; No breaks, constantly in the meeting; Can be active listening without participation; A crucial success factor is the availability of the Internet; Different expectation about participation; Virtual sense of being part of the community in interactions or discussions.	Anxiety at beginning/during meetings; Participation unequal; More chance of hierarchies; Dynamics evident but lost after the event; Listening without participation may be frowned upon; In UJ, the lecture room impacts because of African cultural norms- working in a community. Certain expectations about participation; Immediacy of verbal/non-verbal communication or discussions.

	e-learning	face-to-face learning
Returning	High psychological/emotional stress when wanting to rejoin.	Stress of rejoining not high.
Feedback	Feedback on each individual's piece of work very detailed and focused; Whole group can see and read each other's feedback; Traumatic for first years; Textual feedback only; No one can "hide" and not give feedback; Permanent record of feedback obtained by all; Delayed responses to feedback; Mostly generic; Sometimes little discussion after feedback; Group looks at all participants' work at same time can be embarrassing.	Can cover much detail, based on individual's work; Group hears feedback; Verbal/visual feedback; Possible to "free-ride" and avoid giving feedback; Permanent record of feedback Numerical and in text-; Immediate reactions to feedback possible; Usually some discussion after feedback with tutors and lecturer consultations, looking at wider issues; Group looks at one participant's work at a time.
Divergence /Choice Level	Loose-bound nature encourages divergent talk and adventatious learning; undersells feedback and other participants (receivers) could experience increasing uncertainty.	Contrite, requiring adherence to accepted protocols; Uncertainty less likely due to common understandings about how to take part in discussions.

Table 2: A Comparative Analysis of e-learning and face-to-face learning, adapted from McConnell (2000).

The crucial differences between e-learning and face-to-face learning highlighted in Table 2 are that delivery in e-learning is textual, whereas with face-to-face delivery, the content is verbally interactive and complemented by reprographics. This is important for students who have English as a second or third language, particularly in developing their oral presentation skills. Another important difference is that with e-learning many students feel isolated which results in a high dropout rate. The same can be said of face-to-face learning, but such students are more likely to re-join, as there is more likely to be community spirit, a very important motivational factor for students who have recently left the school environment and joined university.

Section 3: e-learning at the University of Johannesburg

Currently, we are involved in a wide-reaching process of reflection and change, oriented toward promoting e-learning or at the very least hybrid or blended learning at UJ. This leap to change the educational model of most South African universities stems from the global endeavour to be participants in the fourth Industrial Revolution: the Robotic Age. This is the basis of a new knowledge-based economy that responds to the challenges of globalisation and decolonisation underpinned by Africanisation (Olivier, 2016). In line with the title of this book, politics must help drive e-learning practices forward across universities. With both e-learning and traditional classroom teaching, the overarching outcome is that students achieve a level of competence across the Business Communication curriculum.

In Business Communication, various assessments both verbal and written are conducted during the academic year. Their intention is to measure competence; however this cannot be the gold standard of establishing competence. There are various factors that impinge on its (assessment's) absoluteness, particularly in the e-learning space. In keeping with interdisciplinary fruitfulness, the acquisition of English linguistic competence through interaction with lecturer and peers is vital in my Bussiness Communication classes at UJ- Soweto campus; which evidences the need for face-to-face delivery in the acquisition of primarily linguistic skills in Business Communication which makes up the first semester curriculum. This has implications for teaching Business Communication and English skills, as students imitate their peers and teachers, and are influenced by various environments such as visual media. In aspects of the theory of syntax, Chomsky (1965:40) introduces a distinction between what he terms *"competence"* and *"performance"*. Linguistic theory is concerned primarily with an ideal speaker-listener, in a completely homogeneous speech-community, who knows its language perfectly and is unaffected by such grammatically irrelevant conditions as memory limitations, distractions, shifts of attention and interest, and errors (random or characteristic). This manifests itself when my students apply their knowledge of English speaking skills in the Oral Presentation in Business Communication. To study actual linguistic performance, we must consider the interaction of a variety of factors, of which the underlying competence of the speaker-hearer is fundamental. The researcher thus makes a vital distinction between competence (the speaker-hearer's knowledge of English) and performance (the actual use of English in concrete situations). A record of natural speech will show numerous false starts, deviations from rules, changes of plan in mid-course, and so on. The problem for the linguist, as well as for the student learning the language, is to determine from the data of performance the underlying system he puts to use in actual performance (Chomsky, 1965:3f). It becomes imperative then that Business Communication ideally should be offered as hybrid course. In the e-learning component, it must strive for pedagogical excellence by reaching e-learning 3.0 (construction), wherein both teacher and student collaborate to create new knowledge, as expounded by Nygaard (in this volume).

Qualitative data analysis

A purposive sample of Business Communication students were selected. These research tools interrogated students on a range of subjects and learning methods. Using qualitative analysis, the paper analysed students' responses based on personal experiences and their preferred option of learning. The research used the interpretive qualitative research approach. Cohen & Manion (1994:36) assert that interpretive researchers understand *"the world of human experience"*. Interpretivists recognise multiple interpretations as equally valid (Bertram & Christiansen, 2014). In this study, the participants' interpretations of e-learning and traditional classroom teaching methodologies in the context of Business Communication and English skills are sought. Qualitative research was employed to discover and understand a process and the perspectives of the people involved (Merriam, 1998).

The design used for this research was a multiple case study. Creswell (2013:97) posits that case study *"explores a real-life, contemporary multiple bounded system (cases) over time"*. A case study design enables one to gain an in-depth understanding and insight into the problem being investigated (Merriam, 1998; Patton, 2015; Baxter & Jack, 2008). Purposive sampling consisting of two hundred and fifty past and current students were used, because the use of specific participants lends to the richness and relevance of data in relation to the study (Yin, 2006). Data was analysed using content analysis which is a *"technique used to make replicable and valid inferences from different contexts"* (Krippendorff, 2004:18). Henning et al. (2004) procedure for content analysis was applied to analyse the data obtained. The transcripts were read to get a general idea of the content after which a coding technique was used to identify *"segments of meaning"* (Henning et al., 2004:138). Once the transcripts were coded, the codes were grouped into categories and thereafter patterns across categories led to the generation of themes (Henning et al., 2004). Trustworthiness is the *"truth value"* of the study, its applicability, consistency and neutrality (Lincoln & Guba, cited in Mertens, 2003). A measure of triangulation eliminated bias that might result from relying exclusively on one data collection strategy, source or theory .

Case Study data

In *"The Trouble With e-learning Education"*, Edmundson (2012) captures the inadequacy of e-learning courses from the teacher's perspective, and the researcher can corroborate that it applies to students as well. In the blog below, Edmunson (2012:NP) relates his experience with an e-learning mathematics course: *"I was a math-obsessive in high school. To supplement my school's curriculum, I turned to a Stanford programme offering e-learning courses to gifted youth. I started the programme with enthusiasm, but I soon felt alone and unsupported. I had no one to impress or disappoint. I struggled to stay motivated. It was impersonal and transactional, and it nearly destroyed my obsession. A face-to-face meeting in a classroom imposes accountability, inspires effort and promotes academic responsibility in subtle ways that we don't fully appreciate. On a campus, students attend class and stay alert because they worry what the lecturer will think if they don't"*. Once they are in the lecture room, the battle is mostly won. As in life, 80% of education is showing up, in person.

Table 3 compares the content delivery mechanisms between the two instructional modes.

Questions	Themes Challenging aspects about taking an e-learning course	Evidence from Interviews with participants
If given the choice between taking an e-learning or face-to-face course which would you prefer?	Wi-Fi can suddenly be off. Lack of adequate information about the e-learning platform. Stress, time consuming not being able to gain access off-campus.	I have just tried to complete the mcq4 on Emperor Qin and the wi-fi connection cut; since the timer ran out. I could not complete it. I ask for another attempt at the test please sir.
Do you think Business Communication as an e-learning course will prepare you for the workplace?	No, particularly the skills we learn in oral communication. Here we need the lecturer to show us. This also gives us confidence when communicating in the workplace.	120 out of 129 respondents said no.
Do you think it would have been better to do Business Communication as an e-learning course?	Less engagement and no need for practical exams.	20 out of 129 respondents said yes. 107 out of 129 respondents said no. 2 did not respond.
Experiences with technology at UJ	Hard to adjust to the new developments, students weren't consulted.	Only 5 out of 129 students felt that technology was bad at UJ. However, 90% were weary of Business Communication being an online course; they felt contact time is vital, for this course.

Table 3: Data from the questionnaire and interviews.

Students in both e-learning and face-to-face classes were given access to the Blackboard system via UJ's U link platform. In the e-learning classes, all course materials and activities were delivered via Blackboard. In the face-to-face classes, required readings other than the textbook and multimedia resources (mainly video cases for discussion) were made accessible online. In addition, the instructor also required the students to use the assignment function on Blackboard to submit assignments and retrieve feedback. Otherwise, classroom activities such as lectures, discussions, and group projects were carried out in the classroom. The main difference between the two types of class is the mode of interaction between instructor and students as well as that among students. After the protests at UJ in 2015, I wanted to test the efficacy of my teaching, via a questionnaire. I obtained Business Communication students' perceptions about the course. Below is the Business Communication instructor's predetermined teaching objectives, which made up the core of the questionnaire.

Business Communication objectives' effectiveness.

Students will be able to:
1. Comprehend and use appropriately core academic and disciplinary terminology and vocabulary;
2. Identify and solve problems and make decisions using creative and critical thinking;
3. Demonstrate the ability to read textbooks, argumentative texts and entry-level journal articles;
4. Demonstrate familiarity with the Module structure of some academic and professional texts;
5. Use the norms of academic communication in spoken and written form; show some awareness of the norms of professional communication;
6. Express ideas clearly in writing;
7. Demonstrate the ability to produce texts which they have edited for syntactic, grammatical and orthographic correctness;
8. Demonstrate awareness of the differences between academic language, professional language, and every day colloquial language;
9. Understand the role of communication in professional life;
10. Communication skill: Able to debate/discuss/present and write in academic and administrative style;
11. Research ethics: Understandable to practice researcher's code of conduct.

The teaching objectives were communicated to the students via the course syllabus, during the lectures and on Blackboard. The survey asked the students to assess the effectiveness of the class in achieving the objectives on a scale of 1 (poor) to 5 (excellent) and then rank the importance of these objectives on a scale of 1 (very unimportant), to 5 (very important). The result is presented in Table 4. Business Communication students tended to evaluate and rank the ten teaching objectives as more important than the e-learning students did, but they assessed the effectiveness in achieving the five objectives lower than the e-learning students did. The largest discrepancy occurs in the assessment on the effectiveness of improving writing and verbal skills. An explanation for this discrepancy is that e-learning students are required to write more than classroom students, because most communication in the e-learning environment is carried out by writing and then posting that writing. However, all classroom students considered that the learning experience was successful, whereas only 65% of the e-learning students did so.

Learning Objectives	Online		Classroom	
	Effectiveness Mean	Importance Mean	Effectiveness Mean	Importance Mean
Improving my intellectual level	3.37	3.67	3.10	3.78
Improving my analytical skills	3.50	3.47	3.20	3.78
Improving my critical thinking skills	3.47	3.53	3.20	4.11
Improving my writing and oral skills	3.20	3.27	2.80	3.56
Improving my awareness of ethical considerations like plagiarism	3.27	3.07	3.01	4.11
The learning experience was meaningful	65%		100%	

Table 4: Business Communication Student's Evaluation of e-learning and face to face learning effectiveness.

A few design flaws in the research may explain the disparity of findings. First, though the learning objectives were embedded in course material, the instructor noted and emphasized the teaching objectives during the lectures from time to time in the classroom. Second, whereas the survey administered to students who had done an e-learning course was distributed in the middle of semester 2, the face-to-face class survey was distributed at the end of the final examination in 2017, students could have felt stressed. "Face to face" students at that time may have predicted the outcome of the paper, and could have felt that they have accomplished all the learning objectives. However, since the survey was anonymous and the research could not link the grades to the survey responses, the conjecture cannot be proved. To compare the effectiveness of interaction, the e-learning students were also asked to evaluate the different aspects of interaction as compared to their previous classroom experience. Although most of them perceived no change regarding the different aspects of interaction and the learning experience, more students concluded that the traditional classroom instruction experience was better than that of the online. The evaluation regarding the quality of interaction with other students had the most divergent results. Only a small proportion of students commented in the survey that they were pleased or encouraged by other student's responses to their discussion, however, most students felt that a sense of community did not exist.

In comparison to traditional classroom instruction, in this online course	Definitely Decreased	Somewhat Decreased	No Change	Somewhat Increased	Definitely Increased	Mean N = 190
The quality of my learning experience	40	20	60	20	40	30.40
The intensity of my learning experience	10	10	60	40	50	30.47

Chapter 4

In comparison to traditional classroom instruction, in this online course	Definitely Decreased	Somewhat Decreased	No Change	Somewhat Increased	Definitely Increased	Mean N = 190
The amount of interaction with other students	10	20	60	20	75	30.33
The quality of interaction with other students	30	40	50	20	80	30.13
The quality of interaction with the instructor	50	10	80	20	80	30.33
The quantity of interaction with the instructor	40	10	80	20	60	30.33
My motivation to participate in class activities	10	20	60	20	60	30.40
My comfort level of participating in class activities	10	10	40	30	40	20.67

Table 5: Assessment of e-learning interaction.

A few students expressed frustrations about non-responsive group members in any group project setting. The most significant affirmation about e-learning interaction is regarding the comfort level of participation. A small number of respondents (20%) maintained that the comfort level of participation increased in e-learning class work (Table 5). This result is in agreement with previous findings that the classroom environment is less intimidating and may encourage student participation because of friendships and strength in numbers (Citera, 1988; Warschauer, 1997).

Discussion

Given that knowledge of e-learning effectiveness in Business Communication is very limited since research is limited on the effectiveness and trustworthiness of e-learning platforms like Blackboard as an academic tool, this chapter explored student's perceptions about e-learning effectiveness, rather than providing strong empirical evidence supporting theoretical arguments. Although the chapter uses a sample from a single Business Communication programme offered at UJ in South Africa, the study may offer some insights to similar courses and similar programmes. The study controls some critical factors relevant to learning effectiveness, such as course content and face-to-face instruction, but fails to control students' personal traits and other exogenous factors. Despite the limitations, this study points to a number of critical issues about e- learning and raises questions for further study.

First, learning effectiveness is a complex concept with multiple dimensions and it should be assessed with multiple measures. Even though student perceptions do not present significant differences between e-learning and face-to-face classes in this study, the nuanced differences in student's persistence rate and assessment of interaction demonstrate that the two instructional modes are not equal. It is necessary to direct more carefully delineated research efforts to explore the various aspects of learning effectiveness that can be affected by the e-learning instructional mode.

Second, the low persistence rate of e-learning students in the Business Communication class raises the following question: Would e-learning teaching be equally effective in a different course? Some educational programmes may simply not fit into an e-learning setting (medical, physical education and verbal presentation skills in English). Designers of e-learning programmes should take into consideration that the e-learning environment may have different effects on student learning in different courses. The low persistence rate also points to several research questions: What are the specific issues in methodology classes (i.e. theoretical concepts, specialized notations) that may affect students' learning in an e-learning environment? What aspects in the Business Communication curriculum may be a better fit for e-learning rather than face-to-face classes, and vice versa? How could we improve the design of an e-learning course to be effective, especially for some topics that are more challenging in the e-learning environment? The result also points to the importance of pre-registration counselling and post-registration advising. Pre-registration counselling could be used to eliminate students who may not persist through the programme. The counselling may design a module to allow students to self-assess their likelihood of completing the programme. This can be achieved by providing a clearer picture of the estimated time commitment and intensity of the programme. Once students are enrolled, it is also important to retain them in the programme through additional or continued advising. Advising programmes may consider inviting student feedback for improvement, sharing successful student stories, teaching time management skills, and establishing student-to-student or faculty-to-student connections to eliminate the feeling of isolation in the e-learning environment. Frankola (2001) suggests that motivation, realistic expectations, highly integrated live sessions, and application of advanced technologies contribute to persistence in both the academic and corporate distance learning environment. More importantly, counselling and advising may put more emphasis on those courses that present more challenges to students to succeed.

Third, the less intimidating traditional classroom space may be used to enhance collaboration in the virtual domain and in so doing enhance participation. The twenty-first century student is part of the so-called Net Generation that grew up with the Internet. Virtual space has been an integral part of their daily life. Face-to-face classes may exploit this venue to accommodate students who feel intimidated about participating in the classroom. Instructors may design supplemental e-learning discussion modules (e.g., by using Blackboard discussion boards) to extend participation opportunities to those who may not open up as readily in the classroom. This approach may also enhance the quality of participation, because past studies show that an e-learning setting may encourage in-depth and reasoned discussion (Karayan & Crowe, 1997; Smith & Hardaker, 2000).

Last, the difficulties in controlling exogenous factors make the learning effectiveness comparison between e-learning and face-to-face classes a perplexing task, calling for a more concerted research effort. Though this chapter has attempted to control several of those factors—such as instructor, course content, and assignments—some exogenous factors, such as different levels of emphasis in course content and teaching objectives, could have biased the students' self-evaluation of learning effectiveness. Carefully designed and implemented research may discover the subtle differences in learning effectiveness between the two instructional modes.

Conclusion

This study compares the effectiveness of e-learning and face-to-face learning, attempting to go beyond grades and to include a logical assessment of three important aspects of learning: 1) student interaction; 2) achieving learning objectives; and 3) student persistence.

The findings indicate that although student performance is independent of the mode of instruction, if Business Communication were to be a totally online course the throughput rate at the University of Johannesburg would decrease. Student responses indicate clearly that participation is less intimidating and the quality and quantity of interaction is increased in face-to-face classes. The findings have several implications for student learning, course development, and curriculum design.

E-learning interaction can be used to enhance learning, especially for students who tend to be reserved in the classroom setting. In developing e-learning courses, we should realise that some courses may be more challenging to students. Course developers need to diligently examine what are the specific subjects that may hinder persistence and supplement instruction with face-to-face consulting, advising, or tutoring. Although an e-learning class offers a comparably effective learning alternative, we should recognize that e-learning has its unique advantages and disadvantages. In curriculum design, we need to consider how to exploit and integrate the proportional advantages of different modes of instruction to specific courses by offering not only entirely face-to-face or e-learning but also hybrid classes to overcome the constraints of time, place, and resources.

The implications also protrude into the research and practice of gauging e-learning outcomes. This chapter reveals that we can continually determine through observations, surveys, interviews, and analyses of student demography and course design what leads to greater, more effective learning outcomes. The ramifications of this approach is that it will contribute to preparing e-learning instructors in methods and the designing of educational support programmes that allow students to succeed in the e-learning environment. As we continue to assess, improve, and accumulate knowledge of teaching and learning effectiveness in an e-learning environment, we therefore hope that students, too, will achieve a greater understanding of and enjoy greater benefits from this new mode of instruction.

The quote from Nygaard (in this volume) sums up our traditional approach to e-learning. *"This has in many cases led to implementation of unitary stand-alone e-learning systems (CMS and LMS) which at the end of the day have been used as repositories for learning material only. It is my argument that e-learning in Higher Education had been skewed towards e-learning 1.0 (distribution) with a little bit of e-learning 2.0 (dialogue)"*. To guard against being guilty of what Nygaard (in this volume) posits: *"e-learning 1.0 (distribution) with a little bit of e-learning 2.0 (dialogue)"*, Business Communication semester one content requires face to face interaction and should be offered traditionally, with the remaining sections in the curriculum offered as a hybrid course. Interaction will be ensured as student and lecturer collaborate to create new knowledge viz evolve to e-learning 3.0 (Construction). At this level, we can also infuse the curriculum with decolonised content. This will obviate feelings of isolation build an academic community and improve the student persistent rate. Nygaard's, (in this volume) model below gives a clear explanation in tabular format of what we should strive for pedagogically, when migrating from face to face to e-learning.

	e-learning 1.0 (Distribution)	e-learning 2.0 (Dialogue)	e-learning 3.0 (Construction)
Teacher-driven (subject and format decided by teacher)	course website podcast video broadcast online test online quiz online surveys	blogging session chat online conference	online review online assignments online case challenge online collaborative role play games

Table 6: Three types of e-learning (Nygaard, in this volume).

This chapter provided findings regarding e-learning as a teaching and learning method and made recommendations which could possibly streamline teaching and learning for second language English users. It is my hope that the findings influence curriculum designers and help us further shape the Business Communication curriculum at the University of Johannesburg by contributing to the existing body of research on how to teach Business Communication more effectively. Reverting back to the question of the effectiveness of e-learning: *"Do students learn more when using e-learning compared to face-to-face learning?"*, I will conclude that e-learning in Higher Education can act as an innovative platform for teaching which can, if implemented under optimal, circumstances contribute positively to lasting learning.

About the Author

Magas R. Pather is a Senior Lecturer in the Department of Languages, Cultural Studies and Applied Linguistics (LanCSAL), School of Languages in the Faculty of Humanities, at the University of Johannesburg. He can be contacted at this e-mail: magasp@uj.ac.za.

Bibliography

Baxter, P., & Jack, S. (2008). Qualitative Case Study Methodology: Study Design and Implementation for Novice Researchers. *The Qualitative Report*, 13(4), 544–559.

Bertram, C., & Christiansen, I. (2014). *Understanding research: an introduction to reading research.* Pretoria: Van Schaik.

Chomsky, N. (1965). *Aspects of the Theory of Syntax.* Cambridge, Mass.: M.I.T. Press.

Citera, M. (1988). Distributed teamwork: The impact of communication media on influence and decision quality. *Journal of the American Society for Information Science,* 49(9), 792–800.

Clark, R. E. (1983). Reconsidering research on learning from media. *Review of Educational Research.* 53(4), 445–459.

Clark, R. E. (1994). Media will never influence learning. *Educational Technology Research and Development,* 42(2), 21–29.

Cohen, L., & Manion, L. (1994). *Research methods in education.* London: Routledge.

Creswell, J. W. (2013). *Steps in Conducting a Scholarly Mixed Methods Study.* Discipline-Based Education Research Group (DBER) speaker series no. 48.

Davies, J., & Graff, M. (2005). Performance in e-learning: e-learning participation and student grades. *British Journal of Educational Technology,* 36(4), 657–663.

Edmundson (2012). Retrieved June 3, 2018, from https://www.nytimes.com/2012/07/20/opinion/the-trouble-with-online-education.html.

Ekundayo, M. S., & Ekundayo, J. M. (2009). Capacity constraints in developing countries: A need for more e-learning space? The case of Nigeria. Retrieved February 20, 2018, from http://www.ascilite.org.au.

Frankola, K. (2001). Why e-learning drop out. *Workforce,* 80(10), 52–60.

Fulford, C. P., & Zhang, S. (1993). Perceptions of Interaction: The Critical Predictor in Distance Education. *American Journal of Distance Education,* 7(3), 8–21.

Hackbarth, S. (1996). *The educational technology handbook: A comprehensive guide.* Englewood Cliffs, NJ: Educational Technology Publications.

Haertela, G. D., Walberg, H. J., & Haertela, E. H. (1981). Socio psychological environments and learning: A quantitative synthesis. *British Educational Research Journal,* 7(1), 27–36.

Hara, N., & Kling, R. (2000). Students' distress with a web-based distance education course: An ethno- graphic study of participants' experiences. *Information, Communication, and Society,* 3, 557–579.

Harasim, L. M. (1990). *e-learning education: Perspectives on a new environment.* New York: Praeger.

Haythornthwaite, C., Kazmer, M., Robins, J., & Shoemaker, S. (2000). Community development among distance learners: Temporal and technological dimensions. *Journal of Computer Mediated Communication*, 6(1), 54–78.

Henning, E., Van Rensburg, W. A., & Smit, B. (2004). *Finding your way in qualitative research*. Pretoria: Van Schaik.

Hugenholtz, N. I. R., de Croon, E. M., Smits, P. B., van Dijk, F. J. H., & Nieuwenhuijsen, K. (2008). Effectiveness of e-learning in continuing medical education for occupational physicians. *Occupational Medicine*, 58(5), 370–372.

Karayan, S., & Crowe, J. (1997). Student perspectives of electronic discussion groups. THE *Journal: Technological Horizons in Education*, 24(9), 69–71.

Keller, J. M., & Suzuki, K. (2004). Learner motivation and e-learning design: A multinationally validated process. *Journal of Educational Media*, 29(3), 229–239.

Kim K.-J., & Frick, T. W. (2011). Changes in Student Motivation during Online Learning. *Journal of Educational Computing Research*, 44, 1–23.

Kiser, K. (1999). 10 things we know so far about e-learning training. *Training*, 36, 66–74.

Krippendorff, K. (2004). Reliability in content analysis. Some common misconceptions and recommendations. *Human Communication research*, 30(3), 411–433.

Kumari, D. S. (2001).Connecting graduate students to virtual guests through asynchronous discussions: Analysis of an experience. *Journal of Asynchronous Learning Networks*, 5(2), 53–63.

Ludewig-Rohwer, I. (2017). Language Learning in Higher Education through Engaging in Online Role Play. In Branch, J., Hayes, S., Hørsted, A., & Nygaard, C. (Eds.), *Innovative Teaching and Learning in Higher Education*. Oxfordshire, UK: Libri Publishing Ltd., 59–68.

Maki, R. H., Maki W. S., Patterson, M., & Whittaker, P. D. (2000). Evaluation of a web-based introductory psychology course: I. Learning and satisfaction in on-line versus lecture courses. *Behavior Research Methods, Instruments and Computers*, 32, 230–239.

Matthews, D. (1999). The origins of distance education and its use in the United States. *THE Journal*, 27(2), 54–66.

McConnell, D. (2000). *Implementing computer supported cooperative learning*. London: Kogan Page Limited.

McGuigan, A. (2011). A Centralised Tutor System to Support the Affective Needs of Online Learners. In Nygaard, C., Courtney, N., & Holtham, C. (Eds.), *Beyond Transmission – Innovations in University Teaching*. Oxfordshire, UK: Libri Publishing Ltd., 151–166.

Merriam, S. B. (1998). *Qualitative Research and Case Study Applications in Education*. San Fransisco: Jossey-Bass Publishers.

Mertens, D. M. (2003). Mixed methods and the politics of human research: The transformative-emancipatory perspective. In A. Tashakkori and C. Teddlie, (Eds.), Handbook of mixed methods in social and behavioral Research. Thousand Oaks, CA: Sage, 135–164.

Olivier, B. (2016). Gender *Equality in Canada, power and Politics. Canada is listening just as intently as talking about gender equality issues, say Minister for the Status of Women Patty Hajdu*. Retrieved July 23, 2018 from www.cbc.ca/player/play/2685223599.

Patton, C. V. (2013). *Basic methods of policy analysis and planning* (3rd ed). London: Routledge.

Przybylski, A. K. & Weinstein, N. (2012). Can you connect with me now? How the presence of mobile communication technology influences face-to-face conversation quality. *Journal of Social and Personal Relationships*, 30(3) 237–246.

Raiker, A. (2013). Using Computer Supported Collaborative Learning to Enhance the Quality of Schoolteacher Professional Development. In Nygaard, C., Coutney, N., & Bartholomew, P. (Eds.), *Quality Enhancement of University Teaching and Learning*. Oxfordshire, UK: Libri Publishing Ltd., 103–122.

Ramsden, P., & Entwistle, N. (1981). Effects of academic departments on students' approaches to studying. *British Journal of Educational Psychology*, 51, 368–383.

Rovai, A. P. (2002). Sense of community, perceived cognitive learning, and persistence in asynchronous learning networks. *Internet and Higher Education*, 5, 319–332.

Rowley, J. (2011). Innovation and Student Learning: ePortfolio for Music Education. In Nygaard, C., Courtney, N., & Holtham, C. (Eds.), *Beyond Transmission – Innovations in University Teaching*. Oxfordshire, UK: Libri Publishing Ltd., 45–62.

Russell, T. L. (1999). *The no significant difference phenomenon*. Chapel Hill, NC: Office of Instructional Telecommunications, North Carolina State University.

Sherry, L. (1996). Issues in distance learning. *International Journal of Distance Education*, 1(4), 337–365.

Smith, D., & Hardaker, G. (2000). e-learning innovation through the implementation of an Internet supported learning environment. *Educational Technology and Society*, 3, 1–16.

Swan, K., Shea, P., Frederickson, E., Pickett, A., Pelz, W., & Maher, G. (2000). Building knowledge-building communities: Consistency, contact, and communication in the virtual classroom. *Journal of Educational Computing Research*, 23(4), 389–413.

Yin, R. K. (2006). Mixed methods research: Are the methods genuinely integrated or merely parallel. *Research in the Schools*, 13(1), 41–47.

Warschauer, M. (1997). Computer-mediated collaborative learning: theory and practice. *Modern Language Journal*, 8(4), 470–481.

Chapter 5

Using Wordpress, Canvas LMS, Dropbox and Facebook to enhance students' online engagement in postgraduate education

Anne Hørsted

Introduction

With my chapter, I contribute to the book *E-learning 1.0, 2.0, and 3.0 in Higher Education* when I discuss how the use of different technological platforms affects student engagement in a postgraduate training program. The program in focus is named Camp Future. It is a program which helps unemployed university graduates to find a job in a tough job market. Writing about Camp Future is not new to me. I have written about Camp Future in two recent book chapters: 1) from a learning theoretical perspective (Hørsted & Nygaard, 2017a), and 2) from a curriculum design perspective (Hørsted & Nygaard, 2017b). In this book, I will write about Camp Future from an e-learning perspective. Doing so cannot be done without drawing on both learning theory and curriculum theory. Although I will not go into details with these subjects, I will touch upon them, as they are natural elements when choosing e-learning technology. Reading this chapter I hope you will be inspired by the following:

1. an introduction to a postgraduate training program, which actively links unemployed university graduates with private businesses and lead to the creation of jobs;

2. our experiences with the use of different technological platforms to enhance student engagement; and

3. a reflection on strengths and weaknesses of using different e-learning technologies seen in the light of the typology of e-learning 1.0, 2.0, and 3.0.

The chapter has three main sections. In section 1, I give a brief introduction to the Camp Future program to describe the context in which we are using e-learning. In section 2, I describe our use of different technological platforms over time and present some of the pedagogical arguments behind our choices. In section 3, I reflect on our use of e-learning technologies with reference to the e-learning typology developed by my colleague (Nygaard, 2015; Nygaard, in this volume).

Section I: Postgraduate training at Camp Future

Camp Future is a ten-week intensive postgraduate training program, which helps unemployed university graduates land their first/next job. The program was developed in 2012 by professor Claus Nygaard from Copenhagen Business School and the Institute for Learning in Higher Education. His focus was to help students develop an entrepreneurial mindset (Hørsted & Nygaard, 2017a) and encourage them to see themselves as human assets generating additional value for companies rather than seeing themselves as employees. The program has been repeated 22 times. More than 500 unemployed university graduates have participated. On average, 64% of the students find a job during or shortly after having participated in Camp Future.

At Camp Future, each student is matched with a company and asked to solve a real business-challenge formulated by the company. The first six weeks of the program are devoted to learning-centred teaching and case-based fieldwork following an action-learning pedagogy. This is where each student solves "their" company's business-challenge. During the final four weeks of the program, students work full time for their case-company through an internship. In the following subsection, I will briefly introduce the pedagogical philosophy underlying Camp Future and also introduce the curriculum as a learning-centred action plan. I do so to give more detail about the program and the way in which students are expected to study and do fieldwork, because this is important to understand why e-learning technologies have been chosen and changed over the years of the course.

Camp Future as a Learning-Centred Action Plan

The curriculum of Camp Future is best described as a learning-centred action plan (Bolhuis, 2003; Nygaard & Bramming, 2008). It means that students work according to a plan, where their own personal learning is the centre-point. As such students are thrown into deep water on the very first day of the course. Here they are matched with a company, they are given a real business-challenge, and asked to spend the next 7 hours of the first day in self-directed study, during which they have to familiarise themselves with the business-challenge formulated by the company. In addition, they prepare questions for a 1½ hour interview with the manager of the company on the following day. Business challenges are of this kind: "Create a social media strategy for our company"; "Create a marketing plan for our latest product"; "Create an export strategy for our entry into the British market"; "Design a curriculum for our new corporate talent management program"; "Transfer our board game into an app". Students at Camp Future all have a master's degree but come with very different specialities. Language, art, engineering, finance, marketing, culture, politics, theology, accounting, law, and design are some of the most recent backgrounds.

Students are given full agency in their own learning process, as they have to take individual action from the very first day of the course. Their learning is a process of trial and error and they are expected to work as reflective practitioners (Schön, 1983, 1987) as they solve the business-challenge given to them by their case-company. This is what Schön (1983:147) called reflection-in-action. *"When the practitioner reflects-in-action in a case he perceives as unique, paying attention to phenomena and surfacing his intuitive understanding of them, his experimenting is at once exploratory, move testing, and hypothesis testing. The three functions are fulfilled by the very same actions."* Students engage in exploration of their business-challenge. They engage in move testing as they test the boundaries of their solutions in the given business practice; and they engage in hypothesis testing as they come to terms with possible links between the business-challenge and their suggested solutions. Over the first six weeks, students engage deeply in the business-challenge, because much is at stake. Not only do they have to come up with a solution to their case-company, which they present to the manager/management of the company on the second last day of the six-week teaching period, but they also have to make an implementation plan of the solution they propose to the company. That implementation plan will govern their own work during their following four-week internship. It appears that Camp Future succeeds in developing a culture of deep learners (Marton & Säljö, 1976; Ramsden, 1988) where the majority of students are deeply engaged in understanding and solving the business-challenge.

During the six-week period (30 days in total) students meet with their teachers for 10 days. The remaining 20 days are devoted to self-directed work with the case-company.

The mix of learning-centred teaching and case-based fieldwork is apparent throughout the program. On the 10 days where students meet with their teachers the role of the teachers is to help drive the learning-process of students forward.

5 of the 10 days are used to teach tools which students may use to solve their business-challenge. The tools taught at the course are: 1) Wicked—problem analysis; 2) Boston Growth Matrix analysis; 3) Porter's Five Forces analysis; 4) Red Ocean/Blue Ocean analysis; 5) Stakeholder analysis; 6) Scenario analysis; 7) SWOT II analysis; 8) Force Field analysis; 9) Customer value analysis; 10) Customer Journey analysis; 11) Strategy Road Map. Teaching a tool takes between 30–45 minutes. Students are then given 1 hour to have an initial go at using the tool on their own business-challenge.

3 of the 10 days are academic workshops where students work collaboratively to use the tools they have just learnt. Workshops help students to actively apply the tools of the course to their business case under guidance from teachers and inspiration from fellow students.

2 of the 10 days are devoted to supervision, where each student present his or her work and receives individual feedback from teachers. During a day with supervision students also work in groups to help each other with their work.

1 of the 10 days is the exam day, where students present their solution of the business-challenge to the manager/management group of the case-company. All students are present at the exam day, and presentations are therefore given in front of the whole class and possibly also managers/management groups from other case-companies, who are present to

witness their own presentation but decide to come early or hang on after having heard their own student present.

Working with a setup like this, where students spend 20 days away from the classroom and 10 days in the classroom, we have worked with different technological platforms to see if we could find a form of e-learning which could help us engage students throughout the course. In the next section 2, I will briefly present the different technological platforms used during the life span of the Camp Future program.

Section 2: Using different technological platforms to enhance students' online engagement

To begin with no technological platform was used to help further engage students at Camp Future. Students would meet up on the 10 days of teaching. And on the first day they would receive all the course material in two printed compendiums.

Using Wordpress

When it was decided to use a technological platform for Camp Future, Wordpress was chosen. Wordpress was the obvious choice, because it allowed to easily pick an attractive template and make a course website which held all information relevant to students. The installation also had a password protected repository section, where students could download all course materials. So, the two printed compendiums disappeared, and each student could download materials at their own convenience. This comprised academic texts, descriptions of each of the tools taught at the course, and also worksheets for all tools. All students used the same login and password to the site, so it was not possible to distinguish between students, but it was practical and easy to set up. However, as students did not communicate with each other, but only used the platform to access course materials, it was not considered important to track student's use of the platform. The teachers were pleased with the Wordpress installation, and overall students were happy with the easy access to course materials. In course evaluations students expressed satisfaction with the Wordpress installation, although a few complained that they had to print the course material themselves and did not receive physical printouts/printed compendiums. This was compensated for by making a printer available for students to use to print the course materials. After having used Wordpress in three instances of the course, it was decided to change platform. This was done to be able to integrate video presentations into the course material and also to facilitate an online dialogue between students.

Using Canvas LMS

Canvas LMS was an obvious choice as the new platform, because it offered a more flexible platform than the HTML-coded template of Wordpress. In addition, it was an open source platform. Being a LMS (Learning Management System) and not a hardcoded HTML-page, Canvas LMS made it possible to quickly build a course page with all relevant information. It offered more flexible calendar views, where teaching days could be added, and the course materials were presented in a more structured way. It allowed integration of video in a very flexible way, so it was decided to record the teachers' presentations and make them available for students online. Canvas LMS was password protected, and each student got their own login and password, so it was possible to trace students' use of the platform. Added to the course page was also a Q&A-section, where students could ask questions about the course and discuss their work with other students and the teachers. Although the technology allowed for a more interactive use of the platform, students did not make use of this opportunity. They rarely asked questions related to the academic or methodological aspects of their work, and they rarely engaged in discussions of the course material or their business challenges. The Q&A-section was mainly used to ask practical questions about the course such as meeting times, requirements, etc. Although the teachers were pleased with the Canvas LMS installation, they were also a bit puzzled about the lack of online interaction with and between students. On the other hand, students evaluated the technological platform positively, although they mostly used it to access course material and did not make much use of the interactive features the platform offered. After having used Canvas LMS for two instances of the course, it was again decided to change platform. This was done to encourage more online interaction between students and to raise their overall online engagement.

Using Dropbox and Facebook

The third – and current – technological platform chosen for Camp Future is a combination of Dropbox and Facebook. For the latest three instances of the course this setup has been in use. It may seem like an odd choice, because it meant moving away from an integrated online system and onto two disintegrated platforms. Dropbox is used as a repository for the course material, academic articles, worksheets, teachers' presentations, etc. It is also used for students to upload their own work-in-progress and final exam presentations for all to see. The Dropbox then becomes a dynamic repository. One of the main reasons for using Dropbox is that most students make a setup where the Dropbox automatically syncs with their own computer. It means that students don't need to login to an online system to stay updated. When the teacher adds material to the Dropbox it is most probably present on students' computers right away. Facebook was chosen because it is a platform already used by most students. In fact, when the course starts, the teachers introduce Facebook as the online platform for dialogue. And the three times it has now been used, the Facebook Group has been setup by one of the students, who has then invited all other students. By making a private group for the Camp Future course and invite students to join, Camp Future then becomes an integrated part of students' newsfeed when they use Facebook on their smartphones, tablets or computers. All posts and messages added to the Camp Future Facebook Group are then pushed to students and reach them even at times when they are not in "study mode". This means that the students are in much more dialogue now than were the case with the HTML and LMS platforms. Students ask for help, share links, articles, news, etc. Teachers use the Facebook Group to share links and reports, and to inspire and encourage students to work with the tools of the course in a particular way. With Facebook Groups, online engagement of students has been enhanced. They help each other and share ideas and material with each other. The teachers are pleased with this choice of platforms. Dropbox automatically syncs the directory of course materials on their own computers with students' computers, so no login or extra uploading is required. If a file is saved in the Camp Future directory on the teachers' computer, it is automatically sent to all students. Students have evaluated the use of Dropbox and Facebook positively. This includes students who did not have any prior experience of using Dropbox.

Chapter 5

It is perhaps because Dropbox runs in the background and is not seen as yet another system the students has to log into. The task of setting up of the Facebook Group has been given to students, and it seem to have generated a kind of ownership to the platform. Using Facebook also means that students (and students and teachers) can see each other's personal Facebook profiles (if they are public), which allows for a more personal dialogue in coffee breaks or during lunch at teaching days. The online engagement in the Facebook Group may then help to bring both students and students and teachers closer to each other.

As you can see, the technological platforms used at the Camp Future course has changed over the past years. Above I have briefly described the platforms and some of the reasons for choosing them. I have also touched upon the way in which students have used and evaluated the use of the platforms. In the third and final section of the chapter, I will reflect more on the use of the platforms as e-learning technologies. I do so to encourage a dialogue on why and how we use e-learning technologies.

Section 3: Reflections on the use of e-learning technologies

If you look at the use of technological platforms at Camp Future, it appears that the platforms were chosen by the teachers without any prior thorough analysis of their features and use scenarios. It almost appears as if they were chosen because they were the ones already known by the teachers. Although the teachers wanted more online engagement and interaction between students, they chose platforms and used them as repositories of course materials. If we distinguish between teacher-centric education and student-centric education, it seems that the choice of Wordpress was mostly teacher-centric, because the focus was solely on making content available to students. This may be seen as a teacher-centric introduction phase: *"Teachers' introduction to e-learning"*.

When the teachers realised that their Wordpress-design did not enhance student online engagement or accelerate student learning in any particular way, they changed e-learning strategy and used a dedicated LMS, the Canvas LMS. They filmed their own lectures and made them available to students on the platform. And they added a Q&A-section to encourage students to engage online. Again, the approach was mainly teacher-centric, as the focus of teachers was to design a functional platform where students could access the course materials and the videos to use for their homework. This may be seen as a teacher-centric learning phase: *"Teachers' learning to use e-learning"*.

As the teachers found that students did not spend much time watching the videos and did not engage fully in online dialogues, they once again changed e-learning strategy and opted for Dropbox and Facebook. This was done in an attempt to make a more student-centric decision, where the technological platforms can seamlessly integrate with students' everyday use of their computers and the internet. Although using Dropbox was a teacher-centric approach used for distributing course materials, giving editing rights to students and opening the Camp Future Dropbox directories for their own unlimited use means that they can add their own material and also make new folders should they want to. Giving students the task of setting up the Facebook Group and inviting all students to the group has underlined the student-centric approach and helped to make the Facebook Group one that belongs to the students. This third phase of using technology may be seen as a student-centric interaction phase: *"Students interacting using e-learning"*.

Figure 1 shows an e-learning typology proposed by Nygaard (in this volume). He distinguished between e-learning 1.0, 2.0, and 3.0.

	E-learning typologies		
	1.0: Distribution	**2.0: Dialogue**	**3.0: Construction**
Use of e-learning	E-learning is used to distribute information to students	E-learning is used to facilitate a dialogue between students (and teachers and other relevant peers)	E-learning is used to enable construction of new knowledge or innovation of new processes/products

Figure 1: A typology for e-learning (Nygaard, in this volume).

E-learning 1.0 describes situations where technology is mainly used for distribution of information. Here technology is used to establish an online repository of course materials. This is the teacher-centric approach, where teachers decide what information and materials should be made available to students. E-learning 1.0 can be used to describe the use of Wordpress, Canvas LMS and Dropbox.

E-learning 2.0 describes situations where technology is mainly used to facilitate a dialogue between students and teachers. Here technology invites students to engage online in order to share ideas, ask questions, help each other, etc. This is a student-centric approach. E-learning 2.0 can be used to describe the use of Facebook Groups.

E-learning 3.0 describes situations where technology is mainly used to facilitate construction of new knowledge or to guide innovations. This is a student-centric approach where they work together using collaborative online tools. E-learning 3.0 has not yet been used at Camp Future.

In Figure 2 I have summed up some of the advantages and disadvantages – as I see them – from using the various kinds of learning platforms.

	E-learning typologies		
	1.0: Distribution	2.0: Dialogue	3.0: Construction
Use of e-learning	E-learning is used to distribute information to students	E-learning is used to facilitate a dialogue between students (and teachers and other relevant peers)	E-learning is used to enable construction of new knowledge or innovation of new processes/products
E-learning technologies used at Camp Future	Wordpress Canvas LMS Dropbox	Facebook Groups	--- not in use at Camp Future ---
Advantages	Course materials can be distributed to students. Wordpress and Canvas LMS allows for appealing design, categorisations of materials, and cross linking between materials.	The postings in the Facebook Group is automatically pushed to students personal Facebook stream 24/7. Camp Future then becomes a potential part of the students' everyday social life also when they are not studying.	--- not in use at Camp Future ---

	E-learning typologies		
	1.0: **Distribution**	**2.0:** **Dialogue**	**3.0:** **Construction**
	Dropbox allows for seamless synchronisation of learning materials between the teachers' computers and the students' computers and runs in the background with no extra login required.	Interactions between students and teachers get a social and personal touch as they are linked to students and teachers personal Facebook profiles. Students do not have to login to an extra platform to check for new materials, because the Camp Future Facebook Group is integrated into their already existing Facebook account.	
Disadvantages	Wordpress and Canvas LMS are "extra" platforms students have to relate to. They require student login, which may seem like a hindrance to frequent use. If nothing new has been added to the platform students feel their login was a waste of time. Dropbox is a file repository only which runs in the background, and it allows for no further interaction between students.	Dialogues and materials shared are not categorised and cannot be crosslinked. Everything posted in the Facebook Group disappears in the time related feed of the students' Facebook page. If a student is not online for a day or two they may miss the postings in the Camp Future Facebook Group.	*--- not in use at Camp Future ---*

Figure 2: Advantages and disadvantages of the e-learning platforms used on Camp Future.

It is clear that each technological platform has its advantages and disadvantages. Here I situate them in the specific context of their use by Camp Future. Wordpress offers thousands of plugins and design possibilities, which could have helped the teachers design a platform with more flexibility and different use possibilities. However, they did not do so: they changed platform to Canvas LMS. Here the design possibilities were almost endless too. The teachers could have redesigned Canvas LMS rather than changing platform. But they did not do so. My reflection on the use of these platforms, therefore, is solely written to mirror the decisions of the teachers and the implications of those decisions for students' online engagement. They are not written to critique Wordpress or Canvas LMS for being teacher-centric and limited in their offerings. This is how the platforms were designed by the teachers at Camp Future and used by their students. The current combination of Dropbox and Facebook Groups may seem to be a technologically limited solution. Why not use the full power of Wordpress or Canvas LMS and design an interactive learning environment? The choice to use Dropbox and Facebook groups has been made because the technology runs in the background and is an integrated part of what students' already use. It may not be the most technologically advanced solution and it may not be the most impressive setup design-wise. But in the context of Camp Future using Facebook Group in particular has increased students' online engagement and also made the sharing of ideas, materials, links, invitations to meetings, etc. more student-centric, as students are active in the Camp Future Facebook Group at their own initiative. And the use of Dropbox has ensured that any update carried out in the Camp Future file repository on the teachers' computer also appears on students' computers as Dropbox syncs activities real time.

For the time being, the teachers at Camp Future plan to stick to the current technological platforms. If they are to change in the future it should be for further implementation of e-learning 3.0, where students could collaborate and innovate also online.

Conclusion

In this brief chapter, I have aimed to show how a group of teachers have changed their use of technological platforms over a period of three years, and how those changes have affected students' online engagement. I have chosen not to go into technical details, but rather to present these technological choices of the teachers using an everyday language which somewhat mirrors the teachers' own reflections. I wanted to show that sometimes the choice of learning technology happens without thought of their wider use. Teachers first chose Wordpress, because they knew it and had used it to design websites. And it was seen as a good way to make learning resources available to students. This teacher-centric choice led to a platform where student engagement was not a part of the design. The second choice, Canvas LMS, was also a teacher-centric choice chosen to be able to distribute videos to students and to facilitate a Q&A-section. Because nothing new happened at the LMS students only logged in when they had to download materials. The third and current choice, Dropbox and Facebook Groups, allowed for a more student-centric platform, where it is now student initiative that governs the newsfeed in the Facebook Group. The fact that students do not have to login to a platform, where nothing new happens, but can integrate the newsfeed from the Facebook Group in their personal Facebook stream, seems to have made the Camp Future course more present in the minds of students and it has also enhanced students' online engagement compared to the times of using Wordpress and Canvas LMS as technological platforms. With my use of the typology of e-learning 1.0 (distribution), 2.0 (dialogue), 3.0 (construction) (Nygaard, 2015, in this volume) I have aimed at showing the value of discussing the use scenarios of e-learning before a technological platform is used. Had the teachers at Camp Future been aware of e-learning 1.0, 2.0, and 3.0, and had they given themselves time to discuss the use scenarios with former and current students they most probably wouldn't have changed technological platforms three times in three years. At the same time, using this typology of e-learning would have led to a pedagogical discussion of both student engagement and student learning. And it would have implied that they should also reflect on whether their design choices were teacher-centric or student centric. These are two approaches to further understand technological design, which could help refocus the choice of technology from a technical discussion to a pedagogical discussion. I hope this short chapter has given you some food for thought and inspired you to reflect on your own journey using technology to enhance students' online engagement.

About the Author

Anne Hørsted is adjunct professor at the University of Southern Denmark, senior consultant at cph:learning in Denmark, and adjunct professor at the Institute for Learning in Higher Education. She can be contacted at this e-mail: anne@cphlearning.dk

Bibliography

Bolhuis, S. (2003). Towards process-oriented teaching for self-directed lifelong learning: a multidimensional perspective. *Learning and Instruction*, 13(3), 327–347.

Hørsted, A., & Nygaard, C. (2017a). Teaching unemployed university graduates to think like entrepreneurs. In Branch, J., Hørsted, A., & Nygaard, C. (Eds.), *Teaching and Learning Entrepreneurship in Higher Education*. Oxfordshire, UK: Libri Publishing Ltd., 283–296.

Hørsted, A., & Nygaard, C. (2017b). How to design a curriculum for learning. In Hørsted, A., Branch, J., & Nygaard, C. (Eds.), *Learning-centred curriculum design in higher education*. Oxfordshire, UK: Libri Publishing Ltd., 97–120.

Marton, F., & Säljö, R. (1976). On qualitative differences in Learning – Outcome and process. *British journal of Educational Psychology*, 46(1), 4–11.

Nygaard, C. (2015). Rudiments of a Strategy for Technology Enhanced University Learning. In Nygaard, C., Branch, J., & Bartholomew, P. (Eds.), *Technology Enhanced Learning in Higher Education*. Oxfordshire, UK: Libri Publishing Ltd., 31–50.

Nygaard, C., & Bramming, P. (2008). Learning-centred Public Management Education. *International Journal of Public Sector Management*, 21(4), 400–416.

Ramsden, P. (1988). *Improving Learning: new perspectives*. Kogan Page.

Schön, D. A. (1983). *The Reflective Practitioner*. New York: Basic Books.

Schön, D. A. (1987). *Educating the Reflective Practitioner*. San Francisco: Jossey-Bass.

Chapter 6

Using e-learning to improve the student experience of lectures

Rhiannon Evans

Introduction

With my chapter, I contribute to the book *E-learning 1.0, 2.0, and 3.0 in Higher Education* as I address the advantages and disadvantages of using generic recording technology in the lecture theatre—a phenomenon which affects most university lecturers in the 21st century. It also examines the ways in which different ways of providing pre-recorded material might improve upon the one size fits all method of recording lectures which also occur face-to-face (F2F) in real time. The chapter thus seeks to improve the experience of teaching and learning with the use of e-learning technologies, and to describe relatively simple techniques for creating better e-learning materials.

In the chapter, I define e-learning as learning which occurs via web-based digital materials, whether the lecturer records this content or it is created by a third party and provided as a link by the lecturer. It has often been associated with distance learning, and therefore as a 'delivery system' for course content (Li et al., 2009). While this aspect of e-learning continues to be important, it is also increasingly embedded into the learning experience of students who are able to attend some classes on campus, and has therefore taken on supplementary and interactive modes. This more developed use of e-learning fits within Sangrà et al.'s (2012) category of 'Educational-Paradigm-Oriented Definitions', which involves improved access to resources for students, using web resources to give increased support to learners and the potential for asynchronous learning. The focus on the learner suggests that e-learning should enhance the educational experience, rather than simply reproducing established modes of learning for distance students. As this chapter deals primarily with lecturers providing information for students, it is potentially viewed

Chapter 6

as a version of e-learning 1.0 (see Nygaard, in this volume). However, as I show here, it is possible to expand upon the delivery of materials in ways which challenge students and make demands upon them as individual and peer group researchers; thus, this chapter also touches upon aspects of e-learning 2.0 and even 3.0 (see Nygaard, in this volume).

My own experience of e-learning relates mostly to units in Blended or Hybrid mode, but also touches upon Web-Enhanced Course (digital materials as an addition to primarily F2F activity) and entirely Online Courses, with some virtual F2F classes delivered via Zoom technology. This program allows for large groups to meet online in a way akin to a Skype meeting, but with the additional benefit of being able to share screens, divide students into smaller sub-groups ('Zoom rooms') and record sessions. 'Blended' and 'Hybrid' are terms which are sometimes used interchangeably (Ross & Gage, 2006). When they are distinguished, Blended units can be broadly defined as traditionally taught subjects where some elements, such as simple assessments are moved online; while Hybrid mode often indicates units, which move some of the F2F classroom activities into an online space. Hybrid mode is therefore the most relevant to my discussion here, as I consider whether F2F lectures are better supplemented or replaced by online delivery. In any of these scenarios, I would argue that the most significant factor is student engagement: e-learning should enhance engagement, rather than merely supplying information, or even putting up barriers between teacher and student (see Pather, in this volume). When reading this chapter, you will gain the following three insights:

1. The potential gains and losses of theatre-recorded lectures;

2. The means to provide successful pre-recorded material for students;

3. The ways in which pre-recording provides a model for student adoption of e-learning technologies and also allows for customisation of the curriculum.

My chapter has four sections. In the first section, I describe the current situation of institutionalised lecture theatre recording, as well as how and why it is often replaced by other means of content provision. In the second section, I explore two examples of blended units which employ recorded video lectures and other e-learning materials, and show how they support students beyond providing asynchronous learning. In the third section, I consider how e-learning, and specifically the recorded video lecture, might take us beyond merely reproducing or supplementing current teaching modes. Here I examine one aspect of how web-based materials might redefine the way we teach and support student input into the curriculum. In the fourth section, I discuss some ways in which e-learning allows for customisation of the curriculum to support a particular cohort.

E-learning and pre-recording

The problem with recording face-to-face lectures

One of the advantages often claimed for e-learning is its flexibility: it potentially offers asynchronous, segmented communication between teacher and student. One need only look at the marketing of online distance education specialists to recognise this. The Open University proclaims that *"[i]n recent years, we've taken flexibility to a new level by combining our experience of distance learning with the very latest technology....From downloading course materials on your mobile phone to drafting assignments on your iPad, our studies are more portable, accessible and flexible than ever before."* (The Open University, 2018:NP). The positives of flexible e-learning align with the learner control principle (Scheiter, 2014), which can be summed up as allowing the learner to work at their own pace, with the benefit of repeatability, so that previously 'one-time-only' experiences are captured in electronic form and can be reviewed as many times as required by the student.

This is nowhere more obvious than in the recording of lecture presentations by means such as Echo 360, which record the audio and the projected slides of the F2F lecture. Similar technologies are now deployed almost universally at the tertiary level in Australia and elsewhere. The recording device is built into the lecture theatre; it begins and ends recording at a set time and cannot be controlled by lecturers, although they do have the ability to pause the recording if a copyrighted video is being shown—the danger here is that the lecturer may forget to restart the recording. The recording of slides with voice over is then uploaded to a central repository and appears in the class LMS, where it can be accessed by students in that unit.

An audio and screen recording provides a facsimile of the lecture experience, but the 'simile' part of the term is significant here: it is a pale imitation of a live lecture given by a passionate lecturer. Engaging with slides and a voice over is often an alienating experience for the student, as the immediacy and interaction between teacher and students is necessarily missing, and it is hard not to see this as an inferior form of instruction (Tobin, 2018). Further it has been recognised that the 'one-size-fits-all' nature of centrally managed technologies like Echo 360 is unsuited to some disciplines and even some teaching styles (Dona *et al.*, 2017). For example, the actions of a lecturer who gestures or walks around the theatre are not captured, and this may be a key component of their communication with students. This natural movement may no longer even be possible, as the lecturer is locked to the recording desk unless a personal microphone is provided, and thus the lecture experience for those who *do* attend is affected. Furthermore, the recording technology has an impact on the live lecture, as it often constrains lecturers to wait until the automated recording begins and to attempt to finish speaking before it cuts off. Thus, a vicious cycle is created, whereby compromises, which the lecturer must make for the sake of recording, lead to a less compelling live experience, giving students less incentive to attend in person.

Dona *et al.* (2017) questions whether recordings of live lectures have led to the dramatic fall in lecture attendance, but the coincidence is compelling, and has been widely experienced at many institutions. Lecturers fear the empty theatre, but holding forth in an echoing, cavernous space is a near certainty, as university administrators must provide theatres large enough for an entire cohort, even though they know that it will never be filled. However, compelling the speaker, most lectures are attended only by the most die-hard of enthusiastic students by late semester. Data collected from the Echocentre (the 'back end' of Echo 360) at my institution are sobering. This site provides statistics on unique viewers and cumulative views of lecture recordings, and shows that approximately 20% of the student cohort access the lectures in this way. When this is added to the 10–20% of the cohort which attends lectures by mid-semester, it is clear that well over half of the class is not accessing the lectures at all. Indeed, it is possible that these statistics are even worse than they appear, as a small number of highly engaged students use the recording to revisit a lecture which they have attended in person. The Life Sciences department at Imperial College, London found a statistically significant drop in lecture attendance when recordings were introduced in a 2013 survey, although students themselves claimed that they preferred to attend; this survey also found that only a small percentage of students watched the lecture recordings, despite claims that they found this resource useful as a fall-back resource (Sarsfield, 2010). In this study, there is a perceptible gap between students' own ideas of their lecture consumption, or perhaps intention to consume lecture material, and the reality that the recording of live lectures has actually led to fewer students engaging with lecture material. Recording live lectures clearly leads to as many problems as it solves for students (Draper *et al.*, 2018).

These depressing figures show that students who fail to attend in person often do not 'catch up' online by viewing the recording, even though they may have the best of intentions to do so. For example, informal communication at the start of semester demonstrates that students are often willing to enrol in a subject which involves a timetable clash or a lecture on a day when they work *only* if the lecture is to be recorded. Yet, despite checking on this facility, they do not subsequently avail themselves of the opportunity to use the recording. The psychology of the lecture as *having existed* as real-time F2F event, which is now passed, comes into play here: the student knows that there was a scheduled event which they missed; if they are to recover the event through the recorded facsimile, a specific amount of time must be put aside. Meanwhile, in the ever more time-pressured environment of shorter semesters and block mode teaching, the next class, reading or assignment is already upon them. The lecture recording will always be there, so it is easy to imagine that it can be viewed later—but often it is instead left behind.

E-learning and pre-recording lectures

One e-learning solution to this problem is to abandon the live performance entirely and substitute with pre-recorded lectures. Early attempts at my home institution involved high production, time-intensive ventures, filmed in the university's in-house recording studio (Evans & Wurster, 2013). The expense involved was not sustainable, and would not be at most institutions. More recently technologies such as One Button

Studios have been adopted at many universities. These provide an in-house recording 'studio'—in fact, a small room with some sound insulation, a computer, a presentation screen, a ceiling-mounted camera and spot lights. The lecturer uploads a presentation and presses a large button (hence 'One Button') to begin and end the recording (One Button Studio, 2016). This enables the integration of presentation, presenter and audio, and has resulted in a much simpler pre-record facility. Similar results can be achieved with software such as Camtasia (Camtasia, 2018). It is now also possible to record slides, audio and video of the speaker (as a corner icon) in front of a PC, without the need for a studio, in programs such as MS Power Point, although acquiring a good microphone is highly recommended for this method. I used the One Button recording method in two units recently, an introduction to ancient languages (Latin and Ancient Greek) and an ancient Roman history unit on gladiators and emperors. I uploaded the recorded video lectures (hereafter RVL) for these units to online video platforms (such as YouTube or Vimeo) so that they were easily accessible. The lectures were of varying lengths, anything between five and twenty-five minutes, although most were around ten-to fifteen-minutes long—in fact recordings of over fifteen minutes tend to result in large files which break the Vimeo free-version maximum upload of 500 MB per week. One significant advantage, commented on by students, is that these recordings are not an inferior version of another format. They do not pretend to stand in for the live lecture experience, and all students are placed on the same footing, provided that they have access to a reasonably reliable internet facility. The pre-recordings can also be provided in advance, making time-management easier for the student, who does not need to wait until after a scheduled lecture for the recording to appear. Perhaps more importantly, the student is able to look at the size of the lectures in advance and knows the amount of time needed to view the content, before attending a tutorial or taking a quiz. I tried to restrict the total viewing time to between sixty and ninety minutes per week, so students became accustomed to scheduling a set period of online viewing per week.

One benefit for the lecturer is that there is some flexibility in how much content and detail provided each week, as opposed to the two 50–minute lectures in a lecture theatre format. Prerecording allows the lecturer to dictate the amount of content required for a particular topic, rather than shoe-horning that material into a predetermined amount of time. In fact, my experience is that material which might have taken two 50-minute lectures could often be compressed into an hour or less. There are a number of possible causes for this, although they are not all necessarily positives:

- *Class administration*: this is usually omitted as details alter from semester to semester; it then needs to be absorbed into another class setting (such as a tutorial) or platform (such as instructions via an LMS or class forum [see Meier, in this volume, on e-learning to carry out this type of supervision]).
- *Set up time*: switch over time between F2F classes using the same space is often insufficient, particularly if the teachers of both need to set up or close down computers, or if there is a problem with the technology. Such delays and glitches will precede or be edited out of a pre-recorded lecture.
- *Exchanges between teacher and students*: the relationship with students in the room is also absent in the pre-recorded lecture. As the lecturer is usually speaking alone to a camera, there is no opportunity for student questions and interaction, which can be used to advantage in the live lecture, as students make clear on the spot what has not been understood.

This last point demonstrates a major difference between recording and live presentation: lectures in a theatre are dynamic situations which allow the lecturer to self-edit on the spot, providing an efficient way to cater to the current student body. It should be remembered, however, that this sort of interaction translates very badly to the recording of the live lecture—a student catching up with the recording often hears only half of the exchange. So, what might be advantageous for the student in the room, paradoxically further reinforces the *secondary* nature of this experience for those consuming the recording at a later date. Recordings of a live event contain the potential for exacerbating student isolation in a way that a pre-recording watched by the whole class does not.

Short videos can perform a 'substitution' for this lack of immediate interaction: they might provide additional background for students who may not have completed units at foundational level, or act as a reminder to those who have; alternatively, they can be recorded as a response to FAQs coming out of tutorial or a class forum, and build a database of videos which respond to those FAQs. In an earlier online subject, we used this method with audio responses to questions posted by students each week. In both cases, students reacted favourably to the content, as they recognised that course materials were being provided in response to their concerns and blind spots. As Betts (2009) points out, students tend to feel connected to both teachers and fellow students when they perceive that e-learning materials communicate directly with them and serve to support their needs. Particularly in situations where F2F time is limited, some variety of personalised response is essential, as generic pre-recordings alone leave students feeling alienated. Where possible, it is a good idea for the lecturer to customise short recordings for a specific cohort: e-learning tools should create an inclusive experience rather than a visibly remote one.

Examples from Two Blended Units

Here I shall describe the format for pre-recorded content in my two blended units, 'Ancient Languages from the Agora to Harry Potter' and 'Gladiators and Emperors: Spectacle and Society in Ancient Rome'. Both units require that students consume class materials in a variety of media: podcasts, presented by class lecturers or third parties; RVLs made by the class lecturers in the One Button studio, all of which feature the presenter(s) and a screen, rather than simply slides with a voiceover; and, occasionally, third-party documentaries, from high quality providers such as the BBC. The result is that the student hears a multiplicity of voices on a weekly basis, and the evaluation of those different voices is just one of the tasks which might be set for tutorial or forum discussion.

Blended Unit 1: Gladiators and Emperors

For example, one week in 'Gladiators and Emperors' featured three podcasts from the 'Emperor of Rome' series, which traced the narrative of the emperor Caligula's life (Evans, 2014); an RVL on representations of Caligula in ancient and modern sources; some clips from the 1976 BBC television series *I, Claudius*; and an optional viewing of a BBC documentary *Caligula* presented by Mary Beard. Students also read an ancient biography of the emperor (30 pages). Student discussion in tutorial then centres around the differences in emphasis between the ancient sources, a mainstream documentary and a fictional account. In particular, students use the information from the RVL and their reading to critique the modern interpretations of this material, and to evaluate both a documentary by a well-regarded scholar and a television dramatisation. All three appear as digital downloads or streams, yet students begin to recognise that web-based materials supported by firm evidence are more reliable (Midford & Evans, 2017).

The podcasts are quite different from lectures, as they are heavily edited conversations between the class lecturer, Rhiannon Evans, and the podcast host, who is not a Classics expert, and, in a sense 'stands in' for the student in this scenario. The presence of an interlocutor prevents the podcast from becoming a lengthy monologue and also breaks down the flow of information. This is a dialogic format we have occasionally employed for RVLs, but usually the class lecturer uses the video lecture to discuss texts and images on slides in a relatively informal manner—notes are not used. The physical presence of the lecturer is important to us in this class, as the lecturer is often able to teach only one of the tutorial groups, and thus podcasts and slides with voice-over would leave students with a rather disembodied notion of their lecturer—a potentially alienating experience. In addition, this RVL zones in on representation, as the lecturer guides students through methods of interpreting and critiquing texts and material culture. The podcasts have already given the historical background on the emperor's life. In this case, the lecturer also refers frequently to set readings and tutorial activities, making a link with the students' preparation for class and the F2F component of the unit, and knitting them together. On occasion a simple puzzle or question is set up in the RVL, for example the presenter might ask students to build or draw a timeline of the information provided and to bring it to tutorial to contextualise discussion. It is important that the One Button technology allows for a fairly quick and unfussy production process, as, if readings or activities change in future iterations of the unit, it is relatively easy to rerecord the RVL. The podcasts never refer to classroom task or assessment and, barring major changes in the historical record, are reusable resources.

Thus, in this exemplar week, students know that they need to listen to and view material of around 90 minutes duration, with an optional additional 60 minutes available, as well as read a 30–page biography. The data for downloads of these materials shows a much higher download rate than we ever saw with Echo360 lecture capture. In part this may be attributed to setting a class pattern of consuming online before meeting in person. The knowledge that a certain amount of material in pre-recorded format is prescribed each week is psychologically more likely to lead a student to watch the videos in order to prepare for tutorial than they might be to engage in the catch-up recording of the live experience. Firstly, the whole class experiences the content in the same way; secondly, most of the material is accessible on mobile devices, and can be consumed while travelling; it is also available well in advance, rather than only after a live performance; lastly, and perhaps most importantly, none of this material is presented to students as a 'catch-up' or revision option (although in reality it can function as both), but instead as preparation for the class session which they attend in person.

One significant advantage of presenting material in this way—or rather via this variety of media—is that it is possible to section off subject matter and set hierarchies of information and analysis. When studying ancient cultures, some knowledge of basic chronology and power structures is necessary. Even though our Classics program does not frame our study of the past as primarily concerned with dates and facts, or 'war-to-war' history as it is sometimes called, it is not possible for students to analyse ancient societies without information on historical periods and terminology. Most students come to us with a fairly patchy grasp of ancient history; and furthermore, most of our units are electives, so that even advanced units might be taken by students with little background in Classics. We have found that our podcasts are an accessible and easily consumable way of conveying this background information. However, as they were initially produced with the general public in mind, we have had to supplement them with additional materials, notably lists of technical terms and Latin phrases. The advantage of giving students materials which have already been offered freely to a worldwide audience is that some listeners respond with questions, comments and opinions via social media. We are then able to use this feedback in class and ask for students to comment on the public's response to the podcast material.

As our students have access to additional materials, their reading of the historical period tends to be more nuanced, a scenario which inspires confidence and often enables students to see the value in being exposed to multiple sources and interpretations.

The availability of the podcasts as background material has a knock-on effect upon the RVLs, which are free to concentrate on a particular problem or issue, such as 'how has Caligula been represented?' They can be used to model ways of analysing a short passage of text, or focus on one single image to think about how or why it was produced. In short, the RVLs are a flexible format, which enables lecturers to practise the 'segmenting principle', fencing off specific, often higher level, content away from more basic background material (Mayer, 2014; Clarke & Mayer, 2016). In previous iterations, it was often necessary to present both types of content together in the F2F lecture; in such a scenario, it was sometimes difficult for students to separate out and prioritise content. The flexibility of e-learning allows for multiple delivery modes which potentially reflect different types of content.

This format also makes contiguity easier, as students can be referred back to earlier material when it becomes relevant at a later date. In the example used here, it was recommended that students revisit the RVL on representations of Caligula when they read about movies featuring the emperor Nero and that they should compare the two.

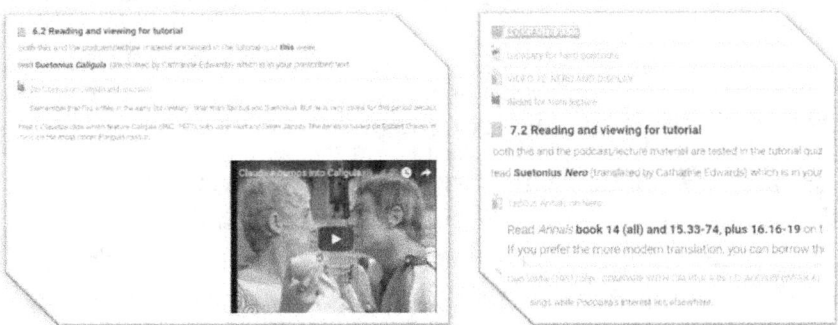

Figure 1: Extracts from two weekly 'blocks' on LMS: section 7.2 reminds students to refer back to section 6.2.

Such a comparison helps students to consider whether there is a common stereotype of the 'bad emperor', and the extent to which each emperor's reputation should be contextualised by their own era and the era in which the evidence was produced The ease with which recordings can be repositioned on an LMS is helpful here: most of these platforms have a 'duplicate' function, so that a file or a link to a recording can reappear in an LMS block a number of weeks after the initial, mandated viewing of the material as a recommended 'listen again'. This is an indication to students that they are likely to see connections between these two segmented chunks of content, and it encourages them to perceive similar links between other, apparently disparate sections of the curriculum. This format touches upon the rhizomatic model of the internet, which allows 'horizontal', and perhaps unexpected, connections to be made between silos of information. Indeed, the rhizome as an e-learning theory has often been applied to MOOCs with varying degrees of success, as the internet provides both a plethora of information and a challenge to verify its authenticity and reliability (Harris, 2016; Midford & Evans, 2017). This is less of an issue within the limited ecosystem of an LMS, which amounts to a body of lecturer-provided materials, including RVLs. Nevertheless, students can be encouraged to see sideways associations between topics, as suggested above, and they might see links which the lecturer has not foreseen. These can be incorporated into the unit as it is taught, by juxtaposing materials which have been drawn together by students, providing a fairly simple way to allow for student agency in the redesign of the curriculum.

Blended Unit 2: Ancient Languages

The Ancient Languages unit features a similarly eclectic combination of RVLs, podcasts and documentaries. It benefits from the fact that there are a number of high quality linguistics podcasts freely available, and one of these in particular, 'The History of English Podcast' is used as a resource to supplement the RVLs in two weeks early in the semester. Here the first-year students are required to listen to one podcast on the development of Latin and to take notes summarising its content. This is a skill many university students find difficult and it is a good idea to assess it as a foundational activity in the first year. In addition, students are asked to assess the reliability of the podcast's content, by assessing the evidence provided to support assertions in the podcast. This is something which can only be done using a third-party presentation, as students are reluctant to critique their class lecturer. It is also something of an artificial construct, as the teaching staff have previously vetted the podcast and regard its content as well researched. However, students need to assess the content and pinpoint the indicators of reliability, such as the provision of sources. We view this task as significant in the world of e-learning, as we know that students will extract material from multiple online sources, and we regard it as part of our duty to teach students to evaluate this material effectively when we produce online content or point students towards digital content.

Redefining the lecture?

The context of these recordings clearly differs from the traditional lecture. Nevertheless, the question arises: is this merely reproducing the lecture experience in a different format? Puentedura (2017) puts forward a model of e-learning in four progressive stages: Substitution, Augmentation, Modification, Redefinition (SAMR). Substitution and Augmentation represent limited use of e-learning's potential, either directly transferring or making a minor addition to materials used F2F and putting them online. As these materials were designed for a different context, they may no longer be as useful for learners. E-learning gives teachers the opportunity to change the curriculum in ways which benefit students (Modification), or even to rebuild it entirely (Redefinition), so that new technology becomes a tool for reimagining unit design, student interaction and assessment, etc.

The word 'substitution' demonstrates the problem with institutionally recorded lectures: digital versions never fully reproduce what was a very personal experience, even in a large lecture theatre. In the unit examples discussed above, the podcasts in both units, to a certain extent, substitute for traditional F2F lectures, by conveying required historical and cultural information. However, aside from being more accessible, they are also used to augment the possibilities of the conventional lecture: firstly, they allow students to interact with the general public's responses to the same material; and secondly, they are tailored as basic introductions which students with some knowledge can use to refresh their memories, while those with less foundational experience can revisit them a number of times.

In addition, one key modification made possible by pre-recording is that it allows the teacher to break away from the mandated time-frame for a traditional lecture (often 50 minutes), and to avoid the attendant problem: a guillotined end-of-lecture enforced by lecture theatre recording. The open-ended format of an independently recorded presentation is one of its most significant advantages, and returns us to the arena of flexibility. In addition, rather than flexibility which solely benefits a student (who can access lecture content anytime and anywhere) here it also operates for the teacher, who is unlocked from a set timeframe, and can develop presentations of different lengths, usually shorter than the traditional lecture, and thus corresponding to Mayer's 'segmenting principle', which asserts that students learn more effectively when learning is broken down into manageable chunks (Mayer, 2014; Clarke & Mayer, 2016). Although Clarke and Mayer's work relates directly to training in the workplace, their concept of 'essentials overload' is applicable in higher education. 'Essentials overload' describes a situation in which students are not able to process basic principles before the lecturer adds more complex processes or analysis. The separation of core historical information (e.g. in a podcast) from more sophisticated readings of the past (e.g. in a RVL) *"allows the learner to manage essential cognitive processing"* (Clarke & Mayer, 2016:223).

The popular conception of millennials as students possessing short attention spans is a distraction here, and not the motivation for producing lecture-presentations of varying length. Instead, the elasticity of the format should be perceived as a positive factor in delivering material: an explanation takes as long as it takes; it can be chopped into broad overview videos, and then presentations which drill down into the detail. This kind of knitting together of material might sit uncomfortably together in one set class period, when the constraints of the curriculum mandate that a F2F 50–minute lecture deals with broad overviews and close analysis together. For example, in the past, an introductory lecture on the emperor Caligula forced students to refocus several times as it had to cover historical background; then it needed to provide an analysis of his self-image through portraiture; and finally, it zoned in on a close analysis of a passage in his biography, in order to model this for students in their own reading. The podcasting and RVL format allows for this content to be separated and subsequently curated by the student. If they choose an assignment on imperial portraiture, they can revisit the RVLs on imperial portraits more easily than searching through recordings of traditional lectures, looking for the ten minutes out of fifty which address this theme. If they need a refresher on possible ways of reading an ancient text, they can look at the 'close reading' RVLs.

Customisation

This format can also operate in the opposite direction, to combine presentations and texts in ways which might not have been anticipated by the lecturer in the initial development of the curriculum, allowing for a degree of curriculum customisation by the students themselves. The lecturer can also respond to student need and direct students to consume two or more videos closely together, in instances where it is clear that the cohort has failed to see parallels between two incidents. Video material can be placed alongside an exemplar text or external content, such as documentaries. The manoeuvrability of the content allows for a personalised experience which can be constructed in a relatively easy manner: that is, the explanatory material is made available to all students, but particular students (who fail an assessment, or struggle to understand a concept) might be directed to pair particular components and review before attempting a further assignment.

Does any of this constitute the 'redefinition' of the traditional lecture? For all of the changes wrought by the digitisation of the lecture, information transfer still lies at the bottom of the examples described here. There are, however, two ways in which we might see the lecture being capable of redefinition through the use of e-learning. The first is that the RVL, as well as being useful for primary information before students read and discuss topics, can also function as a response to class conversations in forums or tutorials. Where it becomes clear that many students have misunderstood or would like more information about a particular issue, the RVL (or, if appropriate, a more low-tech audio recording) allows the lecturer to respond to the class as a whole. For example, in the first week of the Ancient Languages unit, students learn about Proto-Indo-European

(PIE), the putative language from which Ancient Greek and Latin derive, and hear some reconstructions of the language. By week two we move on to the Greek alphabet, but it sometimes becomes apparent that some students regard PIE as an extant language: this is not the case, as no written evidence for the language exists. In the past, we would have to devote a portion of a lecture some weeks later to this clarification, or repeat it several times to each group in tutorials, and perhaps make a note to shift the emphasis in next year's lecture—something of little use to this year's class. By recording and posting a short RVL, we are able to clarify the various theories on PIE, and also to link the current week's content to this proto-language, by giving possible PIE reconstructions to demonstrate the possible origin of that week's Greek vocabulary.

Although this does demand additional work for the lecturer, it can be completed relatively quickly, and the RVL should be kept to a minimal length, as it represents an additional time investment for the student. In many cases, it saves time in the long term, as it deals with questions which may be asked multiple times by individual students, as well as avoiding the ripple effect of misunderstandings, which have long term effects in cumulative disciplines such as languages—if base level material is not clear to students, they will find more complex content very difficult. This method also represents a customisation of the curriculum for a particular cohort, and is something we have often found useful as entry standards are frequently altered regulations, making it impossible for teachers to predict the exact level at which to pitch classes each year. On a more positive note, I think of this procedure as a *sphragis* or 'seal' on a component of the unit, as it allows for the lecturer give a summation of a topic. However, there is a distinction between this format and a periodic 'conclusions' class, which might be mapped into the unit schedule beforehand. Because it answers the needs of a specific class, the *sphragis* encourages the cohort to see their particular imprint on the curriculum. In this way e-learning allows the lecture to become more than a foundational medium and transforms it into a responsive medium, which feeds the needs of specific groups and avoids the conveyer belt mentality of reproducing cookie cutter lectures, with the same material trotted out year after year.

Secondly, in our units, the online lecture has led to a redesign of assessment, beyond the research essay, to which Humanities education in Australia is often exclusively wedded. For it is clear that the RVL does not need to be the sole domain of the lecturer. A further beneficial aspect of widely available recordable lecture technology is that it is repeatable at many levels, allowing for student adoption of the format. In many of our units we now ask students to respond with e-learning productions of their own as a final assessment piece. This might include the creation of a YouTube video, a Sway (a simple presentation format which combines text, images and video), or a Pecha kucha (a slide presentation with a strict time limit). One clear advantage of combining this form of assessment with the pre-recorded lecture is that the method, or a form of it, has already been modelled by the lecturer. In the Ancient Languages unit students complete a more scaffolded task and are asked to find a passage from a particular genre of literary or scientific writing, and to analyse the vocabulary found within it. They then create a recorded presentation in which they determine the percentage of words which derive from Ancient Greek, Latin, Germanic or other roots, and form tentative conclusions about the linguistic origins of that genre. Obviously, this form of assessment differs considerably from the traditional essay, although there is no need to abandon the essay, which does assess vital research, writing and referencing skills. Where appropriate, an essay can easily be contiguous with the recorded presentations. Ancient Languages is a first-year unit and writing is assessed elsewhere in shorter formats, but in more advanced classes students are always required to extend an aspect of their presentation and write it up as an individual research essay.

These presentations are small group performances and encourage students to be collaborative, countering one downside of online and blended learning, which is potential alienation. In both units discussed above the assessment is designed to build on methodologies which have been demonstrated to students, following the concept of 'e-moderating' (Salmon, 2011), which offers a high degree of direction in the early stages of a course, but guides students towards social interaction and independence in the latter stages. Students must come to terms with new technologies and learn skills from peers who have some experience with recording techniques. They benefit from the multimedia principle/effect, which claims that using more than one medium (audio/visual/text) promotes 'deeper learning than using just one' medium (Mayer, 2014). In addition, students also have to map out the best way of presenting the material in an alternative format: in a way, they are forced to empathise with the lecturer and consider why lectures might be framed in a particular way, in terms of ordering information and evidence, so that they can use the pre-recorded lecture as an example of how to frame their own content. Thus, students must think about how best to present their research: are detailed images required? Do quotations need to be read aloud, summarised or presented as written text on a screen? Would the presentation benefit from more than one voice, perhaps demonstrating oppositional perspectives? And while a number of students working together tends to produce higher quality work and to develop a cohort experience, the use of multimedia technologies also allows for student who suffer from anxiety to produce a pre-recorded presentation which can substitute for a group in-class presentation.

Conclusion

A significant aspect of the pre-recorded lecture is that it can feature the lecturer in person, or sometimes more than one presenter in conversation—the latter a feature which would be difficult to reproduce year-on-year in F2F mode due to conflicting schedules. It combines F2F and online or computer-mediated communication, which are often seen as mutually exclusive. The format of the pre-recording however demands a transformation of presentation style and content. On a purely practical level, the lecturer must avoid content specific to that iteration of the class; but the upside is that it can be redeployed as foundational material for higher level classes without the teacher having to repeat content provision. The presentation style necessarily alters, as there is no 'live audience' present. I have found that it is preferable to present in a relatively informal style, in order to recreate some aspects of the in-class dynamic. Engaging students in the presentation by giving them a related task to do is also a means of building a bridge between the teacher in the video and the student at the computer. This might involve instructing them to pause the video and do a task now, or to prepare a response for tutorial (see Lloyd, in this volume, for a nuanced version of this). In-class experience and student evaluations also show that this method works best if the lecturer is also involved in some F2F elements of the unit, whether that be a classroom tutorial or a meeting online (such as via Zoom or Collaborate). This suggests that students are more accepting of e-learning technologies if they can connect the presentation of materials with some form of personal contact.

We should, then, see the potential of e-learning in this form not merely as an efficient form of lecturing to students who are no longer accustomed to be present at a prearranged time in a mandated space, nor as a lecture which can be recorded once and then recycled year after year. Instead, pre-recording can produce a dynamic form of teaching which separates out formative and complex levels of material into the appropriate modes; which is able to quickly and efficiently respond to a specific cohort's need; and which provides students with a coherent and equitable experience, rather than the ad hoc methods of lecture theatre recording for those who cannot attend. Rather than a second-best format, pre-recording can provide an e-learning means to customise the curriculum and to design creative assessment tasks.

About the Author

Rhiannon Evans is Senior Lecturer in Classics and Ancient History at La Trobe University, Melbourne, Australia. She can be contacted at this e-mail: r.evans@latrobe.edu.au

Bibliography

Betts, K. (2009). Lost in translation: Importance of effective communication in online education. *Online Journal of Distance Learning Administration*, 16(2), 55–78.

Camtasia (2018). Retrieved April 27, 2018, from https://www.techsmith.com/video-editor.html

Clarke, R. C., & Mayer, R. E. (2016). *e-learning and the Science of Instruction: Proven Guidelines for Consumers and Designers of Multimedia Learning*. Hoboken: John Wiley & Sons.

Dona, K. L., Gregory, J., & Pechenkina, E. (2017). Lecture-recording technology in higher education: Exploring lecturer and student views across the disciplines. *Australasian Journal of Educational Technology*, 33(4), 122–133.

Draper M. J., Gibbon, S., & Thomas, J. (2018). Lecture recording: a new norm. *The Law Teacher*, DOI: 10.1080/03069400.2018.1450598

Evans, R. (2014). Emperors of Rome Podcast Series – Episodes XIII-XV. Retrieved April 24, 2018, from https://itunes.apple.com/au/podcast/emperors-of-rome/id850148806?mt=2

Evans, R., & Wurster, S. (2013). Roman Politics and Poetry: Cicero and Catullus, Retrieved April 24, 2018, from https://www.youtube.com/watch?v=-1–C5mbV9Lk

Harris, D. (2016). Rhizomatic education and Deleuzian theory. *Open Learning*, 31(3), 219–232.

Li F. W. B., Lau R. W. H., & Dharmendran, P. (2009). A Three-Tier Profiling Framework for Adaptive e-learning. In Spaniol, M., Li, Q., Klamma, R., & Lau, R. W. H. (Eds.), *Advances in Web Based Learning – ICWL 2009*. Berlin & Heidelberg: Springer Verlag.

Mayer, R. E. (2014). Cognitive theory of multimedia learning. In Mayer, R. E. (Ed.), *The Cambridge handbook of multimedia learning*. New York: Cambridge University Press, 42–71.

Midford, S., & Evans, R. (2017). Revitalising the Past: Crafting a Digital Engagement Model to Innovate Humanities Curriculum. In Hørsted, A., Bartholomew, P., Branch, J., & Nygaard, C. (Eds.), *New Innovations in Teaching and Learning in Higher Education*. Oxfordshire, UK: Libri Publishing Ltd., 125–148.

One Button Studio (2016). Pennsylvania, Pennsylvania State University. Retrieved April 11, 2017, from http://onebutton.psu.edu/

The Open University (2018). Retrieved April 27, 2018, from http://www.openuniversity.edu/why-the-ou/flexibility

Puentedura, R. (2017). Defining Goals for Change: SAMR, Learning, and the Road Ahead. Retrieved February 11, 2018, from http://hippasus.com/blog/archives/377

Ross B., & Gage, K. (2006). Global Perspectives on Blending Learning: Insight from WebCT and Our Customers in Higher Education. *The Handbook of Blended Learning: Global Perspectives, Local Designs*. San Francisco: Wiley, 306–335.

Salmon, G. (2011). *E-moderating: The Key to Teaching and Learning Online*. New York and London: Routledge.

Sangrà, A., Vlachopoulos, D., & Cabrera, N. (2012). Building an Inclusive Definition of e-learning: An Approach to the Conceptual Framework. *The International Review of Research in Open and Distributed Learning*, 13(2), 145–159.

Sarsfield, M. (2010). Lecture recordings: examining the evidence. Retrieved June 6, 2018, from http://www.imperial.ac.uk/edudev/flyers/technologies/Life_Sciences_Podcasting.pdf

Scheiter, K. (2014). The learner control principle in multimedia learning. In Mayer, R. E. (Ed.), *The Cambridge handbook of multimedia learning*. Cambridge: Cambridge University Press, 487–512.

Tobin, T. J. (2018). The eLearning Leader's Toolkit for Evaluating Online Teaching. In Piña, A. A., Lowell, V. L., & Harris, B. R. (Eds.), *Leading and Managing e-learning: What the e-learning Leader Needs to Know*. New York, NY: Springer, 235–251.

Chapter 7

The E-CIL framework: An instructional practice for promoting student engagement with content, the instructor, and other learners in online courses

Malinda Hoskins Lloyd

Introduction

With this chapter, I contribute to the book *E-learning 1.0, 2.0, and 3.0 in Higher Education* as I highlight an innovative practice for fostering university students' *engagement*. In particular, I put emphasis on *content*, the *instructor*, and *co-learners* in online environments. Together, engagement (E), content (C), instructor (I) and co-learners (L) constitute what I refer to as the E-CIL Framework. This framework is based on a recent study during which I explored students' preferences, attitudes, and experiences related to online and digital learning in an effort to improve university teaching and, ultimately, student achievement. Within the context of this chapter, I use the terms e-learning and online learning synonymously and define these phrases as any learning environment during which technology is used for instructional purposes, which can include face-to-face, hybrid, or online courses. I define student engagement with respect to students' engagement (E) with course content (C), with the course instructor (I), and with co-learners (L) and present detailed guidelines for implementing the E-CIL Framework. Thus, the rationale for this chapter is to enhance the effectiveness of instruction in online environments by presenting ways to positively impact students' online experiences. To do so, I provide a context in which university students and their instructors become co-facilitators of learning in online spaces.

Chapter 7

The following are questions professors may ask as they plan their instruction for e-learning environments: What are university students' preferences related to online and digital learning? What techniques and activities related to online and digital learning are viewed as beneficial to higher education students? How can university instructors increase a sense of "connectedness" with their students in an online environment? How can university instructors design e-learning experiences so that they resemble the positive characteristics of traditional, face-to-face courses? How can university students engage with course content and their peers in meaningful ways in online environments?

The delivery of online and hybrid courses is commonplace in university settings, and many universities are offering full online degrees. With competition between universities being a key player in enrolment decisions, administrators and faculty are charged with the challenging task of meeting the calls of prospective students. These students, when it comes to actually choosing their courses, seem to favour programs which offer the convenience and flexibility of online accessibility (Young & Norgard, 2006); however, their reported experiences in these online spaces are often far from positive.

I present the findings from a recent study on university students' preferences, attitudes, and experiences related to online learning. Prompted by the findings of the study and considerations of prior scholarly works, I then present an innovative instructional framework for e-learning, E-CIL, which highlights ways to utilise suggested technological applications such as Nearpod, Flipgrid, and Padlet, as explained in subsequent sections. The techniques emphasized in E-CIL are intended to cultivate students' learning as they engage with the content, the instructor, and with co-learners—practices which contribute to the innovative design of online courses, mirroring the positive characteristics of engagement in face-to-face courses.

While reading this chapter, you will gain the following insights regarding the use of novel practices, particularly the E-CIL Framework, in e-learning environments:

1. how they increase students' engagement with content, with the instructor, and with co-learners;

2. how they increase students' sense of belonging to a learning community in an online course; and,

3. how a course can be effectively designed with weekly guidelines of specific components to be included.

The chapter includes the following sections: Introduction, The Background, The Practice, and Conclusion. The introductory section explains the need for novelty in e-learning and includes a definition of e-learning and student engagement and the features of the E-CIL Framework. The background section provides information related to a recent study by the author which highlights university students' preferences, attitudes, and experiences related to e-learning. The practice section presents the E-CIL Framework with recommended guidelines for a week-by-week delivery of an online course, which, although designed with online courses in mind, could be implemented in any e-learning environment including face-to-face, hybrid, and online courses. The conclusion summarizes the main points of the chapter and provides reflections on advancing the integration of novel technology in order to further increase student engagement and achievement with respect to online and digital learning.

Section I: The background

The Literature

The information which follows presents some of the aspects to consider in relation to online learning. I share the history of online learning and then discuss the opportunity for creating a sustainable framework for e-learning delivery. I also discuss the realities of online learning by addressing some of the advantages and disadvantages, students' inclinations for taking online or face-to-face courses, e-learning from a business perspective, the strategical design of online courses, and the importance of active learning in digital environments.

According to "The People History" (www.thepeoplehistory.com/1981), 1981 was a year of firsts around the world—the year that Lady Diana Spencer married Prince Charles, NASA launched its first space shuttle, Post-it notes were invented, Pope John Paul II was shot in the Vatican City, the AIDS virus was identified, and the first university course was delivered online. Fast-forward nearly four decades, and we find that these 1981 occurrences have met varying fates—some have ended, while others continue to evolve. Online learning, in particular, is one of the events which has continued to evolve, especially within the context of higher education. Finding ourselves amidst an extreme evolution of technological luxuries, how have these computer-related advances influenced the changes in online delivery of university courses since the 1981–"maiden voyage?" Although educators strive to remain current with respect to best practices, the mode by which these practices is delivered is continuously advancing. Consequently, higher education institutions must prepare themselves for effective delivery of online courses by remaining current with the latest instructional practices *and* the most effective modes for delivery. Some say we learn about the future by knowing about the past. The trend for online learning is certainly on an upward climb, and, with this in mind, it is evident that online learning is very likely to have a sustainable future. To illustrate, the author presents specific findings related to online learning in the subsequent sections and conveys how these findings can be applied within a pedagogical context using the E-CIL Framework.

Past literature suggests students are inclined to choose online delivery as opposed to traditional face-to-face courses; however, their reasons are perplexing and sometimes either contradictory or in opposition to educational philosophies. For example, according to prior research by Young & Norgard (2006) and the current study that will be discussed in subsequent sections, university students tend to enrol in online courses because of convenience and flexibility, although they claim to prefer face-to-face courses. Students report that they do not learn as much in online courses and claim that online courses require more time than traditional face-to-face courses; yet, they also claim that online courses are not as difficult as face-to-face courses. As suggested by Young & Norgard (2006), students with more experience with online courses reportedly feel more comfortable with engaging in online activities. University students tend to convey mixed emotions regarding online courses, while emphasizing more positive aspects of face-to-face courses. With this in mind, what can we, as university instructors, do to mirror the positive characteristics of face-to-face courses within our online courses in order to increase their appeal to university students? This question will be addressed in subsequent sections, as the E-CIL Framework is presented.

From a business perspective, universities are situated in a position to compete with other universities. Administrative conversations stem from students' requests for online programs. Some universities' enrolment numbers may be in decline due to their rivals offering some of their programs completely online. Again, although students say they prefer face-to-face courses, when it comes to actually choosing a course, they elect to take online options more frequently; therefore, higher education institutions must be prepared to accept students' propensity to take these courses and establish the mission of meeting this challenge. As a result, higher education institutions are confronted with the daunting, if not perplexing, task of targeting their student consumers by offering online programs characterized by effective learning environments. Cautiously, however, if university courses are convenient but ineffective (Young & Norgard, 2006), unfortunately, all stakeholders are at a tremendous disadvantage. Universities, therefore, must proceed cautiously in order to maintain a balance between convenience and effectiveness in the design of these online environments. As shown in later sections, the E-CIL Framework addresses how to effectively design courses in an effort to reach the balance discussed above.

When making decisions regarding e-learning, stakeholders must consider the advantages and disadvantages of online courses. For example, one concern with online courses is students' feelings of social isolation (Dixon, 2010). As stated by Kahn et. al. (2016:205), *"If we are to gain a more comprehensive understanding of student engagement, it is important to consider how individual students determine their own engagement."* In this vein, it is important that university students and faculty demonstrate a reciprocating presence in online learning environments. Joksimović et. al. (2015:97), in their meta-analysis of various studies related to online learning, describe how *"the lack of unity of time and place leads to greater independence between students and instructors"* and that online learning has its advantages including a decrease in overcrowded classrooms, an increase in enrollment, and a reduction in cost for universities. Contrarily, the disadvantages include dealing with technology gaps and feelings of isolation by the students.

Parallel to the findings of the current study presented in this chapter, Young & Norgard (2006) discuss that university students prefer their courses to be designed in a manner which uses extensive structure and contains set dates stated in advance. Strategically designed online courses provide a framework for students to be more in control of their learning with respect to online learning and its relationship to self-regulated learning. Joksimović et. al. (2015:114) argue that online courses *"should provide good support for student-student and student-content interactions."* In addition, they claim that the instructor must serve as moderator in guiding structured online discussions, while providing timely, formative feedback to students. Further, they maintain that instructors must present content in a visually engaging and interactive manner. The E-CIL Framework, as will be discussed in the following sections, provides opportunities for students and faculty to engage and interact in a strategic approach.

Another aspect to consider is how the E-CIL Framework is conducive to active learning. Although active learning is no new concept in education, researchers (Czerkawski & Lyman, 2016) claim that, while both environments—online and face-to-face—have similar goals of creating interactive learning spaces, online learning presents more of a challenge to instructors. Researchers (Park & Choi, 2014; Patrick et al. 2016; Choi & Anderson, 2016; Hudesman et al., 2013; Kim et al., 2013) argue for the vital role of active learning within the context of higher education. Park & Choi (2014), in their study of active learning classrooms, found that students in an active learning environment participate more, show more interest in course content, increase interactions with co-learners and instructors, and voluntarily ask more questions. Students in these active learning spaces also began to show new "ways of knowing" as they shared their knowledge through peer-to-peer interactions. In addition, self-regulated learning (SRL) and active learning environments create learning spaces conducive to high levels of achievement. Researchers such as Hudesman et al. (2013) argue that SRL, even more than students' performance on standardized exams, is a strong predictor of students' grade point average. Again, how can we, as instructors, design online learning environments which mirror these positive attributes of face-to-face courses?

Research Methods

Prompted by the literature and current trends in higher education, the author/researcher delved into further exploration of university students' perspectives of online learning. Valuing students' voices, the researcher's goal was to understand students' viewpoints based on their experiences or, in some cases, lack of experiences related to online learning. In this study, 434 graduate and undergraduate university students completed an online survey entitled *University Students' Preferences, Attitudes, and Experiences Related to Online and Digital Learning*. These student participants represented 17 public and private universities located in the United States and United Kingdom and 44 fields of study including, but not limited to, Biochemistry, Mathematics, Education, Nursing, Computer Science, Accounting, Engineering, Biology, Environmental Science, Physics, Sociology, Psychology, History, Political Science, Pre-Med, and Business.

Utilizing Qualtrics software to disseminate the survey, the researcher recruited university students either directly or by contacting their professors and provided them with an anonymous link to access the survey. Utilizing the survey instrument as the exclusive method of data collection, the researcher inquired about the number of students who had taken an online course and then further probed these students' feelings of "connectedness" in online courses. In addition, the researcher assessed the likelihood of all student participants to enrol in an online course in lieu of a traditional face-to-face course and also asked about students' preferences, if given a choice, between online or paper-and-pencil exams and other assignments.

Students were asked if they would enjoy interacting with their peers in online environments such as discussion boards and how comfortable they would feel submitting a video or audio of themselves in an online course. Students also ranked types of learning environments—online, hybrid, and traditional face-to-face—from favorite to least favorite. Students ranked specific course activities in order from most beneficial to least beneficial. Students then provided open-ended responses to two key questions which asked them to 1) identify the most beneficial activity required of them in an online course and 2) provide a recommendation for instructors regarding the integration of technology.

The researcher analyzed the findings using descriptive and inferential statistics; however, for the scope of this chapter, the researcher has provided primarily descriptive data in the subsequent sections to highlight for the reader the key findings and relevance of the study, particularly with respect to design of the E-CIL Framework.

Chapter 7

Findings of the Study

Reportedly, 58% of the participants had taken an online course, and half of these had taken the course by choice over a traditional face-to-face course. The other half took the online course because it was required of their program of study. In contrast, however, more than 59% of those who had taken an online course stated they would rarely or never choose the online option over a traditional face-to-face course. Even more of those who had not taken an online course (over 71%) said they would not choose an online course over a traditional face-to-face course. These findings raise questions regarding students' reasons and inclinations for taking an online course. Although students claim they do not prefer an online course, perhaps they still take it as a matter of convenience or for other personal reasons. Those who had previously taken an online course were more likely to choose an online course, however, than those who had never taken an online course.

Regrettably, the majority of the university students expressed feelings of being disconnected from their instructor (59%) and classmates (55%) in online courses compared to their experiences in a traditional face-to-face course, possibly contributing to the high percentage of students saying they would rarely or never choose an online course over a traditional face-to-face course. In contrast, almost half of the students indicated they *had* taken an online course as a personal choice. Perhaps this indicates that personal situations at the time of choosing their courses affect their decision, although it may not have been their preference.

In looking at the various classifications and feelings of "connectedness" in online courses, more than 85% of graduate students claimed to feel the most connected, while juniors (65%) seemed to feel the most disconnected. Notably, graduate level students were the only group who represented a majority as feeling connected to their instructor in an online course. The author also noticed a correlation between students' feeling of connectedness and their being inclined to take an online course over a traditional face-to-face course. For example, 80% of students who claimed they felt connected to their instructor in an online course also claimed that they would choose an online course either most of the time or always over a traditional face-to-face course. In contrast, 82.6% of students who claimed to feel disconnected said they would rarely or never take an online course over a traditional face-to-face course. These findings support the importance of the need for students to feel connected, particularly in an era of a high push for online programs in the university setting and also with respect to students' propensity to choose an online course regardless of their preference. As shown in Figure 1 below, these findings represent a positive correlation between connectedness and students' desire to enrol in online courses.

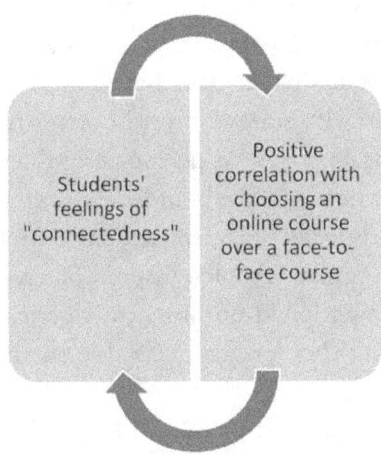

Figure 1: Correlation between students' feelings of connectedness and their likelihood of choosing an online course over a face-to-face course.

The majority of student participants (72%) reported their online experience would be improved if their instructor provided frequent video or audio explanations of upcoming assignments and course content; however, when the roles were reversed, the majority of participants were much less inclined themselves to submit an audio or video of themselves in an online course. In looking further into the data, however, no participant reported to have submitted such an assignment. Perhaps their opinions could be altered if given the opportunity to contribute to a course through video or audio platforms. In addition, 81% of the participants reported that they enjoy their instructors integrating technology in face-to-face courses.

When asked to rank the type of learning environment they preferred, university students (57%) chose traditional face-to-face courses as their favorite, hybrid courses (a combination of online and face-to-face class meetings) as their second choice, and online courses as their least favorite. In fact, 75% of the participants identified online courses as their least favorite. In a related question, 64% of the participants claimed they would rarely or never choose an online course over a traditional face-to-face course if given the option. Surprisingly, though, 50% of the participants who had taken an online course did so as a personal choice rather than as a requirement. In several of the survey data sets, many of the students contradicted their preferences with their experiences. Students' contradictions, for example, were evident when asked about digital assignments compared to traditional paper-and-pencil assignments. Although half of the university students claimed to have taken an online course as a personal choice, about 41% stated they still prefer traditional paper-and-pencil assignments as opposed to online assignments. In a subsequent question, however, when asked about their preferences for online or traditional paper-and-pencil exams, students' preferences were fairly equal and showed no great variance in preference. In their open-ended responses, students mentioned on numerous occasions that they prefer online quizzes, stating they prefer these due to their ability to receive immediate feedback.

University students (approximately 81%) highly favor the integration of technology in face-to-face traditional courses, while 84% also believe their learning is enhanced when the instructor provides online resources and materials. These findings support the need for increased integration of technology in all courses. As the author unveiled in the recent study, university students expressed a desire for timely and detailed feedback from their instructors in e-learning contexts.

When participants were asked to rank activities from most beneficial to least beneficial, 81% reported that electronic class participation in the form of a game-like platform such as Kahoot, clickers, or a digital game show as most beneficial. Students' next favorite was participation in an interactive presentation during which students contribute information to a live presentation such as the use of Nearpod or Poll Everywhere. Another favorite (48%) was watching an online video and reflecting on its content, followed by 47% reporting the completion of an online quiz or test as most beneficial. On the contrary, students' responses indicated a strong aversion for the use of tools such as Skype with 90% of the students identifying this as the least beneficial. Another least favorite activity was participation in discussion boards which was chosen as the least beneficial by 50% of the participants.

The previous section presents students' ranking of beneficial activities when given a choice of specific activities. This section, however, represents students' open-ended responses based on their most beneficial *experiences* in courses. Using open-ended responses, participants were asked to identify the most beneficial course activity or assignment that required them to think deeply about course content. Responses varied across majors and universities; however, some distinct patterns emerged.

Students identified the most beneficial course activities as those that required them to apply course material and generate real-world connections (such as designing lesson plans, speeches, presentations, lab experiments, case studies, and participating in field experiences). This study also revealed that students identified activities that allowed them to engage with content as beneficial. Another commonality was the use of reading-response activities (reading and reflecting on articles, reading a chapter and writing a one-page response, or doing research and writing about it). A third commonality of beneficial activities was the use of videos by the instructor and by the students. Students also stated that pre-session work was beneficial, which included activities such as watching a video before class as an introduction to content. Others valued having access to PowerPoint presentations, mock exams, and supplemental material before attending an upcoming class as a way of preparing in advance. Also, identified as beneficial were step-by-step explanations for assignments and the process for working out problems (provided by the instructor). University students (55%) expressed a strong dislike of discussion boards in online courses, yet some, in their open-ended responses, claimed this was their most interactive online activity. Surprisingly, although the majority of students, with the exception of graduate students, claimed they would not feel comfortable submitting a video as an online assignment, many also acknowledged video assignments as the most beneficial assignments in online courses. This was an interesting finding in that, while students claimed they would be uncomfortable presenting themselves in a video, they contrarily reported that creating a video assignment was beneficial. The previous literature, as well as the findings of the current study, support the notion that student preference may not always align with what students report as beneficial to student learning. This supports the need for instructors to feel confident in situating students within the context of "uncomfortable zones" in order to benefit their learning in online courses. Consequently, in cases such as these, instructors must make instructional decisions which foster student learning. For example, students claimed that being required to create a video presentation and upload it as a YouTube video was beneficial. From the study, the researcher noticed on numerous occasions that student preference and student learning were often conveyed in opposition to each other. A notable topic for future exploration is to investigate the reasons behind this adversarial relationship.

Perhaps the most noteworthy question of the survey was the one in which the researcher asked students to respond to a second open-ended question, making recommendations to instructors regarding the integration of technology. In responding, students made numerous worthy recommendations; however, some commonalities in the data were more prominent than others. First, students recommended that instructors provide avenues for students to engage with the content in the following ways: to provide online access to resources and materials; to provide clear instructions and rubrics for assignments; to choose online resources that are applicable to real life; and, to allow students opportunities to reflect on course content following the viewing of a video or the reading of an article. Students also provided recommendations with respect to engaging with the instructor and other students. These included suggestions such as utilizing instructor-made videos for the students explaining course content or as an overview for the week's content; providing online forums as platforms for students and the instructor to interact; doing live streaming during which students log in and participate in discussions with the instructor and their peers; and, providing online quizzes and assignments through which students can receive timely feedback on their progress.

In general, regarding the use of technology, students recommended that instructors use technology to enhance learning rather than as a distraction and suggested this be achieved by keeping it interesting, yet simple. Students also suggested that instructors provide clear directions for using the technology and to err on the side of "less is more" by utilizing only a few websites, apps, or other digital platforms rather than too many. Students also recommended the use of digital resources that are free of charge to the students and are user-friendly for both the instructor and students, to be organized, and to establish online deadlines at the beginning of the semester so students can work at their own pace and around scheduling concerns.

Overall, students argued that technology should be embraced but should not take centre place in learning. One student's words encompassed the overall mantra of this chapter by saying that technology should "enable the feeling of face-to-face contact." The author aligns the findings of the current study with an instructional practice which takes into account students' recommendations, preferences (although cautiously considered due to the additional findings), attitudes, and experiences. With an emphasis on recognizing and valuing student voice, the author compiled these findings and, as a result, designed the E-CIL Framework, the instructional practice which is detailed in the following section.

Section 2: The practice

Based on prior scholarly works as stated in the literature and the findings of the current study, the researcher designed a framework for practice: Engagement (E) with Content (C), Instructor (I), and Learners (L) (the E-CIL framework) as a means for engaging students in online environments in higher education settings. In looking at the data, the E-CIL Framework takes into account all of these necessary components as mentioned above. Presumably, one or more of these parts may have been missing from online learning environments of the past. With respect to the E-CIL framework, each of these pieces is a valuable component for forging increased learning within online environments. Further, the components of the E-CIL framework are cyclical in nature and rely on all components working in a synergistic manner in order to have an impact on learning. Thus, students must think deeply about course content in order to make connections and apply the information to real-world settings. Students must also experience a sense of "connectedness" with the instructor, which should be accomplished by participating as a co-creator of knowledge situated in a context where everyone's voice is valued. Lastly, students must collaborate and interact with other learners through rich experiences facilitated by the instructor and built on a strong connection to the content. The E-CIL Framework, therefore, transforms online spaces into student-centred learning communities, and its effectiveness would be diminished without one of its parts. Figure 2 below represents the cyclical nature of the E-CIL Framework.

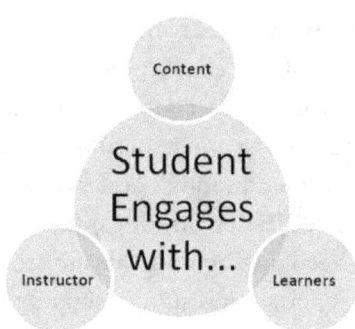

Figure 2: The E-CIL Framework. This figure illustrates the importance of engagement of the student with the content, the instructor, and co-learners in order to establish a sense of connectedness in digital learning environments.

Current Technology Tools

In today's technology-driven world, we are inundated with ever-evolving computer applications, devices, platforms, software, and other computer-mediated tools. In the spirit of simplicity, however, the author provides directives for using three specific applications—Nearpod, Flipgrid, and Padlet—as vehicles for implementing the E-CIL framework. If this framework had been implemented in 1981, although delivery methods would have been less computer-mediated, the premise of the E-CIL Framework would have appeared the same; hence, this framework for instructional practice is sustainable in that it supports student engagement with content, the instructor, and co-learners. (As a disclaimer, the author chose Nearpod, Flipgrid, and Padlet as personal preferences and has no business or financial affiliations to any of these suggested technology tools.) In the sections that follow, the author explains each of the applications. These platforms, however, are *only* suggestions and are not exclusive to the numerous digital tools available to instructors and students.

Nearpod (https://nearpod.com/) is an application which can be used to transform a presentation, such as a PowerPoint, into an interactive presentation. Krahenbuhl (2015) describes Nearpod as an "active, question-driven learning experience," which can be used to deepen students' learning. To do this, the instructor designs a presentation and integrates questions and other interactives. Students then provide responses to the instructor's prompts which enables the instructor to monitor students' understanding of the presentation's concepts. As a formative assessment tool, instructors can use students' responses as a data-gathering method using the Nearpod questions and activities. Questions can be designed using varying formats including selected response and open response. Instructors can also allow students opportunities to be more creative in their responses by drawing and/or writing their responses. Nearpod is a way for students to participate in a presentation through rich interactions with the instructor, the content, and other learners. The instructor can pose a question and then provide immediate feedback to students' responses, an excellent tool for formative assessment.

Flipgrid (https://info.flipgrid.com/) is a platform through which instructors can create a "grid," or a community of learners. Instructors then create topics to which students can respond. To respond, students record a short video (90 seconds or less) of themselves and upload it to the grid. Students may also make their videos unique by adding images and emotion icons. Instructors have control over what other learners can see. For example, instructors can use specific settings allowing other learners to view and respond to videos that have been posted by students. Students can then respond by creating another video. The instructor may also opt to maintain confidentiality of the students by altering the settings enabling only the instructor to access individual students' video submissions. Instructors are also able to provide feedback to students which is sent to the students via email. Flipgrid is an excellent tool for allowing students to engage with the content and their instructor, while also creating a sense of community through meaningful interactions with their peers in the course.

Padlet (https://padlet.com/) is explained as a web-based (or application-based) virtual bulletin board for numerous people to add and share information. The Center for Innovation in Research and Teaching (n.d.) suggests university students use this to share thoughts on assignments and/or to respond to an instructor's questions on a topic. For example, an instructor poses a content-related Padlet question or assignment for students. Students then add their information to the virtual bulletin board using a digital "sticky note." Instructors and students have the freedom to insert text, images, audio clips, video clips, graphs, and other visuals to enhance their Padlet posts. Padlet is an excellent technology tool in that it allows information related to a particular topic to be stored and organized in one central location. The instructor could use Padlet for explaining upcoming projects. Students may then add any further questions by creating a "sticky note" and posting it for the instructor to see. Posts can be anonymous; therefore, instructors could create a "Course Questions" board on which students may anonymously ask questions throughout the course without fear of negative judgements being placed on them. This would be helpful for students who are fearful of asking questions either through email or aloud (in the case of face-to-face courses). Padlet posts could also be used as a way for students to review for upcoming exams. Many instructors use "exit tickets" (student responses to an end-of-class question to gauge student learning) at the end of class, which could be represented on a Padlet board. Overall, Padlet is a useful technology tool which allows content to be represented and shown in visually-appealing ways.

Implementing the E-CIL framework

The following sections provide a detailed plan for implementing the E-CIL framework; thus, regardless of the technology tool chosen, it is important for instructors to emphasize the goal of the framework—to provide numerous opportunities for students to engage with the content, the instructor, and co-learners in an online course. The tools used in attaining this goal, however, could certainly vary from the ones recommended for the scope of this chapter. With this in mind, therefore, it is important for readers to approach the implementation of the E-CIL framework with the mindset of applying the framework to their particular setting. In addition, although this practice was designed specifically for online courses, it is also applicable to traditional face-to-face and hybrid courses and across multiple disciplines.

Student engagement with content

Student engagement with content allows students to interact with the key topics, concepts and vocabulary in meaningful contexts. E-learning environments, when strategically designed, provide students with the opportunity to engage with content in more meaningful ways. For example, instructors can design assignments which require students to explore course content in real-world settings coupled with a reflective piece to be completed online. To this effect, content should be organized for students in the order in which it will be accessed for the course, and a routine should be established which lays the groundwork for clear expectations. For example, instructors create a routine for each week which includes an article or other reading activity for the students to complete; a video for the students to view which shows a real-world connection to the content; an example and/or explanation of a weekly assignment, topic, or problem to be completed; a presentation by the instructor to be viewed by the students; and, numerous opportunities for reflection.

Student engagement with the instructor

The E-CIL Framework was built with the notion of putting students at the centre of learning. For this to happen, students and the instructor must engage in rich conversations and content-related interactions. For this to occur, the instructor serves as the facilitator by intentionally planning activities which allow inclusive opportunities for students to be participants in online courses. Lloyd *et. al.* (2016) presented a similar practice, the Facilitate-Listen-Engage (FLE) Model in which the instructor lays the foundation for engaging students in discourse and creating a community of learners. In this role, the instructor designs learning experiences which are "horizontal" in nature, meaning that the relationship between teacher and student is symbiotic. To add to this, Booker (2008) suggests that students' views are positively altered when they are allowed to voice their opinions, collaborate, and interact with the instructor. Overall, student engagement with the instructor should increase a sense of connectedness and establish a learning community which is conducive to developing two-way communication.

Student engagement with co-learners
In an environment where student engagement with co-learners is nurtured, students are given opportunities for rich interactions with their peers. Sanchez (2008) supports the creation of a community of learners that is inclusive and supportive of all of its members. While online learning in the past has proven to cause students to feel isolated, it is possible to create digital spaces which are conducive to building a sense of community. This is accomplished by intentionally planning assignments and course activities that allow numerous opportunities for students to engage in discourse with their peers.

Introductions in an online environment
Establishing a sense of community in any classroom is imperative; an online classroom is no exception. In an online environment, instructors and students often report a lack of connectedness. In order to encourage rich discussions and interactions, the members of the learning community must first be given opportunities to learn more about each other. To do this, provide an opportunity for you, as the instructor, and for the students to introduce themselves. Allow students to use Flipgrid to create a 90-second video introduction of themselves or Padlet to create a virtual board to introduce themselves. Provide them with some prompts to which they must respond. Allow their introductions to be open-ended and unique; however, for those who are less inclined to be transparent with strangers, provide them with some sentence stems such as those shown in Figure 3. As the instructor of the course, be sure to set an example by posting an introduction yourself.

Next, ask students to access other students' introductory posts and respond to a set number of students' posts. They can choose to do this by creating another video or by writing their response on the post. These introductory activities are important in order to lay the foundation for students' continued interactions in the online course and will help to increase a sense of connectedness. Ask them to respond with at least one statement and one question.

The E-CIL framework

> - One thing you might be surprised to know about me is _____.
> - An event in my life that has had the most influence on my desire to attend university is _____.
> - If I didn't need to sleep, my favourite way to spend my time would be _____.
> - If I could go on any adventure, I would go to _____.
> - The most impressive thing I know how to do is _____.
> - I wish I knew more about _____.

Figure 3: Sentence stems for course introductions.

Weekly outline

Many instructors have access to online portals through their university; however, if this is not available, instructors are encouraged to create one such as an instructor website. Thus, the activities described below are suggested with the notion of students being able to access and upload information to one centralized (digital) location. Consider dividing your course content into weeks. Determine the topics, concepts, and vocabulary or other related information to be addressed each week. As a guideline, the following is a collection of weekly activities designed based on the E-CIL framework, allowing students to engage with course content, with the instructor, and with co-learners in meaningful ways.

Video introduction to course content for the week

As the instructor, provide a video introduction to the week's content. In this video, include an introduction to key vocabulary and concepts, an explanation and recap of the assignments that are due that week, and a "looking ahead" snippet to prepare students for what is to come for the following week. Although any video-creation tool can be used for this, Padlet would be a particularly beneficial tool and would also allow an opportunity for students to post questions related to the content. To ensure students have watched the video, instructors could require that students post a question and/or comment about the video. Instructors could include the following questions to which students are expected to respond: Which vocabulary words or key concepts seem the most difficult to understand and why? Which key vocabulary and concepts are the easiest for you to understand and why? (Note: Flipgrid would not be appropriate for this due to its 90–second limit.)

Instructor presentation of the week
Provide students with a copy of a Nearpod presentation for the week which includes interactive prompts, directives, and/or activities. If desired, include an audio or video clip with the presentation. Using Nearpod, require that students respond to the interactive slides by a particular day of the week. One suggestion is to design the presentation in a manner that includes interactive slides every three or four slides to increase student engagement.

Viewing of a content-related video by students
Provide students with a link to a course-related video (such as one found online or through instructor resource materials). Require students to view the video and then provide a reflection to the video's content. Provide students with a reflection template for completing this task each week. This reflection template could be designed with specific questions to which students reflect and respond, or it could be a general one which could be used for reflecting on any video. This activity could also be completed using Padlet. For example, in this case, the instructor would create a board which contains a link to the course-related video. Students would then provide their reflections directly on the Padlet board by writing on a virtual "sticky note."

Reading-response activity for the week
Require students to respond to a weekly reading-response activity. Determined by the instructor, this weekly reading activity could be in the form of an article from a professional journal, a textbook reading assignment, or a reading requirement from another source. Provide students with a reflection template for completing based on each week's reading

The E-CIL framework

assignment. This could be a specific template for the reading response activity of the week, or it could be one that is more general and could be used for any reading response activity, such as the template shown in Figure 4 below.

Main Points of Article	Your Reflection Based on the Article's Content
	Future Application of the Article's Content
	Questions I Have After Reading the Article

Figure 4: Article summary template.

Video collaborations by the students

Require students to submit a weekly video response through an application such as Flipgrid. Do this by first, as the instructor, posting a weekly higher-order essential question based on the week's course content. Students then create their own video response and are also required to respond to another student's video response (by creating a second video).

Assign each student a partner to whom they will respond (by creating a second video). Partners should vary from week to week and should be determined by the instructor. If desired, provide students with talking prompts to use for their responses such as the ones shown in Figure 5 below. Students are required to support their videos with course-related content and evidence from their weekly readings, the instructor's videos, and/or the weekly PowerPoint presentations. Flipgrid videos have a limit of 90 seconds, so this video assignment is simple and not very time-consuming. The simplicity of this task using Flipgrid maintains the focus on the learning rather than the technology.

My partner this week is _____. I agree with _____ because _____.

My partner this week is _____. I disagree with _____ because _____.

Figure 5: Talking prompts for partner reflections through video collaboration.

Completion of online exit ticket

Require students to submit a weekly post using an application such as Padlet as a summary of the knowledge they gained as a result of the week's activities—also referred to as an exit ticket. Exit tickets are a popular formative assessment tool in that they require very little preparation by instructors, yet they are effective in assessing students' knowledge immediately following a lesson or course session. This assignment is intended to serve as a weekly progress check of students' understanding of the week's concepts. Either provide students with 1–3 questions which assess their understanding of a particular concept of the week, or require students to provide a general statement of what they learned that week. Students are expected to include visuals, related links, and/or text in their posts.

The E-CIL framework

Suggested outline for implementation of the E-CIL Framework on a weekly basis

Table 1 represents the E-CIL framework and is a suggested outline for instructors as they plan weekly instruction in online courses. The author, therefore, highlights how student engagement in e-learning environments can include three dimensions: engagement with the content, with the instructor, and with co-learners through the use of suggested technology tools such as Nearpod, Flipgrid, and Padlet.

Day of the Week	Instructor's Tasks for the Week	Students' Tasks for the Week	Suggested Technology Tool	Alignment with E-CIL Framework, Engagement with…
Day 1	Post a video explanation of assignments due this week.	Ask any questions on the virtual board as they arise this week.	Padlet	Content, Instructor, & Co-Learners
	Post a video intro to this week's course content (introductory explanation of key vocabulary and concepts).	Respond by answering the following questions: Which key vocabulary and concepts seem the most confusing and why? Which key vocabulary and concepts seem the easiest to understand and why?	Padlet	Content, Instructor, & Co-Learners
	Post an interactive presentation representing this week's content.	Respond to interactive slides on presentation by Day 3.	Nearpod	Content, Instructor, & Co-Learners

Chapter 7

Day of the Week	Instructor's Tasks for the Week	Students' Tasks for the Week	Suggested Technology Tool	Alignment with E-CIL Framework, Engagement with...
Day 2	Provide students with a link to a course-related video.	Provide reflections based on course-related video (can be general or specific and will be determined by instructor).	Padlet or Flipgrid	Content, Instructor, & Co-Learners
Day 3	Assign an article reading and/or textbook or other reading.	Complete the article summary template or other reading response activity designed by the instructor.	Padlet	Content & Instructor
Day 4	Post a higher-order question to which students must respond via video.	Respond to higher-order question using a video explanation.	Flipgrid	Content, Instructor, & Co-Learners
Day 5	Design 2 or 3 end-of-the week questions as an exit ticket to assess students' mastery of this week's concepts.	Respond to exit ticket questions (using text, drawings, emojis, etc.).	Padlet	Content, Instructor, & Co-Learners

Table 1: Dimensions of Engagement Through Innovative Technology Practices.

Conclusion

In this chapter, I presented the history of online learning and shed light on the likelihood of online learning being here to stay. I then highlighted the findings of a recent study which explored university students' perceptions, experiences, and attitudes towards online learning. Then, prompted by the findings of the study and particularly by students' perceptions of isolation in online study, I presented an innovative instructional tool—the E-CIL Framework. This framework was designed to promote student engagement with content, the instructor, and co-learners in online learning spaces. I then provided readers with detailed guidelines for implementing the E-CIL Framework using three recommended computer-based applications—Nearpod, Flipgrid, and Padlet—based on a week-by-week plan for teaching key concepts and topics in a university course.

We, in higher education, must embrace the reality of online learning becoming a primary means of program completion for university students. To do this successfully, however, we face the lofty goal of creating learning spaces which parallel those of face-to-face environments. In addition, most noteworthy from the present study, students' experiences contribute to their positive outlook with respect to online learning, while their lack of experiences correlated with negative outlooks toward online learning. This suggests that students who are exposed to more engaging and varied e-learning tools and activities will have more positive attitudes towards online learning. Therefore, the author proposes that instructors view these findings as motivation for creating new learning experiences for students in an effort to transform their perspectives while increasing student learning. This demands that instructors transform teaching and learning in online spaces through the utilization of a more constructivist approach such as the E-CIL Framework.

Based on past and current trends, online learning environments will presumably continue to evolve for decades to come. Fast-forward several decades and imagine a hypothetical timeline representing the future of online learning. How will pedagogical strategies, technology tools, and students' perceptions, experiences, and learning be enhanced by e-learning instructors in higher education settings? What role will we, in higher education, play in "placing" impactful strategies and techniques on this timeline? We, as university instructors, are key players in the creation of future timelines and are charged with the task of "filling in" the events. In response to this call, the author challenges instructors to put aside any reservations related to implementing innovative techniques in online courses and accept the challenge—the challenge of providing new experiences for current and future university students in online courses. As shown in the literature and the current study, positive correlations exist between students' experiences with online learning and their perceptions of online courses. In order for these new experiences to occur for *students*, however, *instructors* must also embrace the notion of new experiences. Therefore, in thinking back to the symbiotic relationship mentioned earlier in the chapter, this call for new experiences with respect to online learning requires action from *all* members of learning communities, including instructors *and* students. This is the trend that needs to continue in higher education—increased experiences for *all* stakeholders of online learning communities, with the end result being a positive outcome!

About the Author

Malinda Hoskins Lloyd, Ph.D., is Associate Professor at Tennessee Technological University in the Department of Curriculum & Instruction in Cookeville, Tennessee, USA. She can be contacted at the following e-mail: MLloyd@tntech.edu.

Bibliography

Booker, K. (2008). The role of instructors and peers in establishing classroom community. *Journal of Instructional Psychology*, 35(1), 12–16.

Center for Innovation in Research and Teaching (CIRT) (no date). *Technology teaching tools*. Online Resource: https://cirt.gcu.edu/ [Accessed on 20 March 2018].

Choi, Y., & Anderson, W. (2016). Self-directed learning with feedback. *Journal of College Science Teaching*, 46(1), 32–38.

Czerkawski, B. C., & Lyman, E. W. (2016). An instructional design framework for fostering student engagement in online learning environments. *Association for Educational Communications & Technology*, 60, 532–539.

Dixon, M. (2010). Creating effective student engagement in online courses: What do students find engaging? *Journal of the Scholarship of Teaching and Learning*, 10(2), 1–13.

Hudesman, J., Crosby, S., & Clay, D. (2013). Using formative assessment and metacognition to improve student achievement. *Journal of Developmental Education*, 37(1), 2–13.

Joksimović, S., Kovanović, V., Skrypnyk, O., Gašević, D., Dawson, S., & Siemens, G. (2015). The history and state of online learning. In Gašević, D., & Dawson, S. (Eds.), *Preparing for the digital university: A review of the history and current state of distance, blended, and online learning*. Online Resource: http://linkresearchlab.org/PreparingDigitalUniversity.pdf [Accessed on 28 March 2018]

Kim, K., Sharma, P., & Furlong, K. (2013). Effects of active learning on enhancing student critical thinking in an undergraduate general science course. *Innovative Higher Education*, 38, 223–235.

Krahenbuhl, K. (2015). Nearpod: A technology tool to engage students in inquiry. *ASCD Express*, 10(9), 45–61.

Lloyd, M., Kolodziej, N., & Brashears, K. (2016). Classroom discourse: An essential component in building a classroom community. *School Community Journal*, 26(2), 291–304.

Park, E., & Choi, B. (2014). Transformation of classroom spaces: Traditional versus active learning classroom in colleges. *Higher Education*, 68(2), 749–771.

Patrick, L., Howell, L., & Wischusen, W. (2016). Perceptions of active learning between faculty and undergraduates: Differing views among departments. *Journal of STEM Education*, 17(3), 55–63.

Sanchez, R. (2008). Integrating community in culturally conscientious classrooms. *Education Digest*, 63(7), 53–57.

The People History (2018). Online Resource: http://www.thepeoplehistory.com/1981.html [Accessed on 26 March 2018].

Young, A., & Norgard, C. (2006). Assessing the quality of online courses from the students' perspective. *Internet and Higher Education*, 9(1), 107–115.

Chapter 8
Experiential learning in premedical education: enhancing students' experience through e-learning

Reya Saliba & Rachid Bendriss

Introduction

With our chapter, we contribute to the book *E-learning 1.0, 2.0, and 3.0 in Higher Education* as we show how we have used e-learning tools to enhance students' experience. We did so by implementing an Experiential Learning project in an English for Academic Purposes (EAP) course. We also used e-learning tools to improve students' English language skills, develop their information literacy skills, introduce them to the medical profession early in their education, and facilitate communication and sharing of knowledge. With the recent curricular and instructional reforms of medical programmes recommended by the Association of American Medical Colleges (aamc.org), and the need to move from traditional learning, based on rote memorization, to more hands-on and interactive activities, medical schools need to revamp their curricula to include more community service that engages students in the real world to build their professional identity.

We define three educational theories: 1) experiential learning theory, 2) transformational learning theory, and 3) service learning theory as the basis for this experiential learning project. Experiential Learning has been incorporated in Medical Education for many years to develop students' health literacy skills by observing medical conditions in a real-life setting and expand their knowledge by inquiring about health issues. In our chapter, we aim to outline the planning, development and implementation of the Experiential Learning project in the spring of 2018 for 22 students enrolled in a foundation year that prepares them to join the six-year medical curriculum at a branch campus of an American medical college in Qatar.

Reading this chapter, you will gain the following insights:
- you will learn how to design an Experiential Learning project as an integral component of a university blended course;
- you will understand the role of e-learning in facilitating knowledge gain and effective communication between instructors and students;
- you will gain insight into the opportunities and challenges that faculty and students encounter while engaging in an e-learning environment.

This chapter is divided into four sections. In section one, we introduce the different educational theories behind the study. Section two describes the Experiential Learning project, its deliverables, and the e-learning method. In section three, we provide the outcomes of the project, and students and instructors' perspectives on the opportunities and challenges met during the implementation of the project. Finally, section four is concerned with future direction and enhancement of the project.

Research Underpinnings

Before laying out the methodological approach adopted for this study, ontological and epistemological underpinnings need to be established. According to Cohen *et al.* (2011:33), ontology or *"the nature of reality or of a phenomenon,"* is a result of an individual's *"politics and interests [that] shape multiple beliefs and values, as these beliefs and values are socially constructed, privileging some views of reality and underrepresenting others"*. Simply put, ontology is a way of viewing the philosophy of research and reflects the lens through which researchers view reality, either adopting a subjectivist or an objectivist position. Grix (2010:61) defines objectivism as *"an ontological position that asserts that social phenomena and their meanings have an existence that is independent of social actors"*. However, constructivism, eliciting an interpretivist epistemology, *"asserts that social phenomena and their meanings are continually being accomplished by social actors"*. If ontology is about what researchers may know or how they view social reality, *"epistemology is about how we come to know what we know"* (Grix, 2010:63). This study will adopt a constructivist ontological approach with an interpretivist epistemology, which will allow the researchers to examine the subjective meanings of student interactions in the social phenomenon of e-learning and their motivating actions. Since Experiential Learning is inspired by an action and reflection pedagogical model (Jacoby, 2003), the interpretivist research philosophy can provide an in-depth understanding of the context of participants in their learning milieu and contribute to our knowledge of human experience in a natural setting.

Section 1: The background

Experiential learning

The American psychologist Carl Rogers (1902–1987) developed the Experiential Learning theory (ELT) in which he describes a learning environment that focuses on students' motivation to initiate a learning project relevant to their personal interest as it is *"more lasting and pervasive"* (Ng & Hagen, 2015:184; Combs, 1982). Rogers' ELT defines the role of the teacher as a facilitator who:

- sets a positive climate for learning;
- clarifies the purposes of the learner;
- organizes and makes available learning resources;
- balances intellectual and emotional components of learning;
- shares feelings and thoughts with learners without dominating.

Later, drawing on the work of John Dewey, Kurt Lewin, and Jean Piaget, David Kolb (1984:41) expanded on the ELT theory by indicating that it is *"the process whereby knowledge is created through the transformation of experience. Knowledge results from the combination of grasping and transforming experience"*. And for this purpose, learners should exhibit four types of abilities:

- concrete experience;
- reflective observation;
- abstract conceptualisation;
- active experimentation.

The learner can start the learning process at any point as long as it is carried continuously so that *"knowledge is constructed through the creative tension among the four modes [...or] aspects of learning: experiencing, reflecting, thinking and acting"* (Lee et al., 2016:222).

Transformational learning

In the early 90s, Mezirow (1991) developed the transformational learning theory that he describes as being *"constructivist, an orientation which holds that the way learners interpret and reinterpret their sense experience is central to making meaning and hence learning"*. The Encyclopaedia of the Sciences of Learning defines transformational learning as *"the process of deep, constructive, and meaningful learning that goes beyond simple knowledge acquisition and supports critical ways in which learners consciously make meaning of their lives"*. It results in fundamental change in our perception of the world as we shift from accepting the information we receive to questioning, reflecting on and assessing new information. It involves our thoughts, feelings, beliefs, and behaviours (Simsek, 2012). Students move from high-school supervised learning to adult self-directed learning once they enter higher education. This transition implies that educators adjust their teaching approach to cater to students' needs. It also entails that students *"manage their behaviors and anxieties to facilitate learning, actively avoiding behaviors and cognitions detrimental to academic success"* (Abar & Loken, 2010:25). However, there is no borderline that would show a clear cut between childhood education and adult education, especially that this might happen to different students at any stage in their education, depending on their individual socio-economic condition. Therefore, it is important to integrate service learning in medical education to develop students' awareness of their community, help them mature, create a sense of responsibility and empathy, and prepare them to become lifelong learners.

Service learning

Considered as an experiential education approach, Jacoby (2003) defines service learning as a pedagogy that is *"grounded in experience as a basis for learning and on the centrality and intentionality of reflection designed to enable learning to occur"*. It emerges from the effort of learning theorists such as *"John Dewey, Jean Piaget, Kurt Lewin, Donald Schön, and David Kolb, who believe that we learn through combinations of action and reflection"* (Jacoby, 2003:4). Through service learning, students get the chance to experience real-life examples. While learning starts in the classroom, students observe, interact and reflect on their experience in an original context that provides them with authentic knowledge. They are actively involved in their learning process, and their knowledge emerges from their interaction with their community and environment. Ehrlich (in Jacoby, 1996:45) describes service learning as *"various pedagogies that link community service and academic study so that each strengthens the other"*. Gaster (2011:19) describes the main goal of service learning as *"to facilitate cognitive, affective, social, and developmental learning within the students"*. She also believes that service learning can be used to build a positive relationship between the community and the educational institution. In fact, it could be argued that service learning strengthens academic learning and makes it even more effective not only in the classroom but also for career prospects. However, unlike volunteering, service learning should be made integral to the academic curriculum, and its outcomes should be explicitly determined throughout the syllabus (Jay, 2008). Deliverables may range from essays, written reflections, and presentations to online discussions. There is a need to:

1. clearly communicate the learning outcomes;
2. set the expected deliverables;
3. *"capture"* the knowledge developed in service learning through assessments;
4. and evaluate the effectiveness of the service learning method.

One way of achieving these objectives is through the implementation and use of e-learning tools.

E-learning

Through e-learning, educational technology enhances the learning process and thus makes it accessible to students outside of the classroom environment. Clark and Mayer (2008:9–10) explain the *What, How* and *Why* of e-learning. *What "include[s] both content (that is, information) and instructional methods (that is, techniques) that help people learn the content"*; *How* is the type of resources, such as text or multimedia, used to deliver the content online; and *Why* is the intent of using e-learning such as helping individuals *"reach personal learning objectives or perform their jobs in ways that improve the bottom-line goals of the organization"*. e-Learning can be asynchronous, when students are in control of their learning and can have a flexible schedule where they can *"log on to an e-learning environment at any time and download documents or send messages to teachers or peers"* (Hrastinski, 2008:52). Synchronous e-learning, on the other hand, is usually led by the instructor in real-time and requires online presence to participate in videoconferencing, chats and group discussions. It helps the learner connect to the learning community and become socially interactive by participating in the virtual classroom (Clark & Mayer, 2008; Hrastinski, 2008).

Section 2: The practice

General introduction

As part of the premedical education curriculum, the EAP course director developed a semester-long project to promote experiential learning among premedical students enrolled in their foundation year at Weill Cornell Medicine-Qatar (WCM-Q). The project aimed to provide future medical students with the knowledge, skills, and abilities to gain an understanding and appreciation of healthcare professions in Qatar.

The purpose of this project was to:
- improve English writing and reading skills;
- reinforce the classroom learning of scientific courses through application in a real-life setting;
- expand knowledge of medical terminology by learning medical terms through reading, discussion and interacting with professionals;
- expand students' knowledge by observing, inquiring, and reflecting about health issues and conditions;
- develop information literacy skills through searching, evaluating, and using academic and scholarly resources to gather information;

- improve students' communication skills by presenting and engaging in discussions to share knowledge;
- develop an understanding of professional identity formation through reading about and observing doctor-patient relationships;
- foster empathy and compassion towards patients and therefore their community.

Description of the project

Based on the four types of abilities described by Kolb (1984), students were assigned to a non-profit healthcare organization specializing in rehabilitation to help provide mental and physical care for patients who suffered from strokes, traumatic brain or spinal cord injuries in Qatar. Over 12 weeks, working in groups of three, students developed a *"concrete experience"* by visiting the facility regularly, learning about patients' conditions by using *"active experimentations"* through researching relevant scientific sources that would inform their *"reflective observations"*, and empower their knowledge and *"abstract conceptualizations"* (Kolb, 1984). Students also interacted with caretakers and patients and observed physician-patient interactions and outcomes. As a capstone, students developed a research project, wrote four reflective journal entries, and delivered a formal presentation to share their Experiential Learning experiences. In collaboration with the Learning and Student Outreach (LSO) Librarian, the EAP course director provided ongoing support to the students throughout the semester by:

- supervising and monitoring the students' progress throughout the project;
- evaluating the students' communication, teamwork, and professionalism skills;
- recruiting health professionals to model their role and share their knowledge and experience in the community with the students through weekly career seminars;
- leading small group discussions for the purpose of enhancing this project for next year.

Deliverables

Deliverables were designed to help students examine their experience by reflecting, questioning, and assessing new information as an essential part of transformational learning and future life-long learners' skills.

Short-term deliverables

Prior to every visit, a book chapter or a scholarly article was shared with the students via the Learning Management System (LMS) – an online platform used to communicate and share the course content with students. Inspired by the flipped classroom modality (Bendriss, Saliba & Birch, 2015), students were required to read the material prior to their Experiential Learning visit. On the day of the visit, students observed and reflected on the specific reading material by engaging in an online group discussion and completing a reflective journal entry.

Long-term deliverables

By the end of this project, students were expected to:
1. Submit a research paper that:
   - included a literature review;
   - documented the research process they undertook to understand the background, conditions, and needs of the community they served;
   - chronicled their experience and observations;
   - included a reflection section in which students demonstrated their critical thinking abilities and skills.
2. Deliver a class presentation that:
   - described their Experiential Learning experience;
   - shared the knowledge they gained by participating in community work;
   - demonstrated their communication and presentation skills.

Description of the use of e-learning method

The college's LMS was used as an e-learning platform through which the EAP course director and the LSO librarian provided the following content and resources:

- a description of the project and the expected outcomes;

- an online course reserve which provided students with reading materials (print and electronic books, scholarly articles, web resources, and other online audio-visual materials available through the library). Four resources were shared with the students, and each one focused on a specific topic: medical students' attitudes toward elderly patients, professional communication and team collaboration in healthcare centers, medical students' professional identity formation, and compassion as an essential component of medical care;

- online discussion forums and online reflective journal entries;

- description of the use and purpose of a literature review and examples for students to use when putting together their first literature review;

- schedules of every visit for each group, deliverables and due dates;

- a description of the final research paper and class presentation.

Students visited the Experiential Learning facility every two weeks while working on the requirements of the project. Regular, weekly, face-to-face class time was also used to facilitate the project. Information literacy outcomes that were covered through online modules and class sessions consisted of:

- writing a literature review;

- citing sources in APA style;

- critically evaluating sources of information;

- producing reflective journal entries.

The use of LMS was essential in delivering the content of the project and centralizing the students' learning experience. It helped in creating one point of access to all information students needed to be aware of or to acquire prior to and following each visit. It was also used by instructors to communicate deliverables and due dates and deliver learning resources that students needed at a certain point during their project. The LMS was also a great tool to follow up on students' progress, check on deliverables and facilitate their engagement in discussions.

Section 3: The outcome

Premedical students need to start building their practical skills at an early stage in their medical education. By getting the opportunity to be exposed to the community through Experiential Learning, they gain new knowledge and develop a sense of responsibility and cooperation. They also establish an understanding of the expectations and behaviours required for a successful medical career. Students gain a real-life insight into the everyday challenges of being a healthcare practitioner and develop a humanistic approach towards establishing a compassionate and caring relationship with their community. It helps them build a patient-centred approach to medicine and see the different dimensions of medicine and health care practice. The outcomes are evaluated from the students' perspectives collected through a questionnaire, their submitted work – literature reviews, reflective journal entries and online discussions – as well as the instructors' perspectives.

Students' perspective

Data gathered through a questionnaire
In order to collect students' feedback on their experience, comments and suggestions to enhance this project, a questionnaire consisting of ten closed and open-ended questions was circulated to 22 students who participated in the Experiential Learning activity. Twenty-one responses were returned. Results from the survey analysis can be divided into benefits, challenges and improvements to the Experiential Learning project. First, the Experiential Learning project helped premedical students gain

insight into the medical field by experiencing real-life settings. Second, it improved their English writing and reading skills, as well as their information literacy skills through finding, evaluating, paraphrasing and citing sources of information.

In addition, the Experiential Learning project helped them understand the challenges of the medical career and develop a humanistic approach to medicine and patient care. Students also believed that the Experiential Learning project improved their communication by observing communication among healthcare providers and through communicating with doctors, nurses and patients. Students were able to expand their *"medical jargon by learning medical terms through reading, discussion, and interacting with professionals"*, as expressed in one of the students' feedback.

In one of the questions, students were asked whether the reading material and online discussions that were due prior to every Experiential Learning visit introduced them to topics and issues relevant to the Experiential Learning project. Participants had mixed feelings about the reading requirement. Although 50% agreed with this statement, all of them referred to the themes of the readings in their research papers and final presentations. They also reflected on the importance of the topics discussed in the reading material, such as professional identity, clear communication, and compassion and quoted the texts in their talks. This ambivalence could perhaps be due to students' lack of desire to read in general.

The last two questions collected open-ended answers. For question 9, students were asked to describe the most challenging component of the Experiential Learning project. Students' answers can be divided into three recurring themes:

1. Communication with healthcare staff including doctors: students found communication with healthcare providers challenging. Most of the responses described the staff and doctors at the facility to be misinformed about the visit and not prepared to receive the students, which initially increased students' anxiety about the experience. However, apparently, this issue helped students understand the essential role communication plays among team members and its importance in delivering positive outcomes. One student commented:

> "The most challenging thing we faced in our Experiential Learning experience is the miscommunication that happened throughout the whole 4 visits. The doctors and consultants there didn't know what to deliver exactly for us. However, it became then again one of the best lessons we all learned".

2. Compassion towards patients: students found it emotionally overwhelming to interact with patients in their first visit. Based on an article on the topic of compassion that was shared with them, students were able to reflect on compassion and even ask the doctors for more insight into the role of compassion in interacting with patients. One student particularly mentioned:

   > "[The most challenging component was] the ability to express our compassion towards patients. In some cases, the doctors asked us to talk with the patients. I found these situations -at first- to be very awkward. I had many things to tell, but I could not simply put it in a well-mannered way. I was anxious of showing pity or the exact opposite, to show attitude. However, it turned out that I was exaggerating most of what happened. If I really did not think about it and just let my heart reach out to theirs, I believe that awkwardness would have been inexistent".

3. Time management: the Experiential Learning visits required students to start their day earlier than usual and then come back by noon to the college to attend their biology lab and chemistry class, which made their day long and exhausting. Here are some students' comments regarding time management:

   > "An organized hour by hour schedule".
   > "More precise and organized schedule".
   > "Time [management]".

Students admitted that the Experiential Learning experience helped them develop time management skills. They were able to plan their visit a day ahead of time, make sure they had enough time to submit their online discussions and reflective journal entries while also completing assignments due for other courses. The concept of time management was also recurrent in students' responses to the online discussions and reflective journal entries.

The last question required students to suggest one possible change to improve the programme. Responses can be divided into six main suggestions. Having the doctors prepared for the Experiential Learning visit was the most recurrent suggestion, followed by providing a more organized schedule for the visit. While many students suggested having the chance to follow up on specific patients and measure their progress, a few students suggested allowing them to change units frequently so they *"try all fields equally"*. Some suggestions included extending the Experiential Learning project period to expand students' experience. Finally, two comments found that *"the programme was successful"* and *"suitable for future [...] students"*.

Data gathered through students' literature reviews
An online module covered the purpose, aims, and techniques of preparing a literature review (see Appendix A for a list of the online modules that were created for the Experiential Learning project). The LSO librarian designed two face-to-face class sessions for students to practice creating a literature review. Students submitted a literature review that covered the topic of their final project. Students' progress was very clear when comparing the first and the final drafts of their literature reviews. In their final papers, the majority of the students were able to summarize, paraphrase, and cite sources correctly using the APA format and citation style. The quality of their resources was much more scholarly and relevant to their topics.

Data gathered through students' reflective journal entries and online discussions
Students' reflective journal entries and online discussions were an important factor in evaluating the effectiveness and value of the Experiential Learning project. Prior to the start of the project, students were introduced to the process of writing a reflective journal entry and were provided, through LMS, with a list of websites, additional reading materials, and more examples on writing reflective journal entries. A module on "Writing a Reflective Journal Entry" was created and made available to students through LMS (see Appendix A). The results of their biweekly online engagement were of a very good quality. Examples include improvement in their English language skills when describing their visits and

their reflection on their experiences, not to forget their in-text citations when referring to the reading material or one-on-one interviews they had with doctors or patients. These were indicators of students' progress throughout the academic year. Students improved their writing, reading and speaking skills, developed and used their information literacy skills, and expanded their knowledge by observing and inquiring about health issues and conditions while interacting with patients and developing a sense of empathy.

The results of students' questionnaire, literature reviews, reflective journals and online discussions, provide concrete evidence of the types of abilities that learners need to demonstrate through their learning. As described in the theory section on Experiential Learning, students internalize the four aspects of learning as described by Lee *et al.* (2016): *"concrete experience"* and *"reflective observation"* in a real-life setting, *"abstract conceptualizations"* of ideas based on their weekly reading materials, and *"active experimentations"* in the healthcare facility, among practitioners and patients.

Instructors' perspective

As a pilot project for first-year students, the Experiential Learning component of the course achieved its set goals and objectives despite the challenges encountered throughout the experience. First, students often reported the lack of communication between the college and the hospital. While this is true, the college representatives wielded no control over the operations of the hospital where the participants completed their Experiential Learning. This was actually a teachable moment for students to realize that poor organization and lack of effectiveness are often considered prevalent challenges in healthcare systems. Students also pondered over ways to enhance communication and made suggestions on process improvement. This was an excellent reflection on the part of the students to go above and beyond the Experiential Learning expectations. Students came to realize that lack of communication in organizations such as healthcare institutions impacts not only the operations of the hospital but also its stakeholders, especially doctors, nurses, patients, and doctors in training (students).

Second, the initial planning stage was somewhat challenging. For instance, the course director needed to identify the objectives for

Experiential Learning and ascertain their alignment with the EAP course outcomes, such as improving reading, writing, and critical thinking. Another objective was to develop students' communication skills through observing communication patterns in the healthcare environment and enhance their communication and collaboration among their groups. Finally, the course director aimed to increase students' motivation in medical school through exploring medical topics, especially from a medical humanities perspective.

In order to provide students with reading materials to prepare them for their experience, the LSO librarian, in collaboration with the course director, identified the topics and located scholarly resources that would cover each of the topics: medical students' attitudes toward elderly patients, professional communication and team collaboration in healthcare centres, medical students' professional identity formation, and compassion as an essential component of medical care. As this project involved first year non-native English speaking students in a medical programme, careful attention was paid to the level of language difficulty used in scholarly articles, the medical jargon, and the breadth of knowledge conveyed in the literature they had to read. To be realistic, we had to keep in mind the time required to complete the deliverables of the Experiential Learning project as well as the learning requirements and assignments of the other courses.

The implementation of this project was relatively less challenging than the design phase. The use of LMS as an e-learning platform facilitated instructors-students' communication outside of the classroom. Some of the e-learning features that optimized this communication included *Announcements* that were made prior to each visit, reading materials that were easily accessible and downloadable under *Files*, and journal entries that were created and uploaded by the students under *Assignments*. More collaborative features such as *Discussions* were also used by the students to engage in group work and share their thoughts and updates on the project. A *Calendar* feature clearly indicated assignments and their deadlines, and *Modules* were created for each topic and served as a repository of all teaching and learning materials to make the Experiential Learning experience complete and successful.

Chapter 8

Section 4: Moving forward

The Experiential Learning project allowed the researchers to adopt and experiment an innovative teaching and learning approach to enhance premedical students' skills. The Experiential Learning project was particularly successful in drawing the following learning outcomes:

- developing students' English language and communication skills by reading relevant resources covering the aims and objectives of the Experiential Learning project, and engaging in online and face-to-face discussions;

- putting into practice their information literacy skills by searching, evaluating, citing sources, and writing a literature review;

- gaining better understanding and broadening their perspectives of the challenges and expectations of a medical career by observing, reflecting, and experiencing medicine in a real-life setting;

- fostering their critical thinking by reflecting on their readings, observations, and interactions within their future community of practice.

It is also worth noting that the implementation of this project presented some challenges that researchers need to address in the future to enhance students' experience. First, the learning outcomes of the Experiential Learning project need to be shared with individual doctors who are supervising the students. This can be pre-arranged by having the course director and librarian meet with the doctors, rather than the upper administration of the healthcare facility, to communicate the outcomes of the Experiential Learning project and students' visit. Second, the schedule should take into consideration the workload the students have. This can be avoided by planning the visits on days when the students do not have labs or lectures to attend in the afternoon. Finally, the Experiential Learning project should bring together other faculty in the department to help the students see the transferability of the skills and knowledge they learn in their science class to the "workplace" and vice versa. An example of that is the physics lesson that students recalled while visiting the physical rehab area in the healthcare facility.

Conclusion

Through this chapter, the authors shared their experience in planning, developing, and implementing the Experiential Learning project. They described the integration of information literacy and critical thinking skills in a blended EAP course, using face-to-face class sessions and LMS as e-learning platform. The benefits, challenges, and opportunities for implementing an Experiential Learning project were presented and discussed. Feedback from students and instructors was used for evaluating the effectiveness of such project in delivering the set learning outcomes. Therefore, based on their experience, the authors would like to share some useful tips with instructors who are considering using Experiential Learning for a successful implementation. The main findings of this chapter could be summarised as follows:

1. when using e-learning, instructors need to provide a detailed description of the objectives, aims, outcomes, and deliverables of every activity the students are engaging in;

2. when creating online modules to cover a specific skill or activity, instructors need to use a variety of resources that would complement students' learning style: reading materials, blogs, websites, videos;

3. instructors need to engage students in online discussions by using prompts to initiate the discussion;

4. students' feedback is essential in evaluating the effectiveness of such projects and modifying the process, the timeline, and the activities for future students, and therefore it is important to listen to their feedback and suggestions;

5. collaboration among faculty and librarians is crucial in supporting students' success. Aligning the outcomes of the information literacy skills and sessions with the outcomes of the EAP class and the Experiential Learning project provides a complete experience for premedical students.

Chapter 8

About the Authors

Reya Saliba is the Learning and Student Outreach Librarian at Weill Cornell Medicine-Qatar. She can be contacted at this e-mail: res2024@qatar-med.cornell.edu.

Rachid Bendriss is an Associate Professor of English as a Second Language and Assistant Dean for Student Recruitment, Outreach, and Foundation Programs at Weill Cornell Medicine-Qatar. He can be contacted at this e-mail: rab2029@qatar-med.cornell.edu.

Bibliography

Abar, B., & Loken, E. (2010). Self-regulated learning and self-directed study in a pre-college sample. *Learning & Individual Differences*, 20(1), 25–29.

Bendriss, R., Saliba, R., & Birch, S. (2015). Faculty and librarians' partnership: Designing a new framework to develop information fluent future doctors. *Journal of Academic Librarianship*, 41(6), 821–838.

Clark, R. C., & Mayer, R. E. (2008). *e-Learning and the science of instruction*. San Francisco, CA: Pfeiffer.

Cohen, L., Manion, L., & Morrison, K. (2011). *Research methods in education*. London, UK: Taylor & Francis

Combs, A. W. (1982). Affective education or none at all. *Educational Leadership*, 39(7), 494–497.

Fu, M., & Jung, J. (2015). Top Medical Schools React to Harvard's Curriculum Change. *The Harvard Crimson*.

Gaster, M. A. (2011). Service learning: where is the emphasis? *Teaching & Learning in Nursing*, 6(1), 19–21.

Grix, J. (2010). *The Foundations of Research*. Basingstoke: Palgrave Macmillan.

Hrastinski, S. (2008). Asynchronous and Synchronous E-Learning. *Educause Quarterly*, 31(4), pp. 51–55.

Jacoby, B. (1996). *Service-learning in higher education: Concepts and practices*. San Francisco: Jossey-Bass.

Jacoby, B. (2003). *Building partnerships for service-learning*. San Francisco, CA: Jossey-Bass.

Jay, G. (2008). Service Learning, Multiculturalism, and the Pedagogies of Difference. *Pedagogy*, 8(2), 255–281.

Kolb, D. A. (1984). *Experiential learning: Experience as the source of learning and development*. New Jersey: Prentice Hall.

Lee, S., Barker, T., & Kumar, V. S. (2016). Effectiveness of a learner-directed model for e-learning. *Educational Technology & Society*, 19(3), 221–233.

Mezirow, J. (1991). *Transformative Dimensions of Adult Learning*. San Francisco, CA: Jossey-Bass.

Ng, D. H. P., & Hagen, T. (2015). Achieving improved learning outcomes in Life Science undergraduate research projects. *Asian Journal of the Scholarship of Teaching and Learning*, 5(3), 180–195.

Simsek, A. (2012). Transformational learning. In *Encyclopedia of the Sciences of Learning* (pp. 3341–3344). Springer: Encyclopedia of the Sciences of Learning.

University of California, Davis. (n.d.). *History of experiential learning*. UCD.

Appendix A

A list of the online modules that were created for the Experiential Learning project:

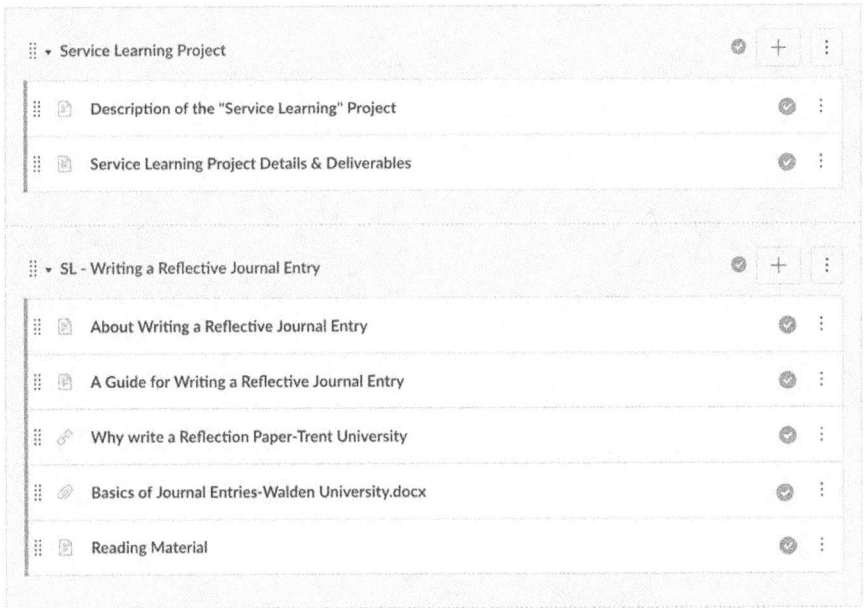

Chapter 8

IL Module 1 - Preparing a Literature Review - Part 1

- What is a Literature Review?
- Example of a Literature Review.docx
- Organizing a Literature Review
- Reviewing a Scholarly Article - In-class Activity
  Jan 7 | 0 pts
- Additional Reading
- Writing Your First Literature Review
- Literature Review - Topic 1 - Draft 1 Due
  Jan 21 | 5 pts
- Preparing a Literature Review-Graded Quiz
  Multiple Due Dates | 5 pts
- Literature Review - Topic 1 - Final Paper Due
  Multiple Due Dates | 10 pts

IL Module 2 - APA Citation Style

- IL Module 2 - Objectives
- American Psychological Association - APA Citation Style
- How to Cite in APA style
- Why you Need to Cite your Resources
- When to Cite your Resources
- What is the Difference between in-text citation and Bibliography?
- Purdue OWL - APA Format
- IL Module 2 - Outcomes
- IL Graded Quiz - APA Style
  7 pts

Experiential learning in premedical education

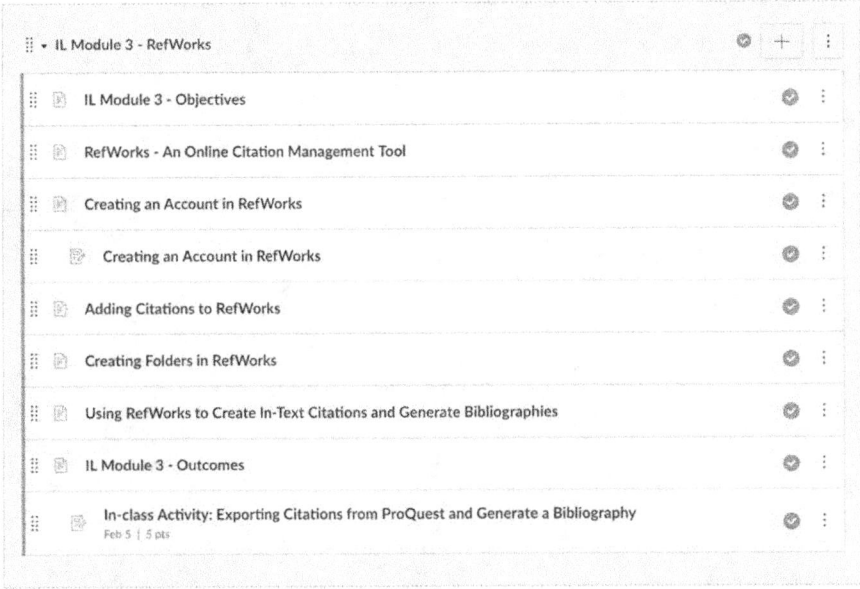

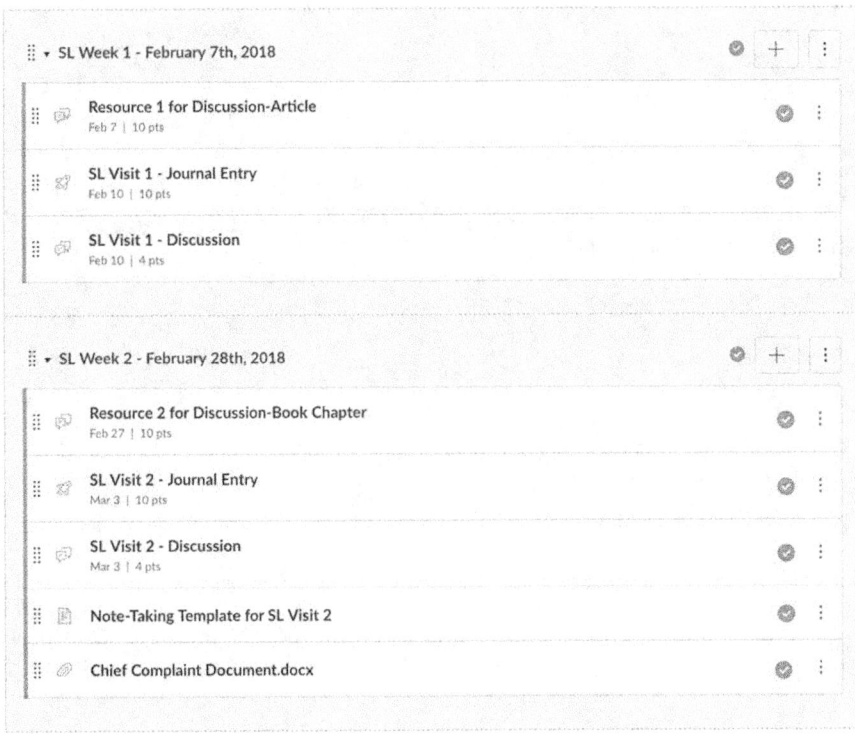

Chapter 8

IL Module 4 - Preparing a Literature Review - Part 2

- Literature Review - Part 2
- Five Steps to Conduct a Literature Review
- How to Organize your Literature Review by Themes
- How to End your Literature Review
- Literature Review - Topic 2 - Draft 1 Due
  Multiple Due Dates | 5 pts
- Example of a Literature Review.docx
- Literature Review - Topic 2 - Final Paper Due
  Mar 25 | 10 pts

SL Week 3 - March 14th, 2018

- Resource 3 for Discussion: Peer-reviewed Article
  Mar 13 | 10 pts
- SL Visit 3 - Journal Entry
  Mar 17 | 10 pts
- SL Visit 3 - Discussion
  Mar 17 | 10 pts
- Note-Taking Template for SL Visit 3

SL Week 4 - March 28th, 2018

- Resource 4 for Discussion: Peer-reviewed Article
  Mar 27 | 10 pts
- SL Visit 4 - Journal Entry
  Mar 31 | 10 pts
- SL Visit 4 - Discussion
  Mar 31

Experiential learning in premedical education

Chapter 9
Ten e-learning technologies to support problem-based collaborative work

Flemming Meier & Claus Nygaard

Introduction

With our chapter, we contribute to the book *E-learning 1.0, 2.0, and 3.0 in Higher Education* as we discuss how e-learning may be used to support problem-based collaborative work. We do so by presenting ten collaborative e-learning technologies, which can facilitate problem-based collaborative work. Engaging students through problem-based collaborative work is not a new practice. It has been described and discussed for more than twenty years. By introducing e-learning into that debate, we aim to show what technological tools and practices are available to support problem-oriented collaborative work. Doing so we may hopefully inspire faculty to use e-learning in such ways. We hope so, because we believe that students learn more from working on both problem-based and collaborative tasks.

Reading this chapter, you will:

1. get an understanding of problem-based collaborative work as a pedagogical practice;

2. familiarise yourself with social learning theory and its understanding of ways in which students learn;

3. see examples of how e-learning may support problem-based collaborative work when being based on social learning theory.

Our chapter is meant to raise an awareness of some of the positive consequences of linking together e-learning technology with learning theory. We say positive consequences because we believe that faculty members and those being responsible for implementing e-learning technologies can use our chapter to frame a wider debate on the choice and use of e-learning technology. Our chapter is introductory rather than exhaustive. We cover problem-based collaborative work, learning theory and e-learning technologies, but we do so to raise awareness of the ways in which they are possibly linked, not to mirror a text-book on any of these issues. We encourage you to read on with that in mind.

The chapter has three main sections. In section one, we present problem-based collaborative work as an educational practice. In section two, we present a theoretical approach to learning which opens for a closer understanding of why and how problem-based collaborative work is included in the curriculum. In section three, we show examples of how we believe e-learning may be used to support problem-based collaborative work.

Section 1: Problem-based collaborative work

Problem-based collaborative work is a learning-centred educational practice in which students are presented with a problem that they need to solve through collaborative practice. Typically, problem-based collaborative work centres on an empirical problem, which guides the work. Usually, the problem is open and complex, meaning that students are challenged to first identify, then analyse and finally solve the problem. In general, there are two ways in which the problem is presented to students: 1) *a desk case*: the problem is buried in a case (which may be written by the teacher, taken from a textbook, downloaded from a case clearing house, etc.). 2) *an empirical case*: the problem is buried in empirical practice (which may be presented to students in a movie, a documentary, or through the observation of practitioners, etc.). Whether it's a desk case or an empirical case, the idea is that students learn through identifying, analysing and solving problems related to practice. Problem-based work may be adequate when the aims are to have students train new research methods and create new knowledge. Problem-based education is different from theory-based education. Typically, problem-based education is inductive, whereas theory-based education is deductive. We believe that problem-based collaborate work helps students develop higher order thinking skills (analysis, synthesis, reflection) for several reasons. First, they need to identify the problem. Second, they need to analyse the problem. Third, they need to come up with a synthesis of their individual understandings of the problem and its components. Fourth, they need to reflect on their conclusions. Fifth, they need to redefine their own work if they come to new understandings during the collaborative process. Figure 1 lists some of the main characteristics of problem-based collaborative work and its possible effects on student learning, as we see it.

Characteristics of problem-based collaborative work	Possible effects on student learning
It requires that student collaborate on solving a problem which is related to practice.	Students learn higher-order thinking skills (analysis, synthesis, reflection) through the identification, analysis and solving of problems related to practice.
It simulates a realistic work environment because students are in charge of their own self-directed collaborative work. Students make their own decisions regarding the collaborative work. They plan and perform on their own behalf.	Students learn to take responsibility for their own learning process, and to prioritise their personal resources (time, knowledge, network, etc.) and make decisions in complex situations.
It puts focus on the unknown (the problem that has to be identified and solved).	Students learn to identify and address problems (this also counts for problems that they might not know existed).
It requires that students develop methodological awareness and research competencies.	Students learn to identify problems and choose the methods they believe is applicable when solving the problem.

Figure 1: Main characteristics of problem-based collaborative work and its possible effects on student learning.

After this brief introduction of problem-based collaborative work and its possible effects on student learning, we will look a little more at student learning from a theoretical perspective. We do so because we think that knowing more about learning is beneficial to our work with e-learning; and because the choice of problem-based collaborative work focusing on real life problems draws on a particular practice-based learning theory. Discussing learning theory helps us choose which type of e-learning to use.

Chapter 9

Section 2: Problem-based collaborative work and learning theory

Nygaard and Holtham (2008) argued for a move *from a discipline-based view to a learning-centred view of higher education*. They meant that the focus of teaching and learning should change from didactic teaching, which delivers pre-defined disciplinary content to students, to a practice where the learning of students – as a process in itself – was centred. In our view, problem-based collaborative work is in line with this move, because it centres the learning process of students. It requires of students that they self-direct and self-manage their learning process, when they have to identify, analyse and solve problems in collaboration. It is impossible to plan and manage problem-based collaborative work without focusing on the learning process itself. Problem-based collaborative work, as we see it, is rooted in social learning theories (Bandura, 1977; Vygotski, 1978; Lave & Wenger, 1991) (see also Nygaard, in this volume). Students construct meaning as they reflect their experiences in relation to the context in which they are embedded. Learning becomes a continuous search to make sense of new situations. This happens when students empirically investigate "real life" problems, and, through that process, construct new meaning and *learn*. Meaning is constructed and reconstructed throughout the process of working with the problem in focus. This is an iterative process where the problem is redefined while it is analysed, and the analysis itself is also redefined as new conclusions are reached. In this way, the learning process becomes an iterative, almost spiralling process.

The understanding of learning as a social process reaches beyond individual cognitive processes. And it opens up a different approach to analysing the learning process. Lave and Wenger (1991) saw learning as a social process embedded in everyday practices. They argued that learning is a process of participating, doing and construction rather than a process of attaining knowledge. And they broadened the understanding of learning by focusing on how learning is affected by the practice being institutionalised in communities. In their view, learning occurs when people with common interest in a subject collaborate and over time, share ideas, determine solutions, and innovate new solutions.

Learning then, should not be perceived as a discipline for schools and universities only, but as a life-long and ongoing personal process which is embedded in communities of practice and from which people learn. The person who learns is in a relationship with significant others. This relationship is thematised in terms of participation, engagement and inclusion, and the social world is thematised in terms of communities, practices and discourses.

Wenger (2008:23) defines a community of practice in this way: *"Communities of practice are groups of people who share a concern or a passion for something they do and learn how to do it better as they interact regularly."* In their theory, Lave and Wenger (1991) and Wenger (2008) put forward three required components which need to be present to talk of a community of practice: 1) a domain; 2) a community; 3) a practice. Whereas these may seem obvious, they are none the less important to know, because they enable us to discuss whether our learning environments (and online learning environments) quality as communities of practice.

First, the community of practice needs a domain. It can be a shared scientific domain, a shared interest, a shared passion, etc. At university, it could be the scientific domain of biology, law, finance, etc. In everyday life, it could be a domain of interest like fishing, cycling, cooking, etc. It could also be a shared passion for music, art, gardening, etc. The existence of the domain and the commitment of the members to the domain distinguishes the community of practice from an aggregate group of people. If you think of a group of students who go to university and follow 15 courses over a period of 5 years, each course may not represent a domain to them. In the area of practice-based learning, we cannot assume that all students are interested in and willing to engage in learning.

Second, the community of practice needs a community. The community is where people with domain interests interact with each other, where they share their domain interests. The community is constituted of relationships between people with domain interests, who interact and learn from each other. Being in the same lecture hall at the same time does not constitute a community. Being on the same e-learning platform at the same time, does not constitute a community either. For a community to exist there need to be people interacting and learning.

Third, the community of practice needs a practice. It is required that people with a domain interest, who meet in a community are also practitioners. By this is meant that they develop a shared practice, a certain repertoire of action so to speak, which helps them deal with tasks and challenges. And it is through their interactive development of this practice that they become holders of a shared repertoire of action, a shared language, a shared meaning, etc. Educating students in a room does not in itself develop a shared practice and thereby constitute a community of practice. Nor does the implementation of an e-learning platform. To have students develop as practitioners within a scientific domain requires domain specific training, ongoing conversations to identify domain interests, support and guidance in forming and maintaining the community, and methods to develop a shared practice. In higher education, such shared practices can be developed through a variety of collaborative methods, such as problem solving, information sharing, coordinating actions, group discussions and group reflections, field work and knowledge mapping.

Lave and Wenger (1991) saw learning as social participation and argued that identity is central to learning. When people become members of communities of practice they construct their own identity through these communities. Identity creation is a continuous process and it evolves as people go in and out of communities of practice over a life time. When we become members of communities of practice and identify with other members, and when we form our identity in the mirror of the domain interests, relationships and practices of the community, we are most likely to get a powerful incentive to learn. Students, when seeing themselves as members of a community of practice with significant others, will feel a desire to learn, when the people they identify themselves with are learning.

In our discussion of how e-learning can best support problem-based collaborative work, we continue to build on the social learning theories. We do so, because we subscribe to social learning theory (see also Nygaard, in this volume), and because we believe that the choice of e-learning technology is qualified by linking it to learning theory. In section three of our chapter, we turn to e-learning technologies and show examples of how we believe e-learning may be used to support problem-based collaborative work.

Section 3: Using e-learning to support problem-based collaborative work

Although e-learning is a matter of using technology to facilitate learning, choosing the right e-learning system is not a matter of technology. It is a matter of learning. Traditional teaching and learning methods (without "e") have their strengths in the personal meeting between students and teachers. For example, the lecture has its strength as the teacher inspires students with an interesting story, example, demonstration, etc. The workshop has its strength as students interact and support each other in their learning endeavour. The assignment has its strength as students are challenged and thus receives feedback about their knowledge and skills. When we think about e-learning, it should be more than just adding an "e" to the traditional teaching and learning methods. We should strive to do more than use technology to distribute recordings of past lectures to students. We should aim for more than transforming assignments into online tests. If we use technology in this way, we only mirror what is already known practice.

We argue that e-learning should be used to transform the ways in which students engage, work, interact and learn. And because of our understanding of learning as being a social and iterative process, we further argue that e-learning should be used in ways which supports the social and iterative processes of learning between students who engage, work, interact and learn. To exemplify our argument, in this chapter we have chosen to focus on problem-based collaborative work as a practice which is designed to have students engage, work, interact and learn.

In this section, we look at ten e-learning technologies, which we as authors are familiar with, and reflect on their use to support problem-based collaborative work. We do so by scoring the e-learning technologies with one to three stars, based on how well they fulfil the three needs of a community of practice: 1) the domain; 2) the community; 3) the practice. The ten e-learning technologies are (in no particular order):

1. Google Docs
2. Canva
3. Padlet

4. Kahoot
5. Realtimeboard
6. Appear.in
7. Facebook Groups
8. Canvas LMS
9. Asana
10. ProWiki

Our short presentation and review of these e-learning technologies are by no means meant to be exhaustive. It is made to inspire e-learning practitioners to reflect on their design and use of e-learning technologies, especially with reflections on the link between e-learning theory and learning theory, and, for the purpose of this chapter, to discuss also whether the e-learning technology supports problem-based collaborative work.

1. Google Docs

We have used Google Docs for collaborative writing of academic texts. It is one of the services linked to Gmail, and once you are logged into your Google-account, you can create a document and invite your contacts to write the document with you. All contacts can work on the document at the same time. They can write, edit, format, etc. at the same time. They can even collaborate on writing the same sentence simultaneously, and words will be added to the sentence in the colour code of each of the authors. So, it is possible to see who contributes to the document.

Ten e-learning technologies to support problem-based collaborative work

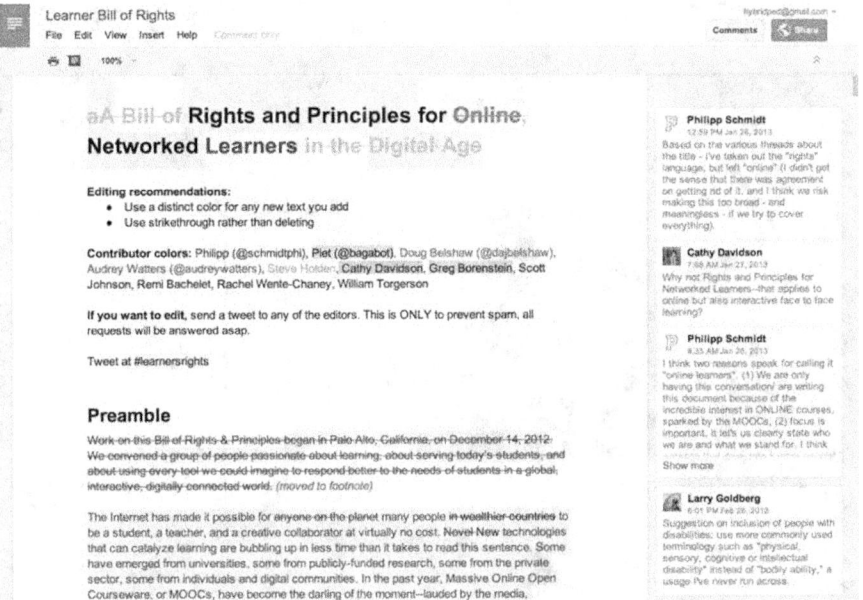

Figure 2: (Frost & Stommel, 2013).

2. Canva

We have used Canva for collaborative design of reports, brochures, e-books, poster presentations, infographics, etc. It is an online design tool, with a workgroup function, which allows more people to work on the same design. Canva has a large number of design templates allowing users with no design-experience to make what looks like a professional design.

Chapter 9

Figure 3: The desktop of Canva (Horne, 2016).

3. Padlet

We have used Padlet to allow students to share digital content and participate in brainstorm sessions. It is an online collaboration tool, where students can share resources, write and discuss.

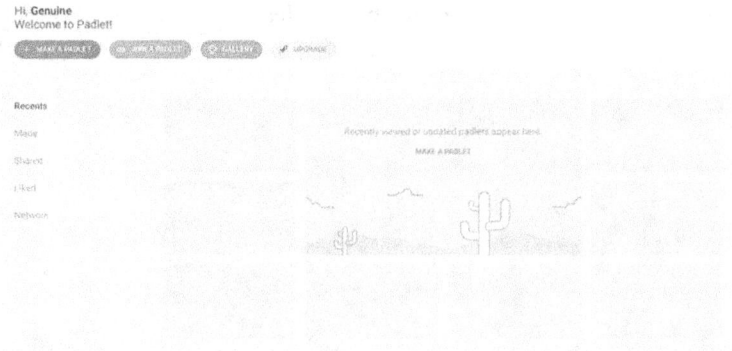

Figure 4: Padlet template for adding content (Rosenberger, 2018).

4. Kahoot

We have used Kahoot to have our students formulate online quizzes as an output of their academic work, and use those quizzes with other students. It is based online and supports individual mode and team mode, so students can work together collaboratively to solve quizzes. One of the benefits of having students make online quizzes is that they activate their individual academic knowledge as they collaborate to formulate questions and answers for the quiz, which is then taken online by fellow students. This could also be extended with peer-grading exercises.

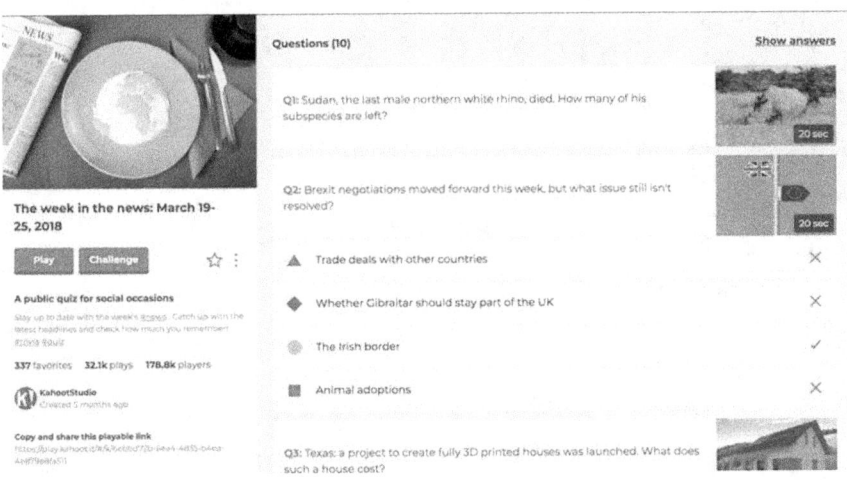

Figure 5: Kahoot in use (www.kahoot.com, 2018).

5. Realtimeboard

We have used Realtimeboard to have our students collaborate on analysing a problem proposed by a company. It is an online collaboration tool which in practice works as an infinite whiteboard, where students can add text, images, pictures, models, figures, etc. One of the advantages of Realtimeboard is that it is open ended, meaning that students can add content to the canvas without limitations. And at the same time, it is possible for students to use pre-defined academic models, which are available as templates. So not all content has to be generated from scratch.

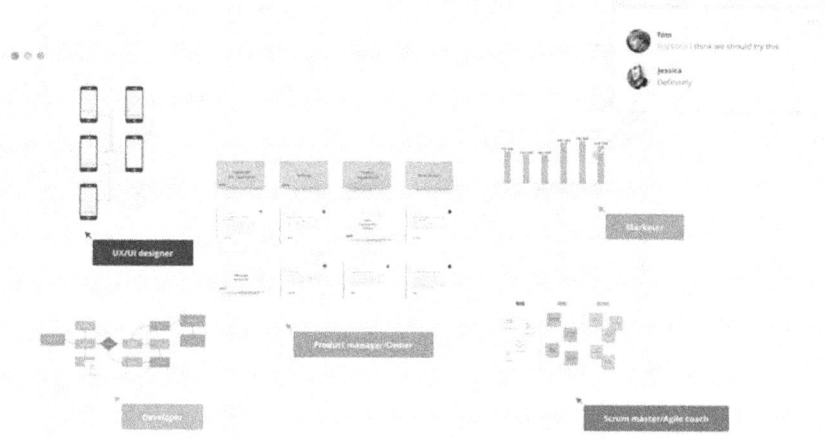

Figure 6: Realtimeboard in use (Realtimeboard, 2018).

6. Appear.in

We have used Appear.in to facilitate virtual meetings between students and their supervisor. It is an online meeting tool, where up to 12 people can be in the same video-meeting. Users can also share their screen. This is a very easy platform to use with no need for signup or downloads. It brings together students and teachers/supervisors via video. It's a quick way of bringing the team together if they are in different physical locations.

Ten e-learning technologies to support problem-based collaborative work

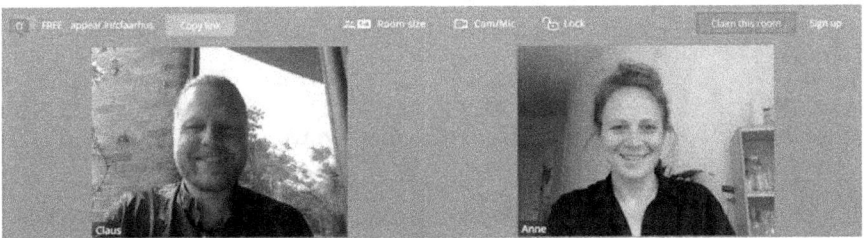

Figure 7: Appear.in in use.

7. Facebook Groups

We have used Facebook Groups to have students share ideas, resources, links, and to facilitate dialogue between students and teachers. Facebook Groups have the advantage that students can easily share ideas, online resources, online links, etc., and comment each other's updates. If you have a Facebook account, you are most probably already a member of an interest group (see Hørsted, in this volume, for a thorough discussion of how to use Facebook Groups with your students).

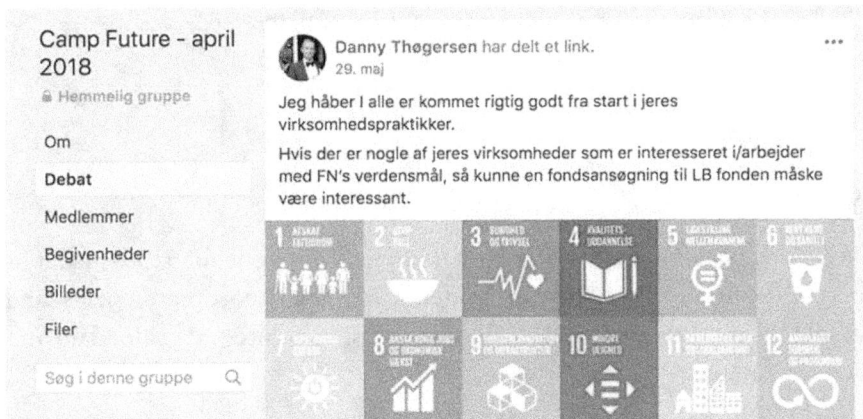

Figure 8: Facebook Group in use.

Chapter 9

8. Canvas LMS

We have used Canvas LMS as e-learning platform for our course. It is an online learning management system, where you can store resources such as links, documents, pictures, videos, audios, etc. You can also setup your LMS with discussion boards, online surveys, learning-logs, etc. There are endless possibilities when using an LMS like Canvas (see Hørsted, in this volume, for a thorough discussion of how to use Canvas LMS with your students).

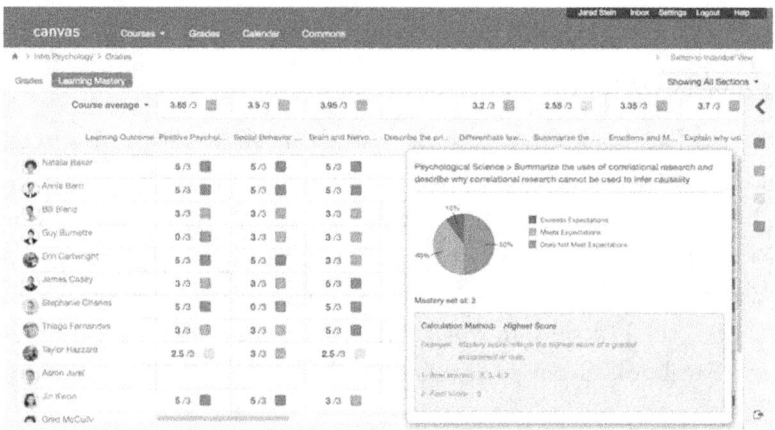

Figure 9: Canvas LMS in use (Carnegie Mellon University, https://www.cmu.edu/canvas/).

9. Asana

We have used Asana as a project management tool for students. It is an online tool, which allows students to plan, coordinate, share and comment on project related tasks. They can also integrate calendars and resource management.

Figure 10: Asana in use (https://asana.com).

10. ProWiki

We have used ProWiki to have students collaborate on writing an online article (Wiki) about a specific scientific topic. Wikis allow students to support each other in their knowledge production and reach a collective output. When given the task to compete a Wiki within an academic area, students can work collaboratively when gathering resources and when writing content for the Wiki. This collaborative nature, as we know from Wikipedia, is a good way of engaging students in collaborative work. There are several software providers, who enable students to write Wikis. ProWiki is one of them.

Chapter 9

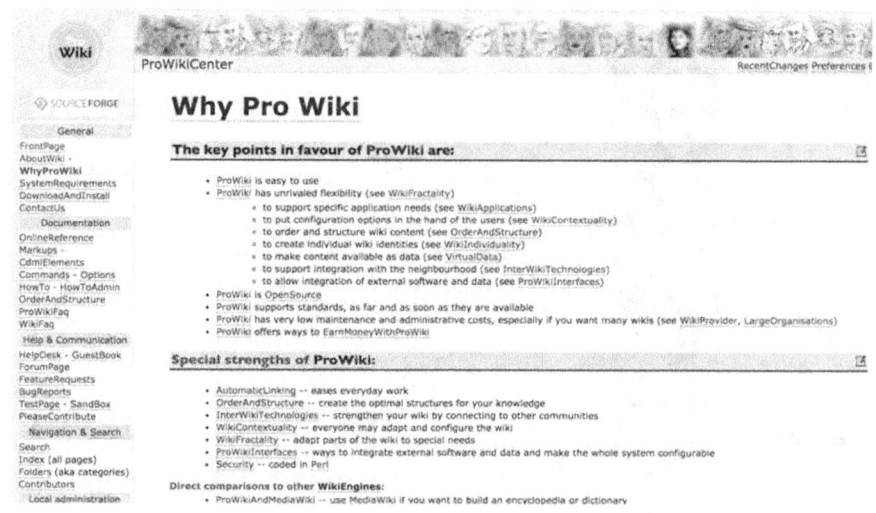

Figure 11: ProWiki in use (www.prowiki.org, 2018).

After this short introduction of the ten e-learning technologies, which are all suitable for supporting parts of the problem-based collaborative work of students, we sum up their characteristics and the score we have given in Figure 12.

Ten e-learning technologies to support problem-based collaborative work

E-learning technology	The domain	The community	The practice
1. Google Docs	*** Students use Google Docs to work with a shared passion for writing.	* Google Docs is not designed to create a sense of belonging to a community. It is a writing tool.	*** Students work on collaborative writing sessions. When they engage in writing sessions they develop their practice.
2. Canva	*** Students use Canva to work with a shared passion for design.	* Canva appeals to students with an interest in design. Canva does not facilitate the forming of a community, although allowing people to work together on a design task.	*** Canva allows for collaborative design, and also makes it possible to invite others to comment and proof a design. It structures a shared practice.
3. Padlet	*** Students use Padlet to work with a shared passion for a scientific topic.	** Padlet allows students to work collaboratively on sharing and developing new knowledge.	*** Padlet allows for collaborative practices such as collaborative brainstorms, collaborative analysis of material, collaborative structuring of material.

Chapter 9

E-learning technology	The domain	The community	The practice
4. Kahoot	* Students use Kahoot to quiz within a scientific domain. If students formulate quizzes themselves it somewhat implies a shared passion for the scientific domain. If teachers form the quiz students may "just" be a student taking the quiz, because it is required by the teacher.	* Using Kahoot to create a quiz or take a quiz does not require or support the forming of a community of practitioners.	* Kahoot is knowledge based and not practice based. It does not help improve a certain practice in relation to problem-based collaborative work.
5. Realtimeboard	*** Students use Realtimeboard to work with a shared passion for a scientific topic. Realtimeboard has templates for innovation and ideation, UX Design, Software development, Business Strategy, etc.	** Realtimeboard allows for students to work seamlessly on sharing and developing new knowledge. Students working together on the Realtimeboard get a sense of belonging to a community.	*** Realtimeboard allows for collaborative practices such as collaborative brainstorms, collaborative analysis of material, collaborative structuring of material.

Ten e-learning technologies to support problem-based collaborative work

E-learning technology	The domain	The community	The practice
6. Appear.in	*** Students and/or teachers/supervisors with a shared passion for an academic subject use Appear.in to cast online video meetings.	*** Online video meetings between students and/or teachers/supervisors constitute communities. When you are invited to an online video meeting, you feel a belonging to the community.	* Appear.in does not imply any collaborative practice. It is a technological platform for hosting online video meetings, and it does not imply or require collective practice apart from taking part in a dialogue.
7. Facebook Groups	* Students and teachers use Facebook as a part of their everyday social life. Being invited to a Facebook Group does not necessarily imply a domain/a shared passion.	** Although Facebook is governed by social relations, it does not imply to constitution of a community to become a member of a Facebook Group. However, membership of a Facebook Group may facilitate communities.	* Facebook Groups do not imply a collaborative practice. Students can be lurkers in the group and not contribute as practitioners.

207

Chapter 9

E-learning technology	The domain	The community	The practice
8. Canvas LMS	*** Canvas LMS supports bringing together students with a shared scientific passion. It is important to remember that the LMS in itself does not build a shared passion. Students without a passion for the scientific domain may be members of the LMS, because they are enrolled as students.	*** Canvas LMS supports the creation of a community, where students take part in collaborative work.	* Canvas LMS does not help students develop their practice or enables them to work together using a specific method.
9. Asana	*** Students with a shared passion for a project work to coordinate their collaboration.	** Asana supports a sense of community through the organisation of collaborative work practices. When students coordinate their collaborative tasks and duties in time and space using Asana, they get a sense of belonging to the community of students.	* Asana does not help students do their collaborative practices. It just helps them coordinate their practice in time and space.

E-learning technology	The domain	The community	The practice
10. ProWiki	*** Students with a shared passion for a topic collaborate on writing a Wiki.	* ProWiki supports students in their writing of a wiki/online article about a certain topic. It does not necessarily support the forming of a sense of community.	*** Using ProWiki to write a Wiki, students work on collaborative writing sessions. When they engage in writing sessions they develop their practice.

Figure 12: Key characteristics and scoring of ten e-learning technologies in relation to social learning theory.

Conclusion

Using e-learning to support problem-based collaborative work requires of the teachers that they see themselves in a new role. The teacher shifts from one who employs traditional didactic teaching to a facilitator, coordinator, supervisor and evaluator. It means that the teacher actively plans and supports activities which are student-driven rather than teacher-driven (see also Nygaard, in this volume). This is a consequence of seeing learning as being social and embedded in communities of practice: we believe that students learn more from being engaged in solving problems which they consider relevant and have a passion for solving (the domain). It also implies that the teacher needs to facilitate students' learning processes. This can be done in a variety of ways, both offline and online. Above we have shown ten e-learning technologies which may help teachers in their planning and supporting of problem-based collaborative work. We hope and believe that by linking together e-learning technologies with learning theory, and exemplifying how e-learning technologies may be used to support students' problem-based collaborative work, we have inspired you to reflect further on your own e-learning practices.

Chapter 9

About the Authors

Flemming Meier is Associate Professor at Aarhus University, Denmark. He can be contacted at this e-mail address: meier@edu.au.dk

Professor Dr. Claus Nygaard is Executive Director of the Institute of Learning in Higher Education and Executive Director of cph:learning. He can be contacted at this e-mail: info@lihe.info

Bibliography

Bandura, A. (1977). *Social Learning Theory.* New York, NY: General Learning Press.

Frost, C., & Stommel, J. (2013). Collaborative and Public Writing Techniques for Google Doc. *Digital Huamities Now.* December 3, 2013.

Horne, K. (2016). Introducing Canva: an accessible graphic design tool. *Sussex Blogs,* 13th December 2016, University of Sussex.

Lave, J., & Wenger, E. (1991). *Situated Learning. Legitimate peripheral participation.* Cambridge, UK: University of Cambridge Press.

Nygaard, C., & Holtham, C. (2008). The Need for Learning-Centred Higher Education. In Nygaard, C., & Holtham, C. (Eds.), *Understanding Learning-Centred Higher Education.* Frederiksberg: Copenhagen Business School Press, 11–30.

Realtimeboard (2018). *Keep everybody in your product developmet team on the same page.* Online resource: https://realtimeboard.com/product-teams/ (Accessed May 14, 2018).

Rosenberger, T. (2018). *How to Use Padlet for Online Collaboration.* Online resource: https://www.maketecheasier.com/use-padlet-for-online-collaboration/ (Accessed May 14, 2018).

Vygotski, L. S. (1978). *Mind in Society. The Development of Higher Psychological Processes.* Cambridge, MA: Harvard University Press.

Wenger, E. (2008). *Communities of practice: learning, meaning, and identity.* Cambridge, UK: Cambridge University Press.

Chapter 10
Using e-learning to supervise students' project work in higher education: some pedagogical requirements

Flemming Meier

Introduction

With my chapter, I contribute to the book *E-learning 1.0, 2.0, and 3.0 in Higher Education* as I discuss possible pedagogical requirements that underlie our use of e-learning to supervise students' project work in higher education. Using e-learning to supervise students' project work is relevant because universities today face demands to economise on the critical face-to-face time used by teachers to supervise students while they work on a project, a thesis or a similarly written assignment. I use the typology of e-learning 1.0, 2.0, and 3.0 (see Nygaard, in this volume) to apply a specific structure to my reflections about ways in which e-learning may help to:

1. mediate distribution of texts and other resources (e-learning 1.0);

2. mediate spaces for conversation and dialogue (e-learning 2.0); and

3. mediate workspaces in which students produce (construct) parts and pieces that go into projects (e-learning 3.0);

In the context of this chapter, I define e-learning as a learning process drawing on digital applications to automatise or mediate certain work-processes – may it be the supervision of project work itself or the students' project-based work-processes. Selecting and implementing e-learning to support supervision of students' project work is not an easy pick. It is my argument that we need to move beyond understanding teaching or supervising as merely a process of transferring information, knowledge

Chapter 10

or wisdom; and also, beyond using standard Learning Management Systems (LMSs), which students mainly access to download course materials (e-learning 1.0). I will unfold this argument as I link the pedagogy of project work with a situated perspective on learning and also link project work to Schön's (1983) vision of contemporary education as a place for educating reflective practitioners. Doing so I come to present some pedagogical requirements with regard to the use of e-learning to supervise students' project work.

I hope to engage you in a reflection of your own supervision practices and also to inspire a discussion of ways in which e-learning may be used when supervising students. Reading the chapter, you may gain the following:

1. knowledge of pedagogy related to project work and supervision;

2. inspiration as to how digital technologies may be integrated into supervision processes.

The chapter has two main sections. In section one, I lay out a general introduction to project work and supervision, and provide some links to learning theory. I do so to show that project work and supervision require certain ways of working, which make demands upon the structures of course modules, upon course (teaching) activities surrounding the project work and upon any technologies used. In section two, I go into detail with e-learning, as I discuss how e-learning may be implemented to facilitate reflective dialogues in students' project work and to improve large group supervision of students during project work.

Section one: a general introduction to project work and supervision

Project work is oriented towards working with a problem. It means that students have to identify/formulate, investigate, and solve a problem in relation to their area of study. This is in contrast to theory based work. However, this is not to say that problem based project work (Meier & Nygaard, 2008) does not draw on theory. Students may well use a theory during project work. In fact, most project work requires students to analyse the problem using theory. This implies that project work has both inductive elements (understanding the problem through empirical investigation) and deductive elements (understanding the problem through application of theory). Being problem oriented means that students primarily engage in investigating and understanding the problem in question, its character, and its relations to other problems, etc. In many projects the formulation of a problem is identical to a research question. It is an identified and delineated problem, which guides the focus of the work process. However, project work may also be centred around 'real life' problems, which means that project work resembles field research, because students often work on a problem as it appears in an empirical setting.

Project work as a reflective practicum

Project work resembles what Schön (1987) characterised as *a reflective practicum*. He had analysed a shift in various professional practice fields and noted: "...*the problems of real world practice do not present themselves as well formed structures..., but as messy, indeterminate situations.*" (Schön, 1987:4). He came to the conclusion that professionals are increasingly faced with indeterminate zones of practice, and what is needed in terms of education is curricula that prepare professionals to be reflective practitioners. This is because the kind of artistry and professional knowledge, that reflective practitioners employ, fits the complex, unstable, uncertain and conflicted worlds of professional practices (Schön, 1987). Universities and Higher Educations institutions have to adjust to this situation, Schön (1987) suggested, by implementing reflective practicums. Schön (1987) described reflective practicums as settings designed for learning the practices of professions. He characterised them as *virtual* worlds relatively free of pressures, distractions and risks of *real* worlds, but with features that approximate real practice worlds. In these settings students "... *learn by undertaking projects that simulate and simplify or they take on real-worlds projects under close supervision.*" (Schön, 1987:37). Further, he noted that: *"It is also a collective world in its own right, with its own mix of materials, tools, languages and appreciations. It embodies particular ways of seeing, thinking and doing that tend, over time, as far as the student is concerned, to assert themselves with increasing authority."* (Schön, 1987:37). Such practicums are reflective in the sense that students have to learn a kind of reflection-in-action that goes beyond stable rules (Schön, 1987). For this reason, teachers or supervisors need to emphasise the indeterminate zones of the practice world (that is unpredictable events) and to set up reflective conversations with the materials (Schön, 1987). Following the outlines of the reflective practicum, we may characterise project work as an arena well suited for contemporary educational purposes. Project work as an educational form is suitable when the aim is to train students to:

1. create new knowledge;
2. develop analytical skills;
3. develop reflective professional identities.

Further, we may describe project work as an educational form where students engage in a complex combination of field studies with various forms of disciplinary knowledge, methodological practices and theoretical perspectives. Thus, it is a rather difficult work process, which involves decisions, dilemmas, experimentation, doubt, reflection, collaboration etc.

This characteristic of problem based project work leads me to raise two central questions:

1. how can e-learning contribute to make available to students a reflective practicum (a virtual world with particular mixes of materials, tools, languages and appreciations) which is also relevant within the real worlds of their disciplinary field?
2. how can e-learning support fruitful reflective processes between students when they work collaboratively in such a reflective practicum?

In the following sections I shall reply to these questions as I look further at student roles in project work and also at the philosophy of constructive alignment.

Student roles: Active and in charge

Sivan *et al.* (2000:381) describe active learning as a teaching method where: "*...students move from being passive recipients of knowledge to being* *participants in activities that encompass analysis, synthesis and evaluation as well as the exploration of values and attitudes."* This description fits that of project work, and points to the kinds of student roles that attract many teachers, curriculum planners, managers and study boards. Leading back to the introductory chapter in this book, it resembles the culture of students as partners or employees rather than pupils or customers. In comparison to traditional forms of teaching, i.e. lecturing or other forms, where students are expected to listen and memorise given content, project work puts students in *more active roles*. They are expected to be in charge of their own project and to work self-directed. In general, problems are not defined by a teacher, but need to be identified, delineated and formulated by students themselves. In this process students often struggle with how to link the academic content of their study program with the problem. Students are presented with theories about 'reality', and enter into project work, where they are to solve a real-life problem while tying together 'theory' and 'reality' in order to perform an academic analysis of the problem at hand.

It is precisely during this struggle to link theoretical assumptions and concepts with investigated real-life problems that supervision plays a crucial role in project work.

For teachers or supervisors this means that their roles are more about facilitating certain kinds of reflective dialogues than delivering answers, knowledge or information. The role of facilitation also includes that of empowering students to engage independently in dialogues and reflective inquiries about problematic situations, materials, tools, methods etc. This could be summarised as using authority to spread authority.

For students, mastering the challenges of being in charge and active, is strongly affected by their expectations, their mindsets and the student culture of a given university. Students often enter university with the expectation that they will 'be taught' what to learn (the culture of pupils as discussed in chapter 1). Such expectations pose a pedagogical challenge for teachers performing supervision of project work. A curriculum based on the premise that students need to be self-directive and have to take responsibility for their own work process requires an institutional culture where students are empowered on many levels, even in areas, where they are not yet experienced.

In continuation of the above and the overall theme here, the question is: *how can e-learning technologies contribute to the legitimisation and staging of such roles?*

In general, project work is organised either as an individual process or as a group process. I will argue that students working together in groups are more likely to develop 'complex' learning outcomes. That is complex in the sense of being constituted by more varied abilities to reflect on their own skills in relation to given situations, challenges and conditions. Collaborative group work requires and enables students to engage in dialogues of inquiry related to challenges and dilemmas in their work process. Dialogues of inquiries may be about how to make use of certain theoretical perspectives or methodologies, they may be about all kinds of small grained practical issues (what to do, how to prioritise time, how to use resources, etc.), and they may be about interpretative issues (how to make sense of situations, data, dilemmas, etc.). Students in project groups have richer opportunities to express their views, argue their standpoints, negotiate their ideas, and reflect on their conclusions in relatively safe relations. Group work thus often leads to a richer dialogue and to a richer process of actions, reflections, experimentations, problem framings, new action, and so on (Meier & Nygaard, 2008).

However, in the present case, the important thing is that group settings and individual settings in project work may result in slightly different requirements when it comes to speculations about supervision of project work. Supervision of individual project work will focus on initiating, facilitating and performing inquiries as mentioned above; whereas supervision of group project work will also focus on mediating and sharpening the dialogical processes between the members of the project group.

Constructive alignment, when project work is the core activity

According to Biggs & Tang (2011) curriculum planning in Higher Education should be performed through constructive alignment. This should be done by aligning examination forms and assessment practices according to intended learning outcomes; formulated as learning objectives. Thus, educational activities should be designed and organised in alignment with examination forms and assessment practices. The rationale in alignment thinking is that building curricula based on assessment practices will result in an adequate mix of 'teaching and learning activities', because it will force or motivate planners, teachers, students and other stakeholders to work towards a situation, where students are passing their exams. The assessment practices will in other words determine stakeholders' expectations and behaviour. This may be criticised for being a deterministic and reductionist way of perceiving curriculum planning. However, there is general agreement that learning objectives, educational activity and examination and assessment should be regarded as interlinked and thus taken into consideration in curriculum design. Project work often emphasise development of qualifications like:

- analytical skills;
- ability to formulate, reflect on and discuss problems;
- ability to apply methodologies by designing tools for data gathering and ability to evaluate and discuss methods in relation to epistemologies;
- knowledge about theories within certain disciplinary fields;
- abilities to use theories to form analytical perspectives on problems and implied phenomena to be investigated and analysed.

The examination will often consist of an assessment of a submitted written report about the project, wherein students demonstrate their abilities to perform skills like the above mentioned. Often this will be combined with an oral exam where students present the project and its findings and participates in a discussion with examiners, and thereby further demonstrate the skills they have acquired. Besides the project work, which, apart from very early phases, is self-directed by students, a course module will also offer lectures, workshops and supervision. The functions of lectures, workshops and supervision is to qualify the project work, which is seen as the core activity of the course module. Thus, the main pedagogical considerations are about *how to design, organise and execute those three surrounding activities so that they support the core activity (project work), provide resources for it and form an infrastructural framework for the self-directedness of it.*

Taking the resemblances of project work to the reflective practicum into consideration and thinking along lines of a situated learning perspective (Lave & Wenger, 1991), this means in general terms, that lectures may be seen as situations where students are introduced to theoretical discourses of disciplinary fields; and that students are being granted access to the discourses-as-practices through participation in reading theoretical texts or research articles, in listening to the lecturer and sometimes through engaging in short directed dialogues with other students and the lecturer in the lecture hall. Students thereby begin to perform the ontological assumptions and concepts of theories.

Workshops then may be seen as situations where students are granted access to participation in practices designed and organised to imitate or simulate practices commonly occurring in academic research work and project work. Students are thereby learning to perform various tasks and procedures, learning to perform with certain tools, methods or techniques, and – because of the distinct character of the situation as an educational setting – they will have opportunities to engage in what Schön (1987) calls *reflections-in-action*. These reflections encompass tasks, procedures, techniques and linkages to theoretical perspectives and they are also a chance to reflect upon their own performance in workshop exercises and specific concrete challenges in their own project work.

Finally, supervision may be seen as situations where a group or an individual engages with a person, who represents a certain authority based on merits and experience in relation to a disciplinary field seen as *a social practice*. Seen this way a disciplinary field is a social context with certain practices and norms regarding project work as well as epistemological assumptions, methodological traditions, inherent technologies and (socio-political) organisational arrangements. Consequently, a supervisor may be seen as a person who is formally recognised as an accomplished practitioner within the disciplinary field. They are also authorised to facilitate conversations and inquiries into concrete challenges, problems and dilemmas experienced by students doing project work. In addition, the supervisor is someone, who can point to choices, 'no-go's and resources; can draw scenarios and simulations, widen scopes and horizons, pass on heuristics and disciplinary lore, all of which may guide students in their decisions and carrying out actions.

In relation to e-learning technologies this raises the question how e-learning technologies can support supervisors in their efforts to perform this role. Another question (although a bit tangential to the main theme here) with regard to both supervision, workshops and lectures is how e-learning technologies might let the surrounding activities support project work better.

Economising with the labour involved in the production of project work

It is costly to have faculty members supervise each project group or student individually. If for example each student could expect to get supervision for 10+ hours each semester of a three-year program, it would require the employment of a considerably higher number of faculty members than is normally provided. Therefore, universities are looking for ways to cut down costs on student supervision. One way of cutting down the costs is to move from individual / small-group supervision to large-group supervision, often in a seminar-, workshop- or Q&A-format, where a teacher delivers general advice and instructions regarding project work and assignments; and take questions from students. In a sense this change actually brings about a change in the mix of teaching activities, by putting less weight on supervision and more on workshops, and it entails a number of problems:

- the main problem is that in such formats it is very difficult to facilitate a supervision process, where concrete dilemmas and challenges in relation to a specific project are addressed, when say 100 students are brought together in a supervision seminar.

- another problem is that not all students will engage in this format and dare to share their own doubts and uncertainties in front of other students.

- a third problem is that only a few students will have the possibility to voice and discuss their problems because of limited time, while some students may be reluctant to invest effort and time in listening to and discussing other students' problems and not their own. Therefore, there is a tendency that the quality of the supervision process goes down as the number of involved students go up.

The challenge addressed in the second section of this chapter is how to provide worthwhile project supervision using e-learning technologies. In addition, bearing in mind that although technologies cannot replicate previous educational practices, it is however worth recognising that specific technologies might actually help to reformulate supervision and peer learning processes, and even produce a better outcome for students – if handled thoughtfully. It might encourage students to address their projects in a new, creative manner and to adopt and adapt new technologies themselves. In section two, I shall take a look at possible applications of e-learning 1.0, 2.0, and 3.0 in supervision of students' project work and also reflect on the pedagogical requirements.

Section two: e-learning 1.0, 2.0, and 3.0 in supervision of students' project work

In line with the tripartite typology of e-learning paradigms (see Nygaard, in this volume), I divide the following discussion into three parts. In each part, I suggest how technologies, that are more or less in sync with each of the three e-learning paradigms, could do something about needs and problems listed above.

That is help to mediate:

1. distribution of resources relevant for the supervision of students' project work (e-learning 1.0);

2. channels for the kinds of conversation and dialogue needed in relation to supervision and in relation to students' project work (e-learning 2.0);

3. workspaces in which students produce (construct) parts and pieces that contributes to their project work (e-learning 3.0).

Other ways of structuring this discussion could have been applied. I could have chosen a more technically inspired structure for instance. Examining how technologies like learning management systems, mobile devices, virtual and augmented reality, gamification and simulation, social network apps, blogs, wikis etc. might be relevant or helpful. But using the e-learning typology proposed by Nygaard (in this volume) to focus on the distribution of resources (e-learning 1.0), design of communication channels (e-learning 2.0), and configuration of workspaces for knowledge construction (e-learning 3.0) allows for a systematic social practice inspired approach (Lave & Wenger, 1991) of the use of e-learning technologies in supervision of students' project work.

E-learning 1.0: distribution of information, texts, instructions, tests and other resources

The prevailing type of e-learning technology at universities comes in the form of Learning Management Systems (LMSs). Examples thereof are Blackboard, Moodle, Fronter, Canvas, Atutor and Claroline. Most LMSs comprise functions like management of user access, course spaces, course content and tests / assessment. LMSs have interfaces for students with links to course materials, discussion boards, assessment or testing functions as well as links to external applications and resources. For teachers and administrators there will be user interfaces, where they can manage course materials, configure students' interfaces (with more or less restrictions) and communicate with students.

This type of e-learning technology has primarily features fit for distribution of content. The features of setting up blogs, discussion fora, chat rooms and sometimes collaborative workspaces within LMSs also have the potential to facilitate communication processes and workspaces in relation to project work. Here I want to emphasise the importance of providing access to a rich variety of resources, which may be useful in relation to project work.

According to Lave & Wenger (1991) the transparency of the sociopolitical organisation of practices and the participatory accessibility to practices are determining conditions for learning processes of participants. Assuming this, it is relevant to consider the potentials of technologies, and here the potentials of LMSs, to mediate access and transparency of all the elements that are part of particular project work practices. In a more detailed account, this could be access to and transparency of (among other things) tools, routines, artefacts, disciplinary discourses, norms, traditions, status hierarchies, manuals, descriptions of partial practices, flows of action and conversation, etc.

Using LMSs to distribute access to resources that represent such elements in the practices of project work may be the most strategic part of implementing e-learning technologies in relation to project work. Two things cause this:

1. LMSs constitute a central management tool at many universities and are thus highly prioritised by stakeholders at a strategic level.

2. LMSs represent a potential for floor level stakeholders (teachers, course coordinators and students) over time to build repositories of resources specifically suited for certain disciplinary fields or a certain course wherein project work is the core activity.

Such repositories may contain texts, videos and audio files, but more interactive resources like tests, wikis and links to games, simulations and external applications are also important to include in efforts to build rich repositories. Of particular importance in this connection is however to build the user interfaces and information architectures of repositories to ensure transparency and easy access, taking into consideration *typical project group work situations* of the specific disciplinary field. This also raises the issue of *devices*, because if students' user interfaces of LMSs can run on mobile devices, it may increase the accessibility and usability of repository resources in many situations.

Not directly connected to the role of LMSs, but crucial to efforts of providing and distributing a rich environment of resources for project work, are training modules designed and produced specifically for given disciplinary fields or courses. It could for example be training modules for:

1. evaluating suggested research questions and problem formulations or inquiring into empirical fields or phenomena;

2. inquiring into and discussing what it might imply to apply a certain specific theoretical framework to form a research strategy or an analytical perspective (for example it could be Actor-Network Theory, Self Determination Theory, Discourse Theory or almost any other theoretical framework);

3. making a plan for conducting an initial Grounded Theory data collection.

However, we need to move beyond standard LMSs in further considerations of ways in which e-learning technologies might be useful in relation to project work and supervision. This is because of the inadequacies of such 'institution-wide' systems. Even when an LMS allows students to upload content or engage in forum activity, the structures of the system enforce limited frameworks upon interactions of teachers and students. They tend to conform to institutional norms and work against students actively creating new models and means of analysis.

E-learning 2.0: setting up channels and fora for discussions, dialogues, reflections and supervision

Technologies, which may be useful in mediating the kinds of communicative processes that occur all the time in project work, and the kinds that occur in relation to supervision, are plentiful. SMS, online chat rooms, blogging, social network apps, online discussion fora etc. are examples of species in that ecology of communication technologies, which have proliferated during the last more than 20 years. However, few of them have been developed specifically with project work or supervision in mind. This has the result that very few attempts have been made to develop applications that have the potential of specifically focusing the communication on dilemmas and challenges and deliberately facilitating inquiring and reflective dialogues. That is however the most urgent need when considering how e-learning technologies might help project work or the reflective practicum as outlined in section one. How such features or virtues or techniques – of detecting and focusing on dilemmas, investigating and inquiring into problematic situations and engaging in reflective dialogues – can be legitimised by and designed into concrete e-learning technologies, is beyond the scope of this text and its author's immediate abilities. It is, however, maybe the issue of facilitating communication channels that becomes central when acknowledging the resemblances between project work and the reflective practicum. In many instances, certain procedures or protocols can take place in existing discussion fora, and these may be a starting point for innovation or updating existing technologies. It is finally worth noting that an abundance of software and applications for planning and managing projects in business and professional contexts exist. Many of these may have features that will make them useful also in educational contexts.

The issue of devices, user interfaces and information architectures are also important here. Because the various situations often occurring in project work may be best supported with very specifically designed user interfaces and information architectures. Group meetings for example may be best supported with a varied set of multitasking applications running on complex user interfaces as on wearable computers. While situations where groups are geographically dispersed, and need to communicate in order to coordinate or to reflect on a problem now and here may require more simplified ones on mobile phones. See also Meier & Nygaard (in this volume) for a evaluation of ten e-learning tools and their abilities to facilitate such dialogues.

As implied above, the implementation of e-learning technologies to develop formats of collective supervision workshops may be a way to gain both cost-efficiency and a supervision process of better quality. The idea suggested here is to integrate e-learning technologies into large group supervision, by:

1. letting technologies help to facilitate a more complex organisation of workshops, where many project groups are supervised in parallel processes by a supervisor or by other project groups;

2. facilitating peer supervision, where two or three project groups supervise each other guided by applications, which helps to focus the discussions on dilemmas and challenges and deliberately facilitate inquiring and reflective dialogues;

3. training certain procedures of evaluating problematic situations in project work via quests in small game-like simulation apps.

A further idea here could be to develop the latter two suggestions into a system, where students or student groups through training and performing peer-supervision achieve some kind of rank or recognition as experienced peer-supervisors and maybe even merits counting in relation to their education.

E-learning 3.0: setting up workspaces for project work

Designing e-learning technologies for project work and supervision may be about imagining digital tools that enable students to construct their project or parts of it in digital forms. In a sense this vision is already reality in almost all areas of Higher Education, where provisions and products come in digital form, for instance, digital formats of texts, spreadsheets, videos, CAD-models, 3D-prints, etc. Most students around the globe already use such tools on computers, mobile phones and tablets; and Microsoft, Apple, Dropbox, Google Apps and others already sell applications which may be used as tools in project work. Moreover, many apps have features relevant for planning, coordinating and communicating around tasks, and dilemmas and problems in relation to work processes. Providing access to an abundance of tools which give adequate workspaces for project work may not be far away. It may be more difficult to link such workspaces with supervision or peer-supervision, but a few existing applications may provide tools for this. For example:

1. online portfolios: these are personal rooms for documenting and reflecting on one's progress as student in relation to the particular project work-phase. Here students can address the important and critical decisions they have taken and reflect on their consequences for their project work and for their own learning.

2. exercises: these could be drilling games and tests, exemplary cases and simulations. In general, the ability to link workspaces to supervision, or rather to let workspaces facilitate supervision, allow supervisors to interact better with student project groups.

3. virtual work spaces: all sorts of technologies outlined above in this section (a multiplicity of resources and applications, communication channels specialized for reflective dialogues, digital tools etc.) are brought together for project groups to work with.

With regard to these work spaces, one assumes that the developers of presently available LMSs have a similar vision for the future of their own systems. The question is whether this development will just lead to an iteration of the conformity and control obsession that characterise present day LMSs.

As already stated in the beginning of this chapter, it is my view that we need to move beyond understanding teaching and supervising as merely a process of transfer of information. I have attempted to show, what such a move would mean for the pedagogical considerations of project work. I suggest we also move beyond using standard LMSs and the very idea of managing learning in a system. I suggest this because most contemporary educational processes (and certainly project work and reflective practicums) require settings that are varied, flexible and complex, and thus reconfigurable and adequate to a multiplicity of practices, discourses, traditions and epistemologies of certain professional, disciplinary and sub-disciplinary fields, as well as certain institutional contexts.

Issues to be addressed when considering e-learning technologies

Summing up on the discussions in this chapter, a number of needs and problems may be listed in relation to supervision of project work:

- group processes may be better guided and supported with a wide variety of tools, communications channels and workspaces for students. E-learning technologies support this;
- certain skills often performed in students' project work may be trained in games or virtual spaces. Such can be applied by e-learning technologies;
- students' efforts of focusing on, framing, inquiring into and making sense of the concrete dilemmas and problems in projects may be helped by *tools, training* and more flexible asynchronous *communication channels* with supervisors. E-learning platforms allows for this;
- students' workspaces for project work may be improved in terms of better suited for the kinds of methodologies, operations and tasks often occurring in certain disciplinary fields. E-learning systems allows online learning workspaces;
- workspaces may also be improved in terms of allowing for more varied and flexible forms of collaboration and for transparent coordination and for easier communication with supervisors and other project groups. E-learning technologies allow for flexibility and transparency in the use of and sharing of data;

- supervisors need to be able to facilitate more differentiated and complex kinds of supervision processes, in order to meet more differentiated project specific needs from students, and in order to make peer supervision processes possible. E-learning platforms and systems allow for such facilitation and interaction.

Conclusion

I have highlighted the challenges of project work for students, and, in particular the issues of supervising individuals and groups in a large class setting. Project work allows students to develop into reflective practitioners, who are able to provide solutions in unpredictable situations by ensuring that they address real-world problems. It is unlikely that students will acquire these skills through knowledge transfer from the teacher alone. However, while project work earns great rewards, it requires a great deal of supervision, and students often feel uncertain about working alone or delivering peer support. In larger class settings, it is essential that e-learning solutions be harnessed in order to support students who are working on projects.

I have demonstrated that current, widespread technology adopted by universities in the form of LMSs have tended to operate largely in an e-learning 1.0 mode of information delivery, as well as, to a lesser extent, e-learning 2.0 by encouraging some communication between students. However, a much less rigid form of technology is needed to guide students through project work and to the e-learning 3.0 stage where they might, for example, create their own formats for dealing with project work. In order to achieve such an outcome, learning designers must think beyond current e-learning formats.

About the Author

Flemming Meier is Associate Professor at Aarhus University, Denmark. He can be contacted at this e-mail: meier@edu.au.dk

Bibliography

Biggs, J., & Tang, C. (2011). *Teaching for quality learning at university: What the student does*. Maidenhead, Berkshire. Open University Press.

Lave, J., & Wenger, E. (1991). *Situated Learning. Legitimate peripheral participation*. Cambridge, UK: University of Cambridge Press.

Meier, F., & Nygaard, C. (2008). Problem Oriented Project Work in Higher Education. In Nygaard, C. & Holtham, C. (Eds.), *Understanding Learning-Centred Higher Education*. Copenhagen: Copenhagen Business School Press, 131–144.

Schön, D. A. (1983). *The Reflexive Practitioner. How professionals think in action*. New York: Basic Books.

Schön, D. A. (1987). *Educating the Reflective Practitioner*. San Fransisco: Jossey-Bass.

Sivan, A., Leung, R. W., Woon, C.-C., & Kember, D. (2000). An Implementation of Active Learning and its Effect on the Quality of Student Learning. *Innovations in Education & Training International*, 37(4), 381–389.

www.ingramcontent.com/pod-product-compliance
Lightning Source LLC
Chambersburg PA
CBHW071340080526
44587CB00017B/2898